Blackstone's

Police Q&A

General Police Duties 2017

Blackstone's
Police Q&A

General Police Duties 2017

Fifteenth edition

Huw Smart and John Watson

OXFORD
UNIVERSITY PRESS

OXFORD
UNIVERSITY PRESS

Great Clarendon Street, Oxford, OX2 6DP,
United Kingdom

Oxford University Press is a department of the University of Oxford. It furthers the University's objective of excellence in research, scholarship, and education by publishing worldwide. Oxford is a registered trade mark of Oxford University Press in the UK and in certain other countries

First published in 2016

Impression: 1

Published in the United States of America by Oxford University Press
198 Madison Avenue, New York, NY 10016, United States of America

British Library Cataloguing in Publication Data

Data available

ISBN 978–0–19–878313–8

Printed and bound by
CPI Group (UK) Ltd, Croydon, CR0 4YY

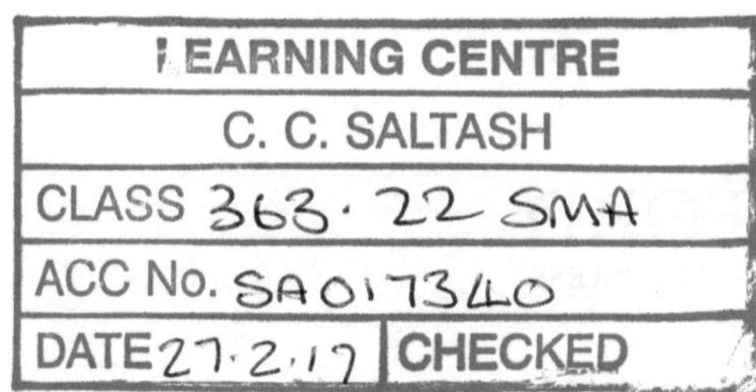

Contents

Introduction

Before you get into the detail of this book, there are two myths about multiple-choice questions (MCQs) that we need to get out of the way right at the start:

1. that they are easy to answer;
2. that they are easy to write.

Take one look at a professionally designed and properly developed exam paper such as those used by the Police Promotion Examinations Board or the National Board of Medical Examiners in the US and the first myth collapses straight away. Contrary to what some people believe, MCQs are not an easy solution for examiners and not a 'multiple-guess' soft option for examinees.

That is not to say that *all* MCQs are taxing, or even testing—in the psychometric sense. If MCQs are to have any real value at all, they need to be carefully designed and follow some agreed basic rules.

And this leads us to myth number 2.

It is widely assumed by many people and educational organisations that anyone with the knowledge of a subject can write MCQs. You need only look at how few MCQ writing courses are offered by training providers in the UK to see just how far this myth is believed. Similarly, you need only to have a go at a few badly designed MCQs to realise that it is a myth nonetheless. Writing bad MCQs is easy; writing good ones is no easier than answering them!

As with many things, the design of MCQs benefits considerably from time, training and experience. Many MCQ writers fall easily and often unwittingly into the trap of making their questions too hard, too easy or too obscure, or completely different from the type of question that you will eventually encounter in your own particular exam. Others seem to use the MCQ as a way to catch people out or to show how smart they, the authors, are (or think they are).

There are several purposes for which MCQs are very useful. The first is in producing a reliable, valid and fair test of knowledge and understanding across a wide range of subject matter. Another is an aid to study, preparation and revision for such examinations and tests. The differences in objective mean that there are slight differences in the rules that the MCQ writers follow. Whereas the design of fully validated MCQs to be used in high stakes examinations, which will effectively determine who passes and who fails, has very strict guidelines as to construction, content and style, less stringent rules apply to MCQs that are being used for teaching and revision. For that reason, there may be types of MCQ that are appropriate in the latter setting which would not be used in the former. However, in developing the MCQs for this book, the authors have tried to follow the fundamental rules of MCQ design but they would not claim to have replicated the level of psychometric rigour that is—and has to be—adopted by the type of examining bodies referred to previously.

These MCQs are designed to reinforce your knowledge and understanding, to highlight any gaps or weaknesses in that knowledge and understanding, and to help focus your revision of the relevant topics.

I hope that we have achieved that aim.

Good luck!

Blackstone's Police Q&As—Special Features

References to Blackstone's Police Manuals

Every answer is followed by a paragraph reference to Blackstone's Police Manuals. This means that once you have attempted a question and looked at an answer, the Manual can immediately be referred to for help and clarification.

Unique numbers for each question

Each question and answer has the same unique number. This should ensure that there is no confusion as to which question is linked to which answer. For example, Question 2.1 is linked to Answer 2.1.

Checklists

The checklists are designed to help you keep track of your progress when answering the multiple-choice questions. If you fill in the checklist after attempting a question, you will be able to check how many you got right on the first attempt and will know immediately which questions need to be revisited a second time. Please visit www.blackstonespoliceservice.com and click through to the Blackstone's Police Q&As 2016 page. You will then find electronic versions of the checklists to download and print out. Email any queries or comments on the book to: police.uk@oup.com.

Acknowledgements

This book has been written as an accompaniment to Blackstone's Police Manuals, and will test the knowledge you have accrued through reading that series. It is of the essence that full study of the relevant chapters in each Police Manual is completed prior to attempting the Questions and Answers. As qualified police trainers we recognise that students tend to answer questions incorrectly either because they don't read the question properly, or because one of the 'distracters' has done its work. The distracter is one of the three incorrect answers in a multiple-choice question (MCQ), and is designed to distract you from the correct answer and in this way discriminate between candidates: the better-prepared candidate not being 'distracted'.

So particular attention should be paid to the *Answers* sections, and students should ask themselves 'Why did I get that question wrong?' and, just as importantly, 'Why did I get that question right?' Combining the information gained in the *Answers* section together with rereading the chapter in the Police Manuals should lead to greater understanding of the subject matter.

The authors wish to thank all the staff at Oxford University Press who have helped put this publication together. We would particularly like to dedicate these books to Alistair MacQueen who sadly passed away in 2008. It was his vision and support that got this project off the ground. Without his help neither Huw nor John would have been able to make these Q&As the success they are. We would also like to show appreciation to Fraser Sampson, former consultant editor of Blackstone's Police Manuals, whose influence on these Q&As is appreciated.

Huw would like to thank Caroline for her constant love, support and understanding over the past year—and her ability to withstand the pressures of being the partner to a workaholic! Special thanks to Lawrence and Maddie—two perfect young adults. Last but not least, love and special affection to Haf and Nia, two beautiful young girls.

John would like to thank Sue, David, Catherine and Andrew for their continued support, and understanding that 'deadline' means 'deadline'.

1 The Police and the Policing Family

STUDY PREPARATION

This chapter covers terms and conditions for regular police officers, under the Police Regulations 2003, as well as the similar conditions for the 'extended policing family' under the Police Reform Act 2002. This includes the introduction of powers to groups of people who are either directly employed by the police, or who work in close liaison with the police.

Under Pt 4 of the Act, the following people may be 'designated' by the relevant chief officer:

- police community support officers (PCSOs);
- investigating officers;
- detention officers;
- escort officers.

A further extension of the policing family comes in the form of accredited employees. Chief officers, in consultation with local authorities, may establish a Community Safety Accreditation Scheme (CSAS).

Further matters covered are the jurisdiction of non-police services and the powers given to special constables.

Attention is also given to 'whistle blowers' under the Public Interest Disclosure Act 1998.

QUESTIONS

Question 1.1

Chief Inspector BRIAR is acting up for Superintendent MICHAELS, who is on leave. Chief Inspector BRIAR works at a police station which has a designated custody office and the superintendent at the station is frequently called upon to conduct 24-hour reviews under the Police and Criminal Evidence Act 1984 (PACE). Chief Inspector BRIAR was promoted to the rank three months ago.

Under what circumstances could Chief Inspector BRIAR conduct PACE reviews in the superintendent's absence, in these circumstances?

A Chief Inspector BRIAR may be authorised by Superintendent MICHAELS.

B Chief Inspector BRIAR must be authorised by the chief superintendent in charge of policing for the area she works in.

C Chief Inspector BRIAR must be authorised by a chief superintendent, but not necessarily one who is in charge of policing for the area she works in.

D Chief Inspector BRIAR may not be authorised to conduct such reviews, until she has been promoted for six months.

Question 1.2

Constable MARGIS is qualified to the rank of sergeant and was working a Sunday morning shift. The officer received a call from the on-duty inspector; she was told that the custody officer at the designated station had suddenly fallen ill and that there were no other sergeants immediately available; also, the nearest custody offices in the force area were full. There were two people detained in the custody office who needed to be booked in and Constable MARGIS was asked to temporarily perform custody duties for these people and the others in custody, while the inspector found a suitable replacement.

Would it be lawful for Constable MARGIS to act as a custody officer in these circumstances?

A Yes, but Constable MARGIS would have to be appointed under PACE by an officer of at least the rank of superintendent.

B Yes, Constable MARGIS has been appointed under PACE to perform the role by an officer of at least the rank of inspector.

C No, a constable may only perform the role of a custody officer at a non-designated station.

D Yes, and there is no requirement for Constable MARGIS to be appointed under PACE to perform this role.

Question 1.3

Sergeant GUNNEY has been a part-time worker for two years. Due to a change in personal circumstances, Sergeant GUNNEY has submitted a report asking to return to full-time working within two weeks as a matter of urgency.

Would the Police Regulations 2003 allow Sergeant GUNNEY to return to full-time working within this time period?

A Yes, if it is considered reasonably practicable to do so.

B No, Sergeant GUNNEY should return to full-time working within two months.

C No, Sergeant GUNNEY should return to full-time working within four months.

D Yes, an officer can return to full-time duties at any time provided a request is made in writing.

Question 1.4

Constable DEERE has recently been appointed to the force, having served as a PCSO for three years. As a PCSO, Constable DEERE was an active member of a trade union and would like to continue this membership, despite being appointed as a constable.

Which of the following statements is correct in relation to Constable DEERE's wish, according to s. 64 of the Police Act 1996?

A Constable DEERE may not remain a member of a trade union and must resign from that organisation.

B Constable DEERE has an automatic right to remain a member of the trade union, because she was a member before being appointed as a constable.

C Constable DEERE may either remain a member of a trade union or become a member of the Police Federation; she cannot be a member of both.

D Constable DEERE may remain a member of a trade union, provided this membership is approved by her chief constable.

Question 1.5

Special Constable PATTERSON is an officer with Northshire Constabulary. Special Constable PATTERSON's home force has a Football League Club in its own area and Special Constable PATTERSON works regularly with the police spotters team, identifying football hooligans. Special Constable PATTERSON has developed an expertise in this area and has been asked to attend away matches to assist regular police officers with preventing crowd trouble.

Would Special Constable PATTERSON enjoy the powers and privileges of a special constable, when working in other police areas?

A Yes, Special Constable PATTERSON would enjoy the powers and privileges of a special constable when working in any police area.

B No, Special Constable PATTERSON would only enjoy the powers and privileges of a special constable when working in an adjoining area, on mutual aid.

C Yes, but Special Constable PATTERSON would only enjoy the powers and privileges of a special constable when working in an adjoining area.

D No, Special Constable PATTERSON would only enjoy the powers and privileges of a special constable when working on mutual aid, but this may be in any police area.

Question 1.6

KYLE works for Eastshire Constabulary as a police community support officer (PCSO) and KNIGHT works as a detention officer in a custody office in the same force, but is contracted to work for the force by a private security company. Under Pt 4 of the Police Reform Act 2002, chief officers of police are given the authority to confer policing powers on non-police officers (such as KYLE and KNIGHT).

What flexibility, if any, does the chief officer of police of Eastshire Constabulary have when it comes to conferring policing powers on the individuals mentioned in the scenario?

A The chief officer is only required to confer such powers on KYLE, as a PCSO.

B The decision whether or not to confer any powers on either KYLE or KNIGHT rests with the chief officer, who has the flexibility to decide whether to grant such powers or not.

C The chief officer is only required to confer such powers on KNIGHT, as a contracted detention officer.

D The chief officer must confer some powers on both KYLE and KNIGHT, but has flexibility to choose which powers are appropriate.

Question 1.7

JENSEN has recently been made redundant; she is a key member of the Residents' Association on the estate in which she lives and regularly undertakes voluntary work with young people in the area. The estate suffers from significant youth annoyance problems and the Residents' Association would like to engage JENSEN on a

Community Safety Accreditation Scheme (CSAS), to work with young people to reduce anti-social behaviour. The Association does not have any funding to employ JENSEN in this role, but she is happy to work as a volunteer.

Would the Residents' Association be able to employ JENSEN on such a scheme, under Part 4 of the Police Reform Act 2002, in these circumstances?

A No, the Residents' Association would have to pay JENSEN to conduct the work; she cannot be accredited under this scheme as a volunteer.

B Yes, JENSEN may be accredited under this scheme as it does not rely on an individual being remunerated for the work they do.

C No, JENSEN must be employed by some organisation, as the local Police and Crime Commissioner must have an employer to agree a contract with.

D No, JENSEN must be employed by a local authority, which must agree a contract with the local Police and Crime Commissioner on the terms of her deployment.

Question 1.8

FLETCHER is employed by Eastshire Constabulary as an investigating officer and has been 'designated' by the chief constable to perform this role. A complaint has been made that FLETCHER committed a serious assault on a suspect during an interview and the matter is being investigated by the Professional Standards Department. The officer in charge of the case is considering making a referral to the Independent Police Complaints Commission (IPCC).

Could the IPCC have jurisdiction over a complaint made against a designated employee, such as FLETCHER?

A No, because FLETCHER is not a police officer and is not covered by the Police (Conduct) Regulations 2012.

B Yes, but only if a joint allegation is made against a police officer and a designated employee.

C Yes, but only because a criminal allegation has been made against FLETCHER.

D Yes, regardless of whether the allegation is of a criminal nature, or whether a police officer was involved.

Question 1.9

Sergeant WHEELER is the custody officer in a designated station. JOHNSTON, aged 12, is in police detention at the station, having been arrested for shoplifting, having stolen property valued at £5. JOHNSTON has been interviewed and has admitted the offence, but has previously been given a youth caution for this offence. JOHNSTON's mother is present and Sergeant WHEELER is considering whether or not it would be appropriate to issue a Disorder Penalty Notice, under the Criminal Justice and Police Act 2001.

Which of the following statements is correct, as to Sergeant WHEELER's intentions?

A Sergeant WHEELER may issue a Notice, because JOHNSTON's mother is present.

B Sergeant WHEELER may issue a Notice, regardless of whether JOHNSTON's mother is present, but must ensure she is given a copy.

C Sergeant WHEELER may issue a Notice, but because JOHNSTON's mother is present, it must be issued to her.

D Sergeant WHEELER may issue a Notice, regardless of whether JOHNSTON's mother is present, but must ensure a copy is sent to her home address.

Question 1.10

BECK is employed as a detention officer in a custody office on the same shift as Sergeant DELGADO. BECK is one of a number of people from a private security company contracted by the force to perform custody detention duties. Sergeant DELGADO has had to warn BECK several times of a failure to conduct visits and update custody records in a timely manner.

Which of the following statements is correct, in relation to whether Sergeant DELGADO can deal with BECK, either under the Police (Performance) Regulations 2012, or the Police (Conduct) Regulations 2012?

A BECK may only be dealt with under the Performance Regulations in these circumstances.

B BECK may only be dealt with under the Conduct Regulations in these circumstances.

C Neither of the Regulations applies in these circumstances, but BECK may be dealt with under police staff Regulations relating to poor performance.

D BECK is not an employee and may not be dealt with under any police officer or police staff Regulations in these circumstances.

Question 1.11

VAUGHAN has been appointed as an accredited employee who works on a large housing estate which has suffered significant anti-social behaviour problems. A Community Safety Accreditation Scheme (CSAS) has been agreed between the police, the local authority and VAUGHAN's employers, a housing association company. A complaint has been made about VAUGHAN's behaviour, alleging that she is aggressive towards residents.

Which organisation has responsibility for dealing with a complaint made about VAUGHAN's behaviour?

A Any of the three organisations could deal with the complaint.

B The complaint should be dealt with by the police.

C The complaint should be dealt with by VAUGHAN's employer.

D The complaint could be dealt with by the police or VAUGHAN's employer.

Question 1.12

KENT is employed as an investigating officer in a police force, in a specialist department that deals with Internet crime. KENT's detective sergeant has obtained a warrant to search the computer of a teacher at a local school, who is suspected of possessing extreme pornography, and has decided KENT should be present when it is executed. All accredited employees in the force are required to wear uniforms and this policy applies to KENT; however, because of the nature of the investigation the detective sergeant would like KENT to attend in plain clothes.

Which of the following statements is correct, as to whether the detective sergeant can lawfully make the decision that KENT is to attend the premises in plain clothes?

A Yes, a police officer can direct an accredited employee not to wear a uniform for the purposes of a particular operation.

B No, only an inspector, or an officer above that rank, can direct an accredited employee not to wear a uniform for the purposes of a particular operation.

C Yes, an accredited employee's direct line manager can direct him/her not to wear a uniform for the purposes of a particular operation.

D Requiring investigating officers to wear uniform is simply force policy and KENT may make the decision to wear plain clothes for any operational reason.

Question 1.13

WALTERS is an accredited employee who works closely with the Neighbourhood Policing Team in an out-of-town shopping centre. WALTERS is employed by one of the larger stores in the centre, as part of a CSAS agreed between the police, the local authority and WALTERS's employers. Sergeant POWELL has received a complaint from a store manager that WALTERS has regularly been seen socialising with people suspected of committing a number of shoplifting offences in the centre. Sergeant POWELL has submitted a report asking for WALTERS's accreditation to be withdrawn.

What process must take place before WALTERS's accreditation may be withdrawn in these circumstances?

A The chief officer of police may withdraw the accreditation, simply by issuing a written notice to WALTERS.

B A meeting must be held between the police and WALTERS's employers and a joint decision must be reached to withdraw the accreditation.

C A meeting must be held between the police and WALTERS's employers, but the final decision to withdraw the accreditation rests with the police.

D A meeting must be held between the police, WALTERS's employers and the local authority, but the final decision to withdraw the accreditation rests with the police.

Question 1.14

SAGNER works in the administration department of an international haulage company based in the United Kingdom. SAGNER has discovered that some of the drivers working for the company are engaged in people trafficking whilst driving on the continent. SAGNER has no evidence that any of the people are being trafficked into, or out of, the United Kingdom, but believes they engage in this activity between other European countries. SAGNER has considered reporting this to the company's management, but believes they may be aware of the activity and would turn a blind eye. SAGNER is considering disclosing this information to someone else.

Which of the following information is correct, in relation to 'protected disclosures', under the Public Interest Disclosure Act 1998?

A A 'protected disclosure' must be made to an employer, as the Act emphasises disclosures of an internal nature.

B A 'protected disclosure' must be made to an employer, or some other body nominated by the Secretary of State.

C This information would not amount to a 'protected disclosure', because it relates to possible criminal activity outside the United Kingdom.

D A 'protected disclosure' should be made to an employer, or some other body nominated by the Secretary of State, but in some cases may be made to another person.

Question 1.15

Constable JOHNSTON was Constable BRIAR's tutor; they were on patrol when Constable JOHNSTON arrested MILES, who was suspected of committing a burglary. When they returned to the station, Constable JOHNSTON persuaded Constable BRIAR to claim credit for the arrest, because it would look good in her probationary report. Both officers submitted statements identifying Constable BRIAR as the arresting officer. MILES was later charged with the offence and bailed to appear in court a week later. The day following the arrest, Constable BRIAR had second thoughts about her statement and was considering reporting the matter to the Professional Standards Department.

If Constable BRIAR were to disclose this information to the Professional Standards Department, would this amount to a 'protected disclosure' under the Public Interest Disclosure Act 1998?

A No, a miscarriage of justice has not yet occurred; therefore, the Act does not apply.

B Yes, because Constable BRIAR is making a disclosure about a serious criminal offence.

C Yes, provided the behaviour amounts to more than a mere disciplinary offence; Police Conduct matters are not covered by the Act.

D Yes, the Act applies to any wrongdoing by another individual.

ANSWERS

Answer 1.1

Answer **A** — Section 107(1) of the Police and Criminal Evidence Act 1984 sets out occasions when an officer of a lower rank can perform the functions required by a higher rank in respect of the investigation of offences or the treatment of persons in police custody. Where a power is exercisable only by or with the authority of a police officer of at least the rank of superintendent, an officer of the rank of chief inspector shall be treated as holding the rank of superintendent if:

(a) he has been authorised by an officer holding a rank above the rank of superintendent to exercise the power or, as the case may be, to give his authority for its exercise, or
(b) he is acting during the absence of an officer holding the rank of superintendent who has authorised him, for the duration of that absence, to exercise the power or, as the case may be, to give his authority for its exercise.

In these circumstances, the chief inspector may be authorised by her own superintendent, whom she is acting up for (s. 107(1)(b)). Answer B is therefore incorrect.

There are occasions when a chief superintendent may make such an authorisation, but these decisions are more likely to be taken in spontaneous circumstances, when a review is required and no other superintendent is available. Answer C is therefore incorrect.

There is no 'probationary' period for the chief inspector who needs to be authorised and answer D is incorrect.

General Police Duties, para. 4.1.2

Answer 1.2

Answer **D** — The Police and Criminal Evidence Act 1984 requires officers of certain ranks to perform roles. The 1984 Act recognises that there may be occasions when officers of the appropriate rank are not readily available and so in limited circumstances allows officers of a lower rank to perform their roles.

Under s. 107 of the Act, chief inspectors who are to perform the PACE duties of a superintendent must be authorised by a superintendent; likewise, a sergeant 'acting up' to inspector may only conduct PACE reviews if they are authorised by a superintendent. However, this prior authorisation is not required for a constable who is to perform custody officer duties (although it is sensible for this to be overseen by an inspector). Answers A and B are incorrect.

Section 36(3) of PACE states that no officer may be appointed as a custody officer unless he/she is of at least the rank of sergeant, but this section refers to the requirement for a chief constable to 'appoint' sufficient custody officers for his/her force area (to avoid the position of having no custody officers available).

Section 36(4) states that an officer of any rank may perform the functions of a custody officer at a designated police station, if a custody officer is not readily available to perform them. Answer C is therefore incorrect.

Note that in *Vince* v *Chief Constable of Dorset Police* [1993] 1 WLR 415, it was made clear that s. 36(4) should only be an exception and that it was not intended that chief constables would be entitled to arrange matters so that as a matter of routine officers below the rank of sergeant performed the functions of custody officers.

General Police Duties, para. 4.1.2

Answer 1.3

Answer **A** — The Police Regulations 2003 set out the required notice period for part-time workers who wish to return to full-time duties. Part-time officers may give notice in writing of their intention to be reappointed as a full-time member and will be appointed within:

- two months of the date the notice is received by the force, where there is a suitable vacancy; or
- when four months have elapsed since the day the notice was received; or
- from an earlier date if reasonably practicable.

The Police (Amendment No. 4) Regulations 2012 extended these timescales in response to proposals contained in the Winsor Review (from one month to two months and three months to four months). Therefore, the normal time period for officers returning to full-time duties would be two months; if there is no suitable vacancy, this may be extended to four months. However, the force may allow such a change in duties from an earlier date if it is considered reasonably practicable to do so. Answers B, C and D are therefore incorrect.

General Police Duties, para. 4.1.4

Answer 1.4

Answer **D** — Section 64(1) of the Police Act 1996 states:

> Subject to the following provisions of this section, a member of a police force shall not be a member of any trade union, or of any association having for its objects, or one of

its objects, to control or influence the pay, pensions or conditions of service of any police force.

However, where a person was a member of a trade union before becoming a member of a police service, he/she may, with the consent of the chief officer of police, continue to be a member of that union during the time of his/her service (s. 64(2)). Answers A and B are therefore incorrect.

There is no mention in the regulations of having to choose between being a member of a trade union or the Police Federation. Membership of the Police Federation is not compulsory and a person may be a member of both provided s. 64(2) applies.

Answer C is therefore incorrect.

General Police Duties, para. 4.1.8

Answer 1.5

Answer **A** — The terms under which special constables may be appointed and deployed are set out in s. 30 of the Police Act 1996. Previously, special constables would only have powers and privileges in their own areas or adjoining police areas, unless they were used in mutual aid schemes, when they would enjoy the powers of a special constable in the area in which they were providing mutual aid.

However, the Police and Justice Act 2006 introduced significant amendments: para. 21 of sch. 2 allows special constables to use their constabulary powers in forces throughout England and Wales, regardless of the duties they are performing. Answers B, C and D are therefore incorrect.

General Police Duties, para. 4.1.9

Answer 1.6

Answer **B** — Under Pt 4 of the Police Reform Act 2002, chief officers of police are given the authority to confer policing powers on non-police officers, such as police community support officers, investigating officers, detention officers and escort officers. Part 4 allows the relevant chief officer to confer certain powers on different groups of people by designating or accrediting them.

The chief officer does not *have to* confer any powers on any such groups and he/she can decide to confer only a reduced number of powers or to place further limitations on those powers: the Act simply gives the chief officer the freedom and flexibility to do so. Answers A, C and D are therefore incorrect.

General Police Duties, para. 4.1.10

Answer 1.7

Answer **C** — Under Part 4 of the Police Reform Act 2002, people may be 'accredited' as part of a Community Safety Accreditation Scheme (CSAS). In order to perform *any* of the roles and exercise *any* of the powers under Part 4 of the Act, an individual must be employed by somebody, because it is through the person's employer that the chief officer or the relevant constable can exercise a degree of control over those auxiliary staff who are not directly employed by the police.

Therefore, if you are unemployed or self-employed, the legislation will not allow you to have these powers or to carry out any of the relevant functions.

Answers A, B and D are therefore incorrect.

General Police Duties, para. 4.1.11

Answer 1.8

Answer **D** — Where designated staff are employees of the relevant force, the chief officer is responsible for dealing with reports of misconduct and complaints against them in the normal way.

The Independent Police Complaints Commission (IPCC) *also* has jurisdiction over any allegations or complaints made against designated staff who are employees of the relevant force. Answer A is therefore incorrect.

This is regardless of whether the allegation is of a criminal nature, or refers purely to a misconduct matter, and there is no requirement for the allegation to be made jointly against a police officer. Answers B and C are therefore incorrect.

General Police Duties, para. 4.1.13

Answer 1.9

Answer **B** — Where a penalty notice is given to a person under the age of 16, the relevant chief officer of police must notify such parent or guardian as he/she thinks fit (Penalties for Disorderly Behaviour (Amendment of Minimum Age) Order 2004 (SI 2004/3166)). Any such notification must be in writing and must include a copy of the penalty notice and may be served *either* by giving it to the parent or guardian personally *or* by sending it to the parent or guardian at his/her usual or last-known address by first-class post before the end of the period of 28 days beginning with the date on which the penalty notice was given (see Art. 3 of the 2004 Order). Since the defendant's mother is present, a copy of the notice should be given to her there and then, and sent to her home address. Answer D is incorrect.

The notice is issued to the person who committed the offence, not the parent, therefore answer C is incorrect.

Finally, a Disorder Penalty Notice may be issued to a person who is under 16, regardless of whether an adult is present; the adult is simply notified of the issue, using the procedure described earlier. Answer A is therefore incorrect.

General Police Duties, para. 4.1.15.1

Answer 1.10

Answer **D** — Under s. 39 of the Police Reform Act 2002, a chief officer of police may enter into a contract with a private company for the provision of services relating to the detention or escorting of people in custody. This allows the chief officer to designate employees of the contractor as either detention officers or escort officers or both.

Although their employee status is the source of control over these employees' activities and performance, the first thing to note is that they are *not* employed by the police force. These contracted-out personnel cannot be given the powers of PCSOs and investigating officers as they are not police employees, but they are given the same powers as police officers to conduct certain functions, such as searching, fingerprinting and photographing.

Because they are neither police officers nor members of police staff, designated employees are not covered by the Police (Performance) Regulations 2012, the Police (Conduct) Regulations 2012 or any other performance regulations relating to police staff employees. Answers A, B and C are therefore incorrect.

Although s. 39 of the Act allows the Secretary of State to make regulations regarding the handling of complaints and misconduct issues arising out of the functions of designated employees, the practical answer to this question is that the police force involved may withdraw BECK's designation by giving the employee notice and asking for his/her services to be withdrawn (s. 42(3)). This power of revocation or amendment is absolute and there is no requirement for any misconduct or poor performance on the part of the employee.

General Police Duties, para. 4.1.16

Answer 1.11

Answer **C** — Under s. 40(9) of the Police Reform Act 2002, it will be the duty of a chief officer of police who establishes and maintains a CSAS to ensure that the employers of the persons on whom powers are conferred by the grant of accreditations under s. 41 have established and maintain satisfactory arrangements for handling complaints relating to the carrying out by those persons of the functions for the purposes of which the powers are conferred.

Therefore, the chief officer of police has responsibility to ensure that VAUGHAN's *employers* have satisfactory arrangements for handling complaints. This implies that the employers actually have responsibility for dealing with the complaint.

Answers A, B and D are therefore incorrect.

General Police Duties, para. 4.1.18

Answer 1.12

Answer **B** — Under the Police Reform Act 2002, designated or accredited employees' powers are only exercisable if the employee is wearing the relevant uniform as determined or approved by the chief officer and identified or described in the designation/accreditation (s. 42(2)). However, given the nature of some investigative functions carried out by investigating officers, they may work in plain clothes for the purposes of a particular operation without any impact on their powers (s. 42(2A)).

An investigating officer who generally works in uniform may only work in plain clothes when directed to do so by a police officer of or above the rank of *inspector*. Answers A and C are therefore incorrect.

If such a direction is given, conditions mentioned in s. 42(2) will not apply in relation to *that* investigating officer for the purposes of *that* operation. This means that not only is KENT not allowed to make the decision not to wear uniform, the direction may only be given on a case-by-case basis and given that this is a legislative requirement, answer D is incorrect.

(Note that the officer giving this direction not to wear uniform must be from the same force as the chief officer who appointed the investigating officer.)

General Police Duties, para. 4.1.19

Answer 1.13

Answer **A** — Section 42(3) allows an accredited employee's designation or accreditation to be withdrawn at any time by a chief officer of police.

There is no requirement to consult with the local authority, or the person's employer; therefore, answers B, C and D are incorrect.

General Police Duties, para. 4.1.19

Answer 1.14

Answer **D** — The Public Interest Disclosure Act 1998 refers to 'protected disclosures', which are generally disclosures made in accordance with the Act of information which, in the reasonable belief of the maker, generally tend to show criminal conduct, or environmental or health and safety breaches.

Because the Act is intended to protect disclosures of an internal nature, the person would normally be expected to report information to an employer. However, in some areas of employment, the Secretary of State has made regulations prescribing those people and bodies to whom some disclosures *can* be made where appropriate (e.g. the Independent Police Complaints Commission (IPCC) or the Inland Revenue, the Charity Commissioners and the Health and Safety Executive).

The Act does not state that it is mandatory to make disclosures to an employer or a body nominated by the Secretary of State; in fact disclosures may be made to other persons, if:

- the employee reasonably believes that he/she will be subjected to a detriment by the employer if the disclosure is made; or
- there is no relevant or prescribed person and the employee reasonably believes that it is likely that evidence relating to the failure will be concealed or destroyed if a disclosure is made; or
- the employee has previously made a disclosure of substantially the same information to the employer or prescribed person.

Answers A and B are therefore incorrect.

Finally, it is immaterial that the relevant behaviour reported occurs or would occur outside the United Kingdom. Answer C is therefore incorrect.

General Police Duties, paras 4.1.21, 4.1.22

Answer 1.15

Answer **C** — The Public Interest Disclosure Act 1998 refers to 'protected disclosures', which are generally disclosures made in accordance with the Act of information which, in the reasonable belief of the maker, tend to show one or more of the following:

- a criminal offence has been committed, is being committed or is likely to be committed;
- a person has failed, is failing or is likely to fail to comply with any legal obligation to which he is subject;

- a miscarriage of justice has occurred, is occurring or is likely to occur;
- the health or safety of any individual has been, is being or is likely to be endangered;
- the environment has been, is being or is likely to be damaged;
- information tending to show any matter falling within any one of the preceding paragraphs has been, is being or is likely to be deliberately concealed.

'Protected disclosures' are not specifically restricted to serious criminal offences (answer B is incorrect).

On the other hand, the Act does not generally apply to 'any wrongdoing by an individual' (and does not generally cover disciplinary offences, unless the behaviour would point to one of the matters listed). Answer D is therefore incorrect.

Finally, the behaviour of the officers *may* amount to an act of perjury, especially if their statements are submitted as evidence in court. Disclosures under the Act are covered where a criminal offence *has been committed, is being committed or is likely to be committed* or where a *miscarriage of justice has occurred, is occurring or is likely to occur.* Therefore, although a criminal offence may not yet have been committed, a disclosure in these circumstances would still be covered (answer A is therefore incorrect).

General Police Duties, para. 4.1.22

2 Complaints and Misconduct

STUDY PREPARATION

Although the concept of police misconduct may seem an unpalatable subject at the start of your course of study, the maintenance of proper professional standards is paramount to all police officers, supervisors and managers—and the communities they serve.

The Police (Conduct) Regulations 2012 set out the procedures for dealing with cases of misconduct or gross misconduct. The conduct procedures are supported by the Standards of Professional Behaviour—which provide the yardstick by which the conduct of police officers is to be judged.

The chapter guides you through the misconduct procedures, including the effect on individual officers and line managers, and misconduct meetings, tribunals, appeals and suspension from duties.

The Independent Police Complaints Commission (IPCC) has an oversight role in complaints against police officers, whether by supervising, managing or independently investigating a matter.

QUESTIONS

Question 2.1

Assistant Chief Constable MOREL was on suspension from duty, having been accused of a criminal offence under s. 2 of the Computer Misuse Act 1990. The officer was being investigated for accessing and using confidential information from a police computer system. Whilst on suspension, Assistant Chief Constable MOREL gave an interview to a national newspaper, claiming to be innocent and that he was being harassed by the force investigating the incident.

Could Assistant Chief Constable MOREL have breached the Standards of Professional Behaviour, under the Police (Conduct) Regulations 2012 (Discreditable Conduct), by giving the interview to the press?

A No, the Regulations only apply to police officers up to and including the rank of Chief Superintendent.

B Yes, the Regulations apply to all police officers, up to and including the rank of Assistant Chief Constable.

C No, the Regulations do not apply to police officers who are suspended, regardless of their rank.

D Yes, the Regulations apply to all police officers, whether they are suspended or not.

Question 2.2

Constable GOULDING is in police detention for providing a positive breath test, having been involved in a fail to stop road traffic collision whilst off duty. The officer in the case intends interviewing Constable GOULDING, who is represented by the duty solicitor.

Is Constable GOULDING also entitled to have a police 'friend' present at the interview, in these circumstances?

A No, a police 'friend' may not be present at an interview in connection with a criminal offence which was committed off duty.

B Yes, Constable GOULDING would be entitled to have a police 'friend' present at the interview, as well as the solicitor.

C No, a police 'friend' may not be present at an interview in connection with a criminal offence.

D No, a police 'friend' may not be present at an interview in connection with a criminal offence, committed whilst off duty, when the offence is not connected to the person's role as a police officer.

Question 2.3

Constable KEMP has been charged with causing the death of a pedestrian by dangerous driving—the officer was pursuing a stolen vehicle at the time of the incident and was not trained to do so. The Independent Police Complaints Commission (IPCC) has decided to independently investigate the incident. Constable KEMP's force (the appropriate authority) is considering whether or not the officer should be suspended from duty.

Which of the following statements is correct, as to the role the IPCC should play in the decision as to whether Constable KEMP should be suspended?

A If the IPCC is independently investigating a matter, it has decision-making powers as to whether police officers should be suspended.

B If it is independently investigating a matter, the appropriate authority should consult with the IPCC, but the decision rests with the force.

C If it is supervising, managing or independently investigating a matter, the appropriate authority should consult with the IPCC, but the decision rests with the force.

D If the IPCC is supervising, managing or independently investigating a matter, it has decision-making powers as to whether police officers should be suspended.

Question 2.4

Constable MURPHY is being investigated for a misconduct matter, but is currently on certificated sick leave, having had a back operation. The officer is not expected to return to work for several months, however, the investigating officer is keen to progress the complaint as soon as possible and wishes to interview Constable MURPHY. The officer's Police Federation representative has emailed the investigating officer, claiming it would be unfair to conduct an interview while the member is on sick leave.

Which of the following is correct, in relation to whether an interview could be conducted while Constable MURPHY is on sick leave?

A Constable MURPHY may be interviewed or alternatively, the investigating officer may send questions to the officer, requesting a written response.

B Police officers may be interviewed while on certified sick leave, if the allegation against them is considered to be serious enough.

C Police officers may not be interviewed while on certified sick leave; this would amount to a breach of the Conduct Regulations.

D Constable MURPHY may be interviewed while on certified sick leave, but the interview must be conducted in person.

Question 2.5

Sergeant VAUGHAN has been asked to attend a misconduct meeting, following a Professional Standards Department (PSD) investigation into a complaint from a member of the public. The allegation was that Sergeant VAUGHAN swore at the complainant, who was reporting an incident at the station. Sergeant VAUGHAN intends denying the incident and has asked for the Station Enquiry Clerk (SEC), who was present during the incident, to attend the meeting as a witness. The investigating officer, on the other hand, has identified an independent member of the public, who was present at the time, and who is prepared to attend as a witness.

Which of the following statements is correct, in respect of witnesses attending misconduct meetings?

A Because Sergeant VAUGHAN has asked for a witness to attend, the person conducting the meeting must ask the SEC to attend.

B The person conducting the meeting is only entitled to ask the independent witness identified by the PSD to attend.

C The person conducting the meeting will decide if witnesses are required, depending on whether or not their attendance is necessary to resolve disputed issues in the case.

D Neither person should be asked to attend; witnesses are only allowed to give evidence in misconduct hearings.

Question 2.6

Constable WOODS is attending a misconduct hearing, having been accused of passing information to a member of the public, which was stored on the force intelligence system. The officer is accused of breaching the 'Confidentiality' standard included in the ten Standards of Professional Behaviour.

Which of the following is correct, in relation to who should hear the misconduct matter, in these circumstances?

A It should be heard by a panel, which may be chaired by a senior police officer.

B It should be heard by a panel, which must be chaired by a legally qualified person.

C It should be heard by a panel, which may be chaired either by a legally qualified person, or a senior human resources professional with sufficient seniority.

D It should be heard by a panel, which may be chaired either by a senior police officer, or a senior human resources professional with sufficient seniority.

Question 2.7

The Independent Police Complaints Commission (IPCC) has conducted an independent investigation into an allegation of misconduct against Constable ATKINS and the officer has been given notification to attend a misconduct hearing. Constable ATKINS has attended a meeting with a Police Federation representative and has been told that consideration is being given to holding the hearing in public. The officer is concerned about this development and has asked about the criteria to conduct the hearing in this way.

Which of the following statements is correct in relation to this issue?

A The hearing may be held in public if the chief officer of police considers it is in the public interest to do so.

B The hearing may be held in public if the appropriate authority considers it is in the public interest to do so.

C The hearing may be held in public if the IPCC considers it is in the public interest to do so.

D The hearing may be held in public if the IPCC considers it is in the public interest to do so; however, Constable ATKINS will be consulted beforehand.

Question 2.8

Constable DAWSON is attending a misconduct meeting, having been accused of being abusive towards the complainant, FROST, during a routine road traffic check. FROST has been asked by the officer conducting the meeting to attend to give evidence of Constable DAWSON's behaviour.

Which of the following statements is correct in respect of FROST's attendance at the meeting?

A FROST must leave the meeting immediately after giving evidence.

B Because this is a misconduct meeting and not a hearing, FROST may remain for the entire proceedings.

C FROST must leave the meeting once the officer conducting it has made a finding.

D FROST may remain at the meeting after giving evidence, but must leave after any character reference/mitigation is given, before the outcome is decided.

Question 2.9

Constable FARRELL has been found guilty of theft and has been sentenced by the court to six months' imprisonment. Constable FARRELL has appealed against the conviction and sentence and has informed the police service of this fact.

Are the circumstances sufficient for the appropriate authority to certify that this is a 'special case' and fast track the misconduct procedures against Constable FARRELL?

A No, they should wait for the outcome of Constable FARRELL's appeal before making this decision.
B Yes, if there is sufficient documentary evidence available to prove the case, and it is in the public interest to dismiss Constable FARRELL without delay.
C Yes, they can proceed with the procedure simply because Constable FARRELL has been convicted of a criminal offence.
D Yes, if there is sufficient oral evidence available to prove the case, and it is in the public interest to dismiss Constable FARRELL.

Question 2.10

Assistant Chief Constable WALL has attended a misconduct meeting with the Deputy Chief Constable. ACC WALL was given a written warning at the meeting and is now seeking legal advice about making an appeal against the finding to a Police Appeals Tribunal.

Is ACC WALL entitled to make such an appeal in these circumstances?
A No, the Police Appeals Tribunal does not hear appeals against the findings or outcomes of a misconduct meeting.
B Yes, an appeal may be made to a Police Appeals Tribunal against any misconduct finding.
C Yes, an appeal may be made by an Assistant Chief Constable against the finding or outcome of a misconduct meeting.
D No, the Police Appeals Tribunal only hears appeals against the findings or outcomes of a special case hearing for gross misconduct.

ANSWERS

Answer 2.1

Answer **D** — The Police (Conduct) Regulations 2012 are supported by a code of ethics—the Standards of Professional Behaviour. The Standards apply to police officers of *all* ranks from chief constable to constable (including special constables). Answers A and B are therefore incorrect. (If you answered A to this question, you may have been confused by the Police (Performance) Regulations 2012, which only apply to police officers (including special constables) up to and including the rank of chief superintendent.)

The Standards of Professional Behaviour do apply to police officers who are subject to suspension; therefore answer C is incorrect.

General Police Duties, para. 4.2.1

Answer 2.2

Answer **D** — A police officer has a right to be accompanied by a police 'friend' at all stages of any misconduct proceedings (under the Police (Conduct) Regulations 2012). This includes interviews, misconduct meetings and hearings.

A police officer is also entitled, in certain circumstances, to be accompanied by a police 'friend' at an interview in connection with a criminal offence. Therefore, answer C is incorrect.

However, the circumstances in which a police officer is entitled to be accompanied by a police 'friend' at an interview in connection with a criminal offence are very narrow. If the officer is arrested or interviewed in connection with a criminal offence committed whilst off duty *that has no connection with his/her role as a serving police officer*, then the police 'friend' has no right to attend the criminal interview of that police officer. Answers A and B are incorrect for this reason.

General Police Duties, para. 4.2.3

Answer 2.3

Answer **C** — In cases where the IPCC is supervising, managing or independently investigating a matter, the appropriate authority will consult with the IPCC before making a decision whether to suspend or not. Answer B is incorrect, as this requirement applies whether the IPCC is supervising, managing or independently investigating a matter.

However, whatever the role the IPCC plays in the investigation, it is the appropriate authority's decision whether to suspend a police officer or not. Answers A and D are therefore incorrect.

Note that the appropriate authority must also consult the IPCC before making the decision to allow a police officer to resume his/her duties following suspension (unless the suspension ends because there will be no misconduct or special case proceedings or because these have concluded) in cases where the IPCC is supervising, managing or independently investigating a case involving that police officer.

General Police Duties, para. 4.2.5.1

Answer 2.4

Answer **A** — Where a police officer is on certificated sick leave, the investigator should seek to establish when the police officer will be fit for interview. It may be that the police officer is not fit for ordinary police duty but is perfectly capable of being interviewed. This is regardless of how serious the allegation is and answers B and C are incorrect.

Alternatively the police officer concerned *may* be invited to provide a written response to the allegations within a specified period and *may* be sent the questions that the investigator wishes to be answered. Answer D is therefore incorrect.

General Police Duties, para. 4.2.5.5

Answer 2.5

Answer **C** — Generally speaking, misconduct meetings and hearings will be conducted without witnesses. A witness *may* be required to attend a misconduct meeting or hearing if the person conducting or chairing the meeting/hearing reasonably believes his/her attendance is necessary to resolve disputed issues in that case. Answer D is incorrect, as witnesses *may* be asked to attend meetings *or* hearings.

The officer concerned *may* ask for witnesses to attend; however, it will be for the person conducting the meeting or hearing to decide whether to allow such witnesses, if their attendance is necessary to resolve any disputed issues in the case. On the other hand, the person conducting the meeting or hearing may decide not to have any witnesses at the meeting/hearing. Answers A and B are incorrect, because either witness could have been asked to attend, but the decision will be made by the person conducting the meeting or hearing.

General Police Duties, para. 4.2.5.9

Answer 2.6

Answer **B** — A misconduct *meeting* for non-senior officers (police officers up to and including the rank of chief superintendent and all special constables) will be heard by a police officer (or other member of a police force) of at least one rank above the police officer concerned.

However, the officer in this case has been invited to a misconduct *hearing*. A misconduct hearing for non-senior officers will consist of a three-person panel. The chair will always be a *legally qualified person* from 1 January 2016.

Answers A, C and D are therefore incorrect.

General Police Duties, para. 4.2.6.3

Answer 2.7

Answer **D** — Where a misconduct hearing (not misconduct meetings) arises from a case where the IPCC has conducted an independent investigation (in accordance with para. 19 of sch. 3 to the 2002 Act) and the IPCC considers that because of its gravity or other exceptional circumstances it would be in the public interest to do so, the IPCC may, having consulted with the appropriate authority, the police officer concerned, the complainant and any witnesses, direct that the whole or part of the misconduct hearing will be held in public.

Since the decision rests with the IPCC and the officer will be consulted, answers A, B and C are incorrect.

Note that in November 2014 the Home Secretary launched a consultation on increased transparency via a far greater number of cases potentially being held in public. The intention is that misconduct hearings for higher level cases that could lead to dismissal will be public by default. This includes both misconduct hearings and special case hearings but does not include lower level misconduct meetings.

General Police Duties, para. 4.2.6.4

Answer 2.8

Answer **C** — A complainant and any person accompanying the complainant will be permitted to remain in the meeting/hearing up to and including any finding by the persons conducting the meeting/hearing, after having given evidence (if appropriate). Answers A and B are therefore incorrect.

However, the complainant and any person accompanying the complainant will *not* be permitted to remain in the meeting/hearing while character references or mitigation are being given or the decision of the panel as to the outcome is being given. Answer D is incorrect, as the person must leave *before* the character reference or mitigation is given (which will also be before the outcome is given).

Note that the appropriate authority will have a duty to inform the complainant of the outcome of any misconduct meeting/hearing whether the complainant attends or not.

General Police Duties, para. 4.2.6.13

Answer 2.9

Answer **B** — The operation of the fast track misconduct procedures, referred to as 'special cases', are set out in Pt 5 of the Conduct Regulations. The special case procedures can only be used if the appropriate authority certifies the case as a special case, having determined that the 'special conditions' are satisfied or if the IPCC has given a direction under para. 20H(7) of sch. 3 to the Police Reform Act 2002.

The 'special conditions' are that there is sufficient evidence, in the form of written statements or other documents, *without the need for further evidence*, whether written or oral, to establish on the balance of probabilities, that the conduct of the police officer concerned constitutes gross misconduct, and it is in the public interest for the police officer concerned to cease to be a police officer without delay. Answer D is incorrect, as the hearing may proceed without oral evidence—in fact, the only oral evidence given at such a hearing will be from the police officer concerned (and the hearing may be heard in the officer's absence if necessary).

There is no requirement to wait for the outcome of the officer's appeal. The panel will merely need to decide, on the balance of probabilities, if it is in the public interest to dismiss the officer. Answer A is therefore incorrect.

A person's conviction for a criminal offence will not automatically provide sufficient grounds for the appropriate authority to certify that this is a 'special case' and fast track misconduct procedures. However, such evidence would certainly be relevant. Answer C is therefore incorrect.

General Police Duties, para. 4.2.8

Answer 2.10

Answer **C** — A police officer has a right of appeal to a Police Appeals Tribunal against any disciplinary finding and/or disciplinary outcome imposed at a misconduct hearing or special case hearing held under the Conduct Regulations. Senior police officers (Assistant Chief Constables and above), in addition, have the right to appeal to a

Police Appeals Tribunal against any disciplinary finding and/or outcome imposed at a misconduct meeting. Since a Police Appeals Tribunal *may* hear an appeal in relation to a finding at a misconduct meeting, answer A is incorrect.

However, since this right is restricted to senior police officers, answer B is incorrect.

Answer D is incorrect because appeals can be made against findings in misconduct hearings *or* special case hearings (or meetings in the case of an ACC).

General Police Duties, para. 4.2.9

3 Unsatisfactory Performance and Attendance

STUDY PREPARATION

The previous chapter dealt with the Police (Conduct) Regulations 2012. In this chapter, we examine the Police (Performance) Regulations 2012.

These Regulations cover both performance and absence management, and the chapter guides you through the procedures for dealing with both aspects of the regulations.

The catalyst for changing these Regulations, initially in 2008, was the Taylor Review. The review recommended simplifying processes, with the emphasis on improving poor performance and attendance, instead of punishing individuals. As a line manager, you will find that the aspects of misconduct and performance are closely related.

The final part of this chapter deals with the offences that can be committed by people in public offices, including police officers, who abuse their powers.

QUESTIONS

Question 3.1

Sergeant GREEGAN is due to hold a first stage unsatisfactory performance (UPP) meeting with Constable O'NEIL in an hour's time, regarding the continued submission of poor paperwork. Sergeant GREEGAN has also been concerned with Constable O'NEIL's poor timekeeping and has recently had to warn the officer several times for arriving at work late. Sergeant GREEGAN is considering discussing the additional matter at the first stage meeting, alongside the original unsatisfactory performance matter.

How should Sergeant GREEGAN proceed in these circumstances?

A The planned meeting should continue and a separate first stage meeting should be arranged to discuss the additional matter. Unconnected UPP matters must always be dealt with separately.

B Sergeant GREEGAN may adjourn the planned meeting and arrange a first stage meeting at a later date to discuss both matters.

C Sergeant GREEGAN may discuss both matters at the planned meeting, because new information has come to light about Constable O'NEIL's performance during the specified period.

D The planned meeting should continue and a separate first stage meeting should be arranged to discuss the additional matter. Matters may only be consolidated if a person reaches stage three of the UPP procedures.

Question 3.2

Sergeant GANT has arranged a first stage unsatisfactory performance (UPP) meeting with Constable RUSH to discuss the officer's poor attendance record. Sergeant GANT intends issuing the officer with an improvement notice, seeking an improvement in the officer's attendance at work. Sergeant GANT is newly promoted and wishes to seek advice on how to conduct the meeting and the possible outcomes.

Which of the following statements is correct, in relation to the advice Sergeant GANT may seek?

A Sergeant GANT may ask a Human Resources (HR) professional to be present, or a police officer with relevant experience, who is independent of the line management chain.

B Sergeant GANT may seek advice from an HR professional, or a police officer with relevant experience, before the meeting, but they may not be present.

C Because the meeting is to do with attendance and not performance, Sergeant GANT must have an HR professional present.

D Sergeant GANT may ask an HR professional to be present, or a police officer who is part of the line management chain, provided the officer is not the second line manager.

Question 3.3

Constable DALE attended an unsatisfactory performance (UPP) meeting with her line manager, Sergeant MALIK. The officer had previously been given a written improvement notice at a first stage meeting, relating to her paperwork submission, and was subject to a three-month action plan. Sergeant MALIK considered that her performance had not improved in that period. At the meeting, Constable DALE asked her sergeant if there was any way her action plan could be extended, rather than proceeding to the next stage.

Would Sergeant MALIK be in a position to agree to the request to extend the improvement period?

A Yes, for up to three months, unless there are exceptional reasons for extending the period beyond six months in total.

B Yes, for up to six months, unless there are exceptional reasons for extending the period beyond nine months in total.

C Yes, for up to nine months, but the period must not exceed 12 months in total.

D Yes, for up to nine months, unless there are exceptional reasons for extending the period beyond 12 months in total.

Question 3.4

Constable POUNDS has been subject to a three-month action plan for poor attendance, following the issue of an improvement notice at a first stage unsatisfactory performance (UPP) meeting. Constable POUNDS has not reported sick during this period and is now meeting Sergeant HALES to discuss the next steps. Sergeant HALES has informed the officer he needs to maintain attendance during the 'validity period' now that the current action plan has been achieved.

Which of the following statements is correct, in relation to the 'validity period' during which Constable POUNDS has to maintain attendance?

A Constable POUNDS has to maintain attendance for another three months to avoid moving to the next stage.

B Constable POUNDS has to maintain attendance for another six months to avoid moving to the next stage.

C Constable POUNDS has to maintain attendance for another nine months to avoid moving to the next stage.

D Constable POUNDS has to maintain attendance for another 12 months to avoid moving to the next stage.

Question 3.5

Detective Sergeant OPIE is under investigation for failing to investigate a suspicious sudden death correctly. The officer was called to the scene and missed several basic investigative opportunities which, had they been recognised at the time, would have led the police to conclude that the deceased had been murdered. During the inquiry, the Professional Standards Department (PSD) interviewed Detective Sergeant OPIE's line manager, Detective Inspector PURDY, who disclosed that she had been gathering negative evidence relating to the officer's performance and attendance, with a view to placing Detective Sergeant OPIE on an action plan. The investigating officer concluded that Detective Sergeant OPIE's investigation of the sudden death was 'grossly incompetent'.

The Police (Performance) Regulations 2012 allow for procedures to be initiated immediately at the third stage, when an officer is deemed to be 'grossly incompetent'. In respect of these Regulations, which of the following statements is correct?

A The appropriate authority may take into account the current investigative failures, as well as any other similar, recent performance matters, when deciding whether or not procedures should be initiated immediately at the third stage.

B The appropriate authority may only initiate procedures at the third stage immediately in respect of a single incident, which could include the investigative failures at the sudden death.

C The appropriate authority may take into account the current investigative failures, as well as any other recent performance or attendance matters, when deciding whether or not procedures should be initiated immediately at the third stage.

D The appropriate authority should take into account the current investigative failures, any recent performance matters and any other acts over a period of time, when deciding whether or not procedures should be initiated immediately at the third stage.

Question 3.6

A meeting is being held between Inspector HATTORI and JENNINGS, a human resources adviser, regarding the performance of Special Constable ANDERSON who works on the inspector's team. Special Constable ANDERSON is currently at the second stage of the unsatisfactory performance procedures (UPP) and has recently failed an action plan. Inspector HATTORI is seeking advice on what should happen next and whether it is appropriate for the officer to progress to the third stage of the procedures.

Which of the following statements is correct in relation to special constables and third stage meetings?

A Because special constables are unpaid volunteers, it is inappropriate for Special Constable ANDERSON to attend a third stage meeting.

B Special Constable ANDERSON may be required to attend a third stage meeting, but a senior special constable will be appointed to attend the meeting to advise her.

C Special Constable ANDERSON may be required to attend a third stage meeting, but a senior special constable will be appointed to attend the meeting to advise the panel.

D Special Constable ANDERSON may be required to attend a third stage meeting, but a senior special constable will be appointed to attend the meeting to form part of the panel.

Question 3.7

Constable PARKER has been on sick leave for 11 months having suffered a broken leg playing football. The officer has had two operations and is still unfit to return to work. Constable PARKER is currently at the second stage of the unsatisfactory performance (UPP) procedures and has failed an action plan which required him to return to work. Consideration is being given to serving Constable PARKER with a notice to attend a stage three meeting; however, the officer's Police Federation representative has stated that he is unfit for duty, which renders him unable to attend a meeting, quoting the provisions of reg. 33 of the Police Regulations 2003 (sick leave).

What impact does Constable PARKER's injury have on the panel being able to require him to attend the meeting?

A The Regulations do not apply; Constable PARKER may be unfit for duty, but he must attend the meeting.

B The Regulations will apply; when a constable is unfit for duty, he/she will also be unfit to attend a meeting.

C When an officer is incapacitated, the meeting must be deferred until he/she is sufficiently improved to attend.

D The Regulations do not apply; the meeting may be held at a location convenient to Constable PARKER, or if necessary, in the officer's absence.

Question 3.8

JESSOP has recently joined Eastshire Constabulary as a constable. Before joining, JESSOP was an active member of the Conservative Party, attending regular political fundraisers and meetings with other members.

In relation to sch. 1 to the Police Regulations 2003 (SI 2003/527) (restrictions on the private lives of officers), what would JESSOP's position now be, as a member of this party?

A Constable JESSOP would have to give up membership of this party, but could still attend political meetings.

B Constable JESSOP may remain a member of this party, but could not attend political fundraisers and meetings.

C Constable JESSOP would have to give up membership of this party and could not attend political meetings: all political parties are proscribed by the Secretary of State for police officers.

D Constable JESSOP could still attend political meetings and remain a member of this party, provided it does not become proscribed by the Secretary of State.

Question 3.9

An investigation by the Professional Standards Department (PSD) found that Constable ROBBINS had become fixated with a victim of a crime and had then sent over 100 emails to that person, which were of an extreme sexual nature. A pre-charge meeting between the PSD and the Crown Prosecution Service (CPS) concluded that there was sufficient evidence to charge the officer with offences under the Protection from Harassment Act 1997, or the Malicious Communications Act 1988; however, it was felt that the maximum sentence for either of these offences (six months' imprisonment and/or a fine) was insufficient, bearing in mind the nature of the offence. Consideration was being given to charging Constable ROBBINS with Misconduct in a Public Office, under common law.

Would it be appropriate to charge Constable ROBBINS with this common law offence, in these circumstances?

A No, there is sufficient evidence to prosecute Constable ROBBINS with another statutory offence.

B No, this offence should only be charged when there is no relevant statutory offence to account for the behaviour of the suspect.

C No, this offence should only be charged when there are evidential difficulties in proving the statutory offence (which is not the case in these circumstances).

D Yes, if it is considered that the maximum sentence for the statutory offence would be entirely insufficient for the seriousness of the misconduct.

Question 3.10

The police had attended several calls during the week relating to a domestic disagreement between FRENCH and HOLLOWAY. On each occasion, the incidents had been classified as 'verbal arguments' and no action was taken. Both FRENCH and HOLLOWAY were usually very drunk. One evening, Constable NAPIER was contacted by the control room and told that FRENCH had telephoned to say that HOLLOWAY had threatened to kill him and asked for the police to attend urgently. Constable NAPIER refused to attend the call on the grounds that previous calls to the address had been a waste of the police's time. Approximately an hour later, the police received a call that HOLLOWAY had actually killed FRENCH.

Could Constable NAPIER be guilty of the common law offence of misconduct in public office, in these circumstances?

A No, this offence cannot be committed because of a failure to do something; it relates to the actions a person actually took.

B Yes, but only if it can be shown Constable NAPIER was aware of the duty to take particular action, and failed to do so.

C Yes, if it can be shown Constable NAPIER was aware of the duty to take particular action, and failed to do so, or was reckless as to the existence of the duty.

D No, this could not amount to a criminal offence; however, Constable NAPIER could be guilty of gross incompetence or misconduct.

Question 3.11

Sergeant LORING was approached by Special Constable MALLET who was concerned about the behaviour of HEBDON who had recently resigned as a special constable. Special Constable MALLET told the sergeant that before he resigned, HEBDON falsely claimed to have lost his warrant card and obtained a duplicate. HEBDON had recently been overheard in a pub boasting that he had a police warrant card that he could use to get favours.

If HEBDON is in possession of a warrant card in these circumstances, which of the following is correct in relation to offences under the Police Act 1996?

A HEBDON is guilty of impersonation, because of his possession of the warrant card.

B HEBDON cannot be guilty of an offence under this Act because he is not in possession of a police uniform.

C HEBDON cannot be guilty of an offence under this Act unless evidence is available that he has used the warrant card to impersonate a police officer.

D HEBDON may be guilty of an offence under this Act because he does not have possession of the warrant card for a lawful purpose.

ANSWERS

Answer 3.1

Answer **B** — Generally, a police officer can only move to a later stage of the UPPs in relation to unsatisfactory performance or attendance that is similar to, or connected with, the performance or attendance referred to in any previous written improvement notice. Where failings relate to different forms of unsatisfactory performance or attendance it will be necessary to commence each UPP at the first stage (unless the failing constitutes gross incompetence). If more than one UPP is commenced, then, given that the procedures will relate to different failings and will have been identified at different times, the finding and outcome of each should be without prejudice to the others.

However, there may be circumstances where procedures have been initiated for a particular failing and an additional failing comes to light prior to the first stage meeting. In such circumstances it is possible to consolidate the two issues at the planned meeting provided that there is sufficient time prior to the meeting to comply with the notification requirements. Answer A is therefore incorrect.

If there is insufficient time to comply with the notification requirements (as was the case in this scenario), either the meeting should be rearranged to a date which allows the requirements to be met or a separate first stage meeting should be held in relation to the additional matter.

Therefore, Sergeant GREEGAN would have the option to adjourn the first stage meeting to discuss both matters at the same meeting, but should not discuss the additional matter at the planned meeting. Answer C is therefore incorrect.

On the other hand, there would be no requirement to wait until the officer reaches stage three of the UPPs to consolidate the unsatisfactory performance matters; this may be done at the first stage and answer D is therefore incorrect.

General Police Duties, para. 4.3.8

Answer 3.2

Answer **A** — The formal procedures to deal with unsatisfactory performance and attendance are set out in the Police (Performance) Regulations 2012 and are referred to as 'UPPs'. There are potentially three stages to the UPP process, each of which involves a different meeting composition and possible outcomes. However, the process is the same whether the officer is being asked to account for their poor performance or their attendance. Answer C is therefore incorrect.

A line manager may ask an HR professional or police officer (who should have experience of UPPs) to attend a UPP meeting to advise him/her on the proceedings at the first stage meeting. Answer B is therefore incorrect. The line manager may also seek such advice before the meeting and answer C is also incorrect in this respect, because attendance at the meeting is optional and not mandatory.

If the experienced police officer is to attend the meeting, he/she must be independent of the line management chain (and not part of it at any level). Answer D is therefore incorrect.

General Police Duties, para. 4.3.9

Answer 3.3

Answer **D** — It is expected that the specified period for improvement would not normally exceed three months. On the application of the police officer or otherwise (e.g. on the application of his/her line manager), the appropriate authority may extend the 'specified period' if it considers it appropriate to do so.

In setting an extension to the specified period, consideration should be given to any known periods of extended absence from the police officer's normal role, e.g. if the police officer is going to be on long periods of pre-planned holiday leave, study leave, or is due to undergo an operation. The extension should not lead to the improvement period exceeding 12 months; therefore, answers A and B are incorrect.

However, if the appropriate authority is satisfied that there are exceptional circumstances making it appropriate, the period may be extended beyond 12 months; therefore, answer C is incorrect.

General Police Duties, para. 4.3.9.2

Answer 3.4

Answer **D** — The 'validity period' of an improvement notice describes the period of *12 months* from the date of the notice within which performance or attendance must be maintained (assuming improvement is made during the specified period). If the improvement is not maintained within this period, the next stage of the procedures may be used.

Answers A, B and C are therefore incorrect.

General Police Duties, para. 4.3.9.2

Answer 3.5

Answer **B** — There may be exceptional circumstances where the appropriate authority considers the performance of the police officer to be so unsatisfactory as to warrant the procedures being initiated at the third stage for 'gross incompetence'.

'Gross incompetence' is defined in the Police (Performance) Regulations 2012 as:

> ...a serious inability or serious failure of a police officer to perform the duties of the rank or role he is currently undertaking to a satisfactory standard or level, to the extent that dismissal would be justified, except that no account shall be taken of the attendance of a police officer when considering whether he has been grossly incompetent.

This Regulation is about performance and not attendance and answer C is therefore incorrect.

It is not envisaged that an appropriate authority would initiate the procedures at the third stage in respect of a series of acts over a period of time, whether similar or not; this Regulation is meant to deal with a *single* incident of 'gross incompetence', therefore, answers A and D are incorrect.

General Police Duties, para. 4.3.11.1

Answer 3.6

Answer **C** — First, special constables may be required to attend a third stage meeting to deal with unsatisfactory performance (UPP). In arranging a third stage meeting involving special constables, due consideration should be given to the fact that special constables are unpaid volunteers and may therefore have full-time employment or other personal commitments. Answer A is therefore incorrect.

In cases where a special constable is required to attend a third stage UPP meeting, the force will appoint a member of the special constabulary to attend the meeting to advise the panel (as opposed to the officer—this is for the purpose of fairness). Answer B is incorrect.

The special constable advising the panel must have sufficient seniority and experience of the special constabulary to be able to advise the panel; however, he/she will not form part of the panel and will not have a role in determining whether or not the police officer's performance or attendance is unsatisfactory. Answer D is therefore incorrect.

General Police Duties, para. 4.3.11.3

Answer 3.7

Answer **D** — Attendance at any stage meeting is not subject to the same considerations as reporting for duty and the provisions of reg. 33 (sick leave) of the Police Regulations 2003 do not apply. In other words, an officer may not claim that because he/she is unfit for duty, he/she is also unable to attend a meeting—of course, it will depend on the individual's illness, but a broken leg is a physical injury and should not prohibit the person from discussing a return to work plan. Answer B is therefore incorrect.

If the police officer is incapacitated, the meeting *may* be deferred until he/she is sufficiently improved to attend. Every effort should be made to make it *possible* for the police officer to attend; however, this is not mandatory and a meeting will not be deferred indefinitely because the police officer is unable to attend. Answer C is therefore incorrect.

Whilst the 2003 Regulations may not apply, advice and guidance suggest that the chair of the meeting should make efforts to help the officer to engage in the meeting, which could include holding the meeting at a location convenient to him/her. It will be the officer's force's duty to find a way to communicate with him/her and forcing the officer to attend a meeting will play into their hands, when it may be possible to communicate with them in some other way, such as using video, telephone or other conferencing technology. Answer A is therefore incorrect.

General Police Duties, para. 4.3.12

Answer 3.8

Answer **B** — Schedule 1 to the Police Regulations 2003 (SI 2003/527) provides that a member of a police force:

- shall at all times abstain from any activity which is likely to interfere with the impartial discharge of his/her duties or which is likely to give rise to the impression amongst members of the public that it may so interfere;
- shall in particular—
  - — not take any active part in politics;
  - — not belong to any organisation specified or described in a determination of the Secretary of State.

For this purpose, the Secretary of State has determined that no member of the police force may be a member of the British National Party (BNP), Combat 18 or the National Front. Since these are the only proscribed organisations at this time, answer C is incorrect.

The wording of sch. 1 does not actually prohibit police officers from being members of other political parties and answer A is incorrect.

However, police officers *are* prohibited from taking an active part in politics. This means that Constable JESSOP could be a member of this political party, but *could not* attend political meetings and fundraisers. Answers A and D are incorrect for this reason.

General Police Duties, para. 4.3.16.1

Answer 3.9

Answer **D** — It is a misdemeanour at common law for the holder of a public office to do anything that amounts to a malfeasance or a 'culpable' misfeasance (*R* v *Wyat* (1705) 1 Salk 380). Such offences can only be tried on indictment and the court has a power of sentence 'at large', that is, there is no limit on the sentence that can be passed. The conduct can be separated into occasions of *mal*feasance and *mis*feasance. The first requires some degree of wrongful motive or intention on the part of the officer, while the second is more likely to apply where there has been some form of wilful neglect of duty: both are notoriously difficult to prove.

The question is: when should this offence be charged?

Generally, where there is clear evidence of one or more statutory offences, they should usually form the basis of the case, with the 'public office' element being put forward as an aggravating factor for sentencing purposes. In *R* v *Rimmington, R* v *Goldstein* [2005] UKHL 63 at para. 30, the House of Lords confirmed this approach, saying:

> Good practice and respect for the primacy of statute require that conduct falling within the terms of a specific statutory provision should be prosecuted under that provision unless there is good reason for doing otherwise.

It concluded that the use of the common law offence should therefore be limited to the following situations:

- where there is no relevant statutory offence, but the behaviour or the circumstances are such that they should nevertheless be treated as criminal;
- where there is a statutory offence but it would be difficult or inappropriate to use it. This might arise because of evidential difficulties in proving the statutory offence in the particular circumstances;
- because the maximum sentence for the statutory offence would be entirely insufficient for the seriousness of the misconduct.

Therefore, the common law offence *could* be charged in the case examined (because the maximum sentence for the statutory offence would be entirely insufficient for the seriousness of the misconduct) and answers A, B and C are incorrect.

General Police Duties, para. 4.3.17.1

Answer 3.10

Answer **C** — It is a misdemeanour at common law for the holder of a public office to do anything that amounts to a malfeasance or a 'culpable' misfeasance (*R* v *Wyat* (1705) 1 Salk 380). The conduct can be separated into occasions of *mal*feasance and *mis*feasance. The first requires some degree of wrongful motive or intention on the part of the officer while the second is more likely to apply where there has been some form of wilful neglect of duty: both are notoriously difficult to prove, but either could constitute an offence. Answers A and D are therefore incorrect.

A death in police custody has led to a clarification as to the nature of the criminal common law offence of misconduct in public office (see *Attorney General's Reference (No. 3 of 2003)* [2004] EWCA Crim 868). The elements of the offence were summarised by the Court of Appeal (Criminal Division) as follows:

A public officer acting as such [who]:
- wilfully neglects to perform his duty and/or wilfully misconducts himself,
- to such a degree as to amount to an abuse of the public's trust in the office holder,
- without reasonable excuse or justification [may be guilty of the criminal offence.]

Since the offence requires 'an awareness of the duty to act or a subjective recklessness as to the existence of the duty', answer B is incorrect.

General Police Duties, para. 4.3.17.1

Answer 3.11

Answer **D** — There are several offences under the Police Act 1996 connected to such behaviour. First, there is impersonation under s. 90(1), but you would have to prove the person, with intent to deceive, impersonates a member of a police force or special constable, or makes any statement or does any act calculated falsely to suggest that he/she is such a member or constable. There is no clear evidence that this has happened in this question, therefore, answer A is incorrect.

There are further offences under the 1996 Act: under s. 90(2) (wearing an article of police uniform of a member of a police force as to be calculated to deceive) and s. 90(3) (possessing an article of police uniform).

Under subs. (3), a person can commit an offence by simply possessing the article of uniform unless he/she proves that he/she obtained possession of that article lawfully and has possession of it for a lawful purpose (which HEBDON cannot do in these circumstances). Answer C is incorrect because an offence may be committed even if the person has not tried to impersonate a police officer.

Finally, an 'article of police uniform' for the purposes of s. 90(3) includes any article of uniform, any distinctive badge or mark or any document of identification usually issued to members of police forces or special constables (s. 90(4)). HEBDON is guilty of this offence and answer B is incorrect.

General Police Duties, para. 4.3.17.2

4 Human Rights

STUDY PREPARATION

It is generally accepted that the introduction of the Human Rights Act 1998 (which incorporated the European Convention on Human Rights into our domestic law) had the largest effect on the use of police powers since the Police and Criminal Evidence Act 1984.

Many of the questions contained in this chapter are based on decisions made in the European Court of Human Rights. Under s. 2 of the Human Rights Act 1998, domestic courts and tribunals are under an obligation to take such decisions into account. However, it is important to remember that the Convention, as a 'living instrument', is constantly evolving.

When looking at the Convention rights in detail, it is also important to recognise the difference between an *absolute* right under the Convention (such as the right to freedom from torture under Art. 3), and a *qualified* or *restricted* right (such as Art. 5, the right to liberty). Probably, the most important consideration is to recognise how the 1998 Act sets out to *balance* the rights of the individual against the needs of a democratic society.

The 'three tests' must be learned, namely 'prescribed by law', 'legitimate objective' and 'proportionality', as well as who will be a 'victim' and who may be in breach of the Act. Lastly, there are several Articles contained in the Convention which directly affect the police, such as the right to life, freedom from torture, right to liberty and security, right to a fair trial and right to respect for private and family life. Other Articles, such as right of freedom of expression and freedom of assembly, also have a significant effect on everyday policing.

Human rights law does not exist in isolation. Therefore, although it is specifically addressed in this chapter, every aspect of the law contained in this book should be viewed with the 1998 Act in mind.

QUESTIONS

Question 4.1

MARSDEN was arrested and charged with an offence under s. 5 of the Public Order Act 1986, during a protest march against the Government's austerity measures. The arresting officers were Constable MILLER and Special Constable DEERE. MARSDEN was subsequently found not guilty of the offence in court and is considering taking a case to the European Court of Human Rights (ECtHR), alleging a breach of Art. 5 of the Convention (the right to liberty and security).

Section 6(1) of the Human Rights Act 1998 outlines that it is unlawful for a public authority to act in a way that is incompatible with a Convention right. In relation to the term 'public authority', which of the following statements is correct?

A Both Constable MILLER and Special Constable DEERE are individuals and neither could be classified as a 'public authority' under the Act.

B Both Constable MILLER and Special Constable DEERE would be classified as a 'public authority' under the Act as they were exercising functions on behalf of a police force.

C Both officers could be classified as a 'public authority' under the Act; however, in Special Constable DEERE's case, only because she was assisting a sworn officer with their duties.

D Only Constable MILLER would be classified as a 'public authority' under the Act; as a volunteer, Special Constable DEERE is not employed by a police force.

Question 4.2

A demonstration at the site of a new out-of-town shopping centre had been authorised under ss. 12 and 14 of the Public Order Act 1986; however, the police had received intelligence that passengers on a coach attending the demonstration intended causing disorder at the site. They responded by stopping the coach and escorting it to the other side of the city. The demonstration organiser, QUINN, was not on the coach and was intending to meet the demonstrators at the site later on. Instead, QUINN met the coach on the other side of the city and was told by the senior police officer that if the coach tried to return to the site now or in the future, the occupants would be arrested for a breach of the peace. Most of the occupants of the coach voted to call it a day and went home. QUINN has sought legal advice in order to challenge police action under Arts 10 and 11 of the European Convention on Human Rights (ECHR).

In relation to whether QUINN may use the ECHR to challenge the actions of the police, which statement is correct?

A QUINN should be advised that the pressure group should pursue a case under the ECHR on behalf of the coach passengers, as this would have more effect.

B QUINN was not directly affected by the police actions and may not pursue a case under the ECHR; an individual who was on the coach would need to do so.

C Although not directly affected by the police actions, QUINN was at risk of being so affected and may pursue a case under the ECHR.

D Neither QUINN nor the coach passengers may pursue a case under the ECHR at this stage; however, they would be able to do so if they returned to the site and the police carried out their threat to arrest people.

Question 4.3

MENCE had been charged with grooming a young child over the Internet, but the case was dismissed in the Crown Court. The defence had discovered that six months previously, while the police were investigating MENCE's laptop, they accessed items which were subject to legal privilege and had failed to disclose this to the defence. MENCE intends bringing proceedings against the police for infringing Art. 8 of the European Convention on Human Rights (the right to private and family life).

Assuming the infringement occurred six months ago, are there any time limits imposed on MENCE to bring proceedings under the Human Rights Act 1998?

A Yes, MENCE has only six months in which to bring the proceedings.

B Yes, MENCE has 12 months in which to bring the proceedings.

C Yes, MENCE has six months in which to bring the proceedings, but the court or tribunal may extend this period if it is necessary to do so.

D No, there are no time limits because the police were legally obliged to disclose the information and failed to do so.

Question 4.4

Constable ANDERSON is an authorised firearms officer who was responsible for the fatal shooting of a suspect whilst on duty and was called to give evidence in the Coroner's Court. Constable ANDERSON applied to give evidence anonymously on the grounds that she was a member of the local community and if her identity were revealed, it would represent a risk of serious harm to herself and her family. The court rejected the application by the officer.

Would there be any restriction on Constable ANDERSON bringing proceedings against the Coroner's Court (a public authority) for infringing Art. 2 of the European Convention on Human Rights (the right to life) in these circumstances?

A Yes, Constable ANDERSON was acting in the execution of her duty, which makes this an employment matter.

B No, this is not an employment matter and Constable ANDERSON may bring proceedings.

C No, there are no restrictions on police officers relying on the Convention rights.

D No, the only restriction on police officers relying on the Convention rights is in relation to recruitment proceedings.

Question 4.5

LAWTON was the father of an 8-year-old boy who was murdered by his neighbour, PEARSON, a convicted sex offender. Prior to the murder, LAWTON had made several complaints to the police that PEARSON had been seen pestering his child. Following PEARSON's conviction, LAWTON brought an action against the police under Art. 2 of the European Convention on Human Rights, alleging that the police had failed to prevent his son's death.

What must LAWTON prove to the court in order to convince it that the police failed to prevent the death of his son?

A Nothing—the police have an absolute obligation to protect life under Art. 2.

B That the police actually foresaw the risk to life, and that they failed to act upon it.

C That the police failed to see a risk to life which would have been obvious to a reasonable person.

D That the police did not do all that was expected of them to avoid a real and immediate risk to life.

Question 4.6

YADAV is bringing proceedings against the United Kingdom in the European Court of Human Rights for a breach of Art. 3 of the Convention (prohibition of torture). YADAV had been arrested under the Terrorism Act 2000 and was being held on remand in prison, however, no charges were brought against him and he was eventually released. YADAV claimed that while he was in prison, somehow, several prisoners managed to gain access to the secure area where he was being held and tortured him for being a terrorist. YADAV's case centres on the fact that the public authority holding him in prison had a duty to prevent his torture and that it failed to act to protect him.

Which of the following statements would be correct, in relation to any statutory defence the public authority might have, if YADAV brings such a case?

A The only defence to a breach of Art. 3 is 'lawful authority', which would not be available in this case.

B There is no defence to a breach of Art. 3; the public authority would have to rely on the Court finding that YADAV's case was untrue.

C The public authority may be able to rely on the defence of 'reasonable excuse', which is available in torture cases.

D The public authority could rely on the fact that their actions were neither 'willful' nor 'intentional', as a defence for a breach of Art. 3.

Question 4.7

SAADI is taking a case to the European Court of Human Rights (ECtHR), alleging a breach of Art. 5 of the Convention (the right to liberty and security). The circumstances are that SAADI had been arrested for attempting to enter the United Kingdom illegally and had been detained in a temporary centre, pending an application to enter the country as an asylum seeker. SAADI's argument is that his arrest and detention were unnecessary because he had family with strong roots in the United Kingdom and that he was not a flight risk.

What does Art. 5 of the European Convention on Human Rights state about the 'necessity' of such an arrest, in these circumstances?

A The State is not required to demonstrate that an arrest is 'necessary' in these circumstances.

B The State is required to demonstrate that all arrests are 'necessary', even in these circumstances.

C The State is required to demonstrate that all arrests are 'necessary', for the purposes of bringing the person before the competent legal authority.

D The State is required to demonstrate that all arrests are 'necessary', for the purposes of bringing the person before the competent legal authority on reasonable suspicion of having committed an offence.

Question 4.8

FOX was arrested for an offence under s. 4 of the Road Traffic Act 1988 (unfit to drive through drink or drugs). FOX was taken to a police station where subsequent blood tests proved negative. FOX is now considering bringing a case of unlawful arrest against the police, under Art. 5 of the European Convention on Human Rights (the right to liberty and security). The basis of FOX's case is that the arresting officer had formed a suspicion that she was drunk based on evidence provided by a member of the public. FOX claims that this suspicion was not 'reasonable' and, consequently, the arrest was unlawful.

In considering FOX's case, how should the court assess the officer's 'reasonable suspicion' that an arrest was necessary?

A Whether the officer was satisfied that the information received about FOX prior to the arrest amounted to a 'reasonable suspicion' that she was drunk.

B Whether an ordinary person would be satisfied that the information received about FOX prior to the arrest amounted to a 'reasonable suspicion' that she was drunk.

C Whether an objective observer would be satisfied that the information received about FOX prior to the arrest amounted to a 'reasonable suspicion' that she was drunk.

D Whether the witness in the case had formed a 'reasonable suspicion' that she was drunk.

Question 4.9

MENDEZ, a Premiership football player, is being taken to civil court by his estranged wife, who is seeking a non-molestation order due to alleged harassment committed by MENDEZ against her and their children. Following legal advice, MENDEZ intends asking the court for the hearing to be held in private. MENDEZ believes that any publicity generated by the case may prejudice the outcome, because of his celebrity status.

Which of the following statements is correct, in respect of whether the hearing should be held in public or private?

A The case may be held in private, if it is adjudged that the publicity would prejudice the interests of justice.

B The case may not be held in private; this facility is only available in criminal courts.

C The case may be held in private, but only if it is being heard in front of a jury.

D The case may be held in private, but only if it is adjudged that the interests of a juvenile need to be protected.

Question 4.10

MORTON is a well-known public figure and is taking legal advice about bringing a case against the police, under Art. 8 of the European Convention on Human Rights (respect for private and family life). The circumstances were that MORTON reported to the police her suspicion that someone was trying to hack into her emails. MORTON alleges that the police failed to act and as a result, the hacker subsequently managed to download several photographs of her with no clothes on, from emails sent by a friend. The photographs were displayed on the Internet and MORTON claims this was potentially ruinous to her career.

Which of the following statements is correct, in relation to MORTON's potential claim?

A The aim of Art. 8 is to protect a person's life from interference by 'public authorities': it therefore does not apply in these circumstances.

B The State has a positive obligation to prevent others from interfering with an individual's right to private and family life; therefore, Art. 8 may apply in these circumstances.

C The State has a positive obligation to prevent others from interfering with an individual's right to private and family life, but this does not extend to a person's correspondence; therefore, Art. 8 would not apply in these circumstances.

D The State has a positive obligation to prevent others from interfering with an individual's right to private and family life, but this duty only extends to maintaining public safety; therefore, Art. 8 would not apply in these circumstances.

Question 4.11

CLAYTON is appearing in the Crown Court, having been charged with an offence of stirring up racial hatred under s. 18 of the Public Order Act 1986. He had displayed a picture in his shop window, indicating that he would not serve refugees. He is pleading not guilty, claiming that his human rights have been interfered with, as he is entitled to express his opinions freely.

Would CLAYTON be able to use Art. 10 of the European Convention on Human Rights (freedom of expression) as a defence in these circumstances?

A No, as his actions are probably not proportionate to the crime committed.

B Yes, every person has a right to express themselves freely.

C No, but he could use Art. 9 (freedom of thought) as a defence.

D Yes, provided he held a genuine belief that his rights had been interfered with.

Question 4.12

The Westford anti-hunt lobby arranged a demonstration outside a farm where a fox hunt was being organised. The organisers of the hunt arranged for marshals to be present and the local police were also in attendance. Demonstrators protested peacefully in the road nearby but, on the instructions of the hunt organisers, the marshals attempted to move the protestors away from the scene. The demonstrators felt intimidated by the marshals, but the police did nothing.

In these circumstances, do the police officers at the scene appear to have infringed Art. 11 of the European Convention on Human Rights (freedom of assembly and association)?

A No, as they have not interfered with the rights of the protestors or the members of the hunt.

B Yes, they should have stopped the protest; it breached the rights of the hunters and the farm owner.

C Yes, they had a duty to prevent the unlawful interference with the rights of the protestors by the marshals.

D No, they would have a duty to act only if public order offences were imminent.

Question 4.13

HAWKINS and GREER are in a same-sex relationship and have sought legal advice about an incident that occurred recently. HAWKINS works for a local authority and has been selected to attend a team-building weekend at premises owned by the local authority, aimed at developing junior managers in the organisation. Staff were told that they could take partners along for the weekend and that double rooms were available for couples. When they arrived, HAWKINS and GREER were told that double rooms were only available for married couples. They are considering taking legal action against HAWKINS's employers on the grounds that they had been indirectly discriminated against due to their sexual orientation (i.e. they were unable to fulfil the criteria of being a 'married couple' as defined by the policy). They have asked their legal adviser whether or not the policy amounted to a breach of Art. 14 of the European Convention on Human Rights (prohibition of discrimination).

Which of the following statements is correct, in respect of HAWKINS and GREER's inquiry?

A The behaviour may amount to discrimination; however, Art. 14 does not extend to cases of indirect discrimination.

B The behaviour may amount to discrimination; however, Art. 14 does not extend to cases involving discrimination based on a person's sexual orientation.

C The behaviour may amount to discrimination; however, while Art. 14 *does* extend to cases of indirect discrimination, this is only applicable to a person's race, colour, language or religion.

D The behaviour may amount to discrimination and Art. 14 extends to all cases of discrimination, whether direct or indirect.

Question 4.14

PUGACH returned from working abroad to find that people were squatting in his flat. PUGACH obtained documentation from the court proving that he was a protected intending occupier, but used all his money doing so. PUGACH contacted the police, asking for assistance to remove the trespassers, but was told this was a civil matter and the police would not get involved. PUGACH tried several times over a six-month period, explaining that he had no money to go to court, but the police did not help. PUGACH eventually contacted a solicitor, who advised him that the police may have breached his human rights and that he should sue them.

Given that PUGACH was a protected intending occupier and the police *could* have used their powers under s. 7 of the Criminal Law Act 1977 to deal with the squatters, could they be in breach of Protocol 1, Art. 1 to the European Convention on Human Rights (right to enjoy possessions), in these circumstances?

A No, the police did not take possession of PUGACH's property at any time.

B Yes, the police could be liable in these circumstances.

C No, 'possessions' do not include land or premises for the purposes of this Protocol.

D No, the police cannot be held liable for a matter which is civil and not criminal.

ANSWERS

Answer 4.1

Answer **B** — Section 6(3) of the Human Rights Act 1998 states that a 'public authority' includes:

(a) a court or tribunal, and
(b) any person certain of whose functions are those of a public nature, but does not include either House of Parliament or a person exercising functions in connection with proceedings in Parliament.

Not only are police organisations public authorities, but so are individual police officers—whether they are regular officers or special constables—and others who are employed by the police to exercise policing powers. Both Constable MILLER and Special Constable DEERE would be classified under s. 6 and answer A is therefore incorrect.

It is irrelevant that in Special Constable DEERE's case, she was 'assisting' with the arrest, or that she was not a paid employee; she is responsible for her own actions and was exercising 'functions' on behalf of a police force. Answers C and D are therefore incorrect.

General Police Duties, para. 4.4.3.5

Answer 4.2

Answer **C** — Under s. 7(1) of the Human Rights Act 1998, a person who claims that a public authority has acted (or proposed to act) in a way that is incompatible with his/her human rights (s. 6(1)) may bring proceedings against the authority in the appropriate court or tribunal.

In order to rely on s. 7, however, a person must first be a 'victim', and must show that he/she is either directly affected or at risk of being directly affected. Section 7 will not enable public interest groups to institute proceedings, only individuals. Therefore, answer A is incorrect.

Answer C is correct (and answer B is incorrect) because QUINN was an individual who was at risk of being directly affected (i.e. by attending the site, QUINN faced being arrested). This was confirmed in *Dudgeon* v *United Kingdom* (1983) 5 EHRR 573, where the petitioner was able to challenge the law proscribing consensual homosexual activity even though he had not been prosecuted under the legislation himself.

The circumstances in this question are similar to those in *R (On the application of Laporte)* v *Chief Constable of Gloucestershire* [2006] UKHL 55. In *Laporte* a lawful assembly had been arranged under the provisions of ss. 12 and 14 of the Public Order Act 1986 in connection with protests against the war in Iraq. As the result of a stop and search order made under s. 60 of the Criminal Justice and Public Order Act 1994, the police stopped a number of coaches en route to the lawful assembly at Fairford US Air Force base, and then escorted them back to London. Intelligence had been received that the passengers would cause disorder at the base. The Court of Appeal held that the police actions were reasonable to apprehend a breach of the peace. However, the House of Lords ruled that the police had acted unlawfully because a breach of the peace was not imminent when the coaches were stopped. This action interfered with the passengers' rights under Arts 10 (freedom of expression) and 11 (freedom of assembly and association) of the European Convention on Human Rights and therefore answer D is incorrect.

General Police Duties, paras 4.4.3.6, 4.12.2.2

Answer 4.3

Answer **C** — Section 7(5) of the Human Rights Act 1998 states that proceedings under subsection (1)(a) must be brought before the end of—

(a) the period of one year beginning with the date on which the act complained of took place; or
(b) such longer period as the court or tribunal considers equitable having regard to all the circumstances...

Therefore, since there is a specified time period, commencing one year from the date of the alleged breach, answers B and D are incorrect.

However, this period may be extended under s. 7(5)(b), which would account for any delays in the information of the alleged breach coming to light. Answer A is therefore incorrect.

General Police Duties, para. 4.4.3.6

Answer 4.4

Answer **B** — There are restrictions on police officers relying on the Convention rights in the context of recruitment *and* disciplinary procedures. Answers C and D are therefore incorrect.

The European Court of Justice regards police officers in Member States as being government servants and as such they cannot generally rely on their Convention rights against the employer (see *Pellegrin* v *France* (2001) 31 EHRR 26). Since the officer was not seeking to bring proceedings in an employment context, answer A is incorrect.

There are certain circumstances where police officers *may* be able to rely on their Convention rights, for example in *R (On the application of A and B)* v *HM Coroner for Inner South District of Greater London* [2004] EWCA Civ 1439, where the coroner refused to allow police officers to give evidence anonymously in a fatal shooting case. The Divisional Court held the risk of serious harm to the officers and their families was sufficient to engage Art. 2, and the coroner ought to have protected their anonymity.

General Police Duties, paras 4.4.3.6, 4.4.5

Answer 4.5

Answer **D** — The circumstances are similar to those in the case of *Osman* v *United Kingdom* (2000) 29 EHRR 245, where a man had been killed by a person who had become fixated with him. Although there the European Court of Human Rights dismissed the case, it examined the positive obligation of the State to protect life under Art. 2.

First, the positive obligation on the State to protect life is not an absolute one (and answer A is therefore incorrect). Other factors should be taken into consideration, such as the source and degree of danger and the means available to combat it. The court said in *Osman* that it will be enough for the applicant to show that the authorities did not do all that could reasonably be expected of them to avoid a real and immediate risk to life of which they have or ought to have knowledge. Answer B is incorrect, as there is no need to show that the State actually saw the risk and failed to act upon it. Answer C is incorrect, as the 'reasonable person' test is not mentioned in this ruling.

General Police Duties, para. 4.4.5.2

Answer 4.6

Answer **B** — Article 3 of the European Convention on Human Rights states:

> No one shall be subjected to torture or to inhuman or degrading treatment or punishment.

Torture is a criminal offence under s. 134 of the Criminal Justice Act 1988 but, whereas that offence has a statutory defence of 'lawful authority, justification or excuse', the prohibition contained in Art. 3 is absolute.

Irrespective of the prevailing circumstances, there can be no derogation from an individual's absolute right to freedom from torture, inhuman or degrading treatment or punishment.

Since there are no statutory defences available for the public authority, answers A, C and D are incorrect.

General Police Duties, para. 4.4.6

Answer 4.7

Answer **A** — Article 5(1) of the European Convention on Human Rights states:

> Everyone has the right to liberty and security of person. No one shall be deprived of his liberty save in the following cases and in accordance with a procedure prescribed by law.

Under Art. 5(1)(c), it must be demonstrated that the arrest or detention of a person was effected for the purpose of bringing him/her before the competent legal authority on reasonable suspicion of having committed an offence or when it is reasonably considered necessary to prevent his/her committing an offence or fleeing after having done so.

However, other subsections in Art. 5 do not require the arrest to be made for the purpose of bringing the person before the competent legal authority. Under Art. 5(1)(f), the lawful arrest or detention of a person may be made:

> to prevent his effecting an unauthorised entry into the country or of a person against whom action is being taken with a view to deportation or extradition.

Answers C and D are therefore incorrect.

In the case of *R (On the application of Saadi)* v *Secretary of State for the Home Department* [2002] UKHL 41, the House of Lords ruled that, unlike part of Art. 5(1)(c), Art. 5(1)(f) does *not* require that detention has to be necessary in order to be justified. As a result, the temporary detention of asylum seekers, pending their application to remain in the United Kingdom, is not of itself unlawful. Answer B is therefore incorrect.

General Police Duties, para. 4.4.7

Answer 4.8

Answer **C** — 'Reasonable suspicion' will be assessed objectively and the court will look for 'the existence of facts or information which would satisfy an *objective observer* that the person may have committed the offence' (see *Fox* v *United Kingdom* (1991) 13 EHRR 157)).

Answers A, B and D are therefore incorrect.

General Police Duties, para. 4.4.7.4

Answer 4.9

Answer **A** — Article 6(1) of the European Convention on Human Rights states that:

> In the determination of his civil rights and obligations or of any criminal charge against him, everyone is entitled to a fair and public hearing within a reasonable time by an independent and impartial tribunal established by law.
>
> Judgment shall be pronounced publicly but the press and public may be excluded from all or part of the trial in the interest of morals, public order or national security in a democratic society, where the interests of juveniles or the protection of the private and family life of the parties so require, or to the extent strictly necessary in the opinion of the court in special circumstances where publicity would prejudice the interests of justice.

Since there are several reasons for determining whether a case can be heard in private, answers C and D are incorrect.

Article 6(1) does not distinguish between civil and criminal cases; therefore, answer B is incorrect.

Note that even where the press and/or the public have been excluded from all or part of the trial, the judgment must always be pronounced publicly.

General Police Duties, para. 4.4.8

Answer 4.10

Answer **B** — Article 8 of the European Convention on Human Rights states:

> 1. Everyone has the right to respect for his private and family life, his home and his correspondence.
> 2. There shall be no interference by a public authority with the exercise of this right except such as is in accordance with the law and is necessary in a democratic society in the interests of national security, public safety or the economic wellbeing of the country, for the prevention of disorder or crime, for the protection of health or morals, or for the protection of the rights and freedoms of others.

The provisions of Art. 8 extend a right to respect for a person's correspondence (as well as their private life, family life and home). Answer C is therefore incorrect.

Whilst the main aim of the Article is to protect these features of a person's life from arbitrary interference by 'public authorities', the State *does* have a positive obligation to prevent others from interfering with an individual's right to his/her private and family life (see *Stjerna* v *Finland* (1994) 24 EHRR 194), and this duty extends beyond simply maintaining public safety. Answers A and D are therefore incorrect.

General Police Duties, para. 4.4.10

Answer 4.11

Answer **A** — Under Art. 10 of the European Convention on Human Rights, everyone has a right to freedom of expression. However, as with all aspects of human rights, this has to be balanced against other social needs. In the case of *Hutchinson* v *DPP* The Independent, 20 November 2000, a conviction for criminal damage was upheld when it was decided that there were other ways in which the defendant could have expressed her opinions without committing a crime. Answer B is incorrect for this reason.

Because his actions were probably not proportionate, CLAYTON would not be able to use Art. 9 as a 'shield' for the same reasons noted previously (making answer C incorrect).

A person's belief, no matter how genuine, that his/her rights had been interfered with, will not provide an automatic defence to a criminal offence if that belief is not proportionate to the crime committed. Answer D is therefore incorrect.

General Police Duties, para. 4.4.11

Answer 4.12

Answer **C** — Under Art. 11 of the European Convention on Human Rights, everyone has the right to freedom of peaceful assembly. Therefore, the protestors had the right to protest, provided they were going about it peacefully. They do not appear to have interfered with the rights of the members of the hunt or the farm owner on these facts. Answer B is incorrect for this reason.

The State (or public authority) has two main obligations in these circumstances. In the first instance, it must not interfere with the protestors' rights to peaceful assembly. However, equally important, it has a positive duty to prevent others from interfering with that right (which is why answer C is correct).

Therefore, even though the officers at the scene did not actively prevent the protest, arguably they should have acted to stop the marshals from doing so (which is why answers A and D are incorrect).

General Police Duties, para. 4.4.12

Answer 4.13

Answer **A** — Article 14 of the European Convention on Human Rights states that:

> The enjoyment of the rights and freedoms set forth in this Convention shall be secured without discrimination on any ground such as sex, race, colour, language, religion, political or other opinion, national or social origin, association with a national minority, property, birth or other status.

Article 14 simply provides a guarantee that access to the Convention's other provisions must be enjoyed equally by everyone under the jurisdiction of the particular State. The list set out in the Article is not exhaustive and other categories of people or grounds of discrimination may be added by the courts (and have been added by the European Court of Human Rights). It does cover a wider range of behaviour than simply discrimination based on a person's race, colour, language or religion. Answer C is therefore incorrect.

A person claiming a breach of Art. 14 must show that his/her own individual circumstances are similar to those of another person who has been treated differently in relation to the enjoyment of Convention rights.

The open-ended wording of Art. 14 means that a wide range of categories of people who can be grouped by reference to their status may be protected. That protection certainly extends to a person's sexuality (see *Mendoza* v *Ghaidan* [2004] UKHL 30). Answer B is therefore incorrect.

However, it does not make express provision for *indirect* discrimination and the Divisional Court has expressed considerable doubt as to whether Art. 14 provides protection against indirect, as opposed to direct, discrimination (see *R (On the application of Barber)* v *Secretary of State for Work and Pensions* [2002] EWHC 1915 (Admin)). Answer D is therefore incorrect.

General Police Duties, para. 4.4.13

Answer 4.14

Answer **B** — First of all, we need to examine whether PUGACH had a right of occupation of the premises. The Criminal Law Act 1977, s. 7(1), states that:

> subject to the following provisions of this section and to section 12A(9) below, any person who is on any premises as a trespasser after having entered as such is guilty of an offence if he fails to leave those premises on being required to do so by or on behalf of—
> (a) a displaced residential occupier of the premises; or
> (b) an individual who is a protected intending occupier of the premises.

By obtaining written evidence that PUGACH was a protected intending occupier of the premises, the police could certainly have dealt with the squatters for a criminal offence.

However, this question mainly deals with whether or not PUGACH's human rights were violated by the police's failure to take action on his behalf. Protocol 1, Art. 1 to the Convention states that every natural or legal person is entitled to the peaceful enjoyment of his possessions.

An example of how this right might be used against a public authority can be seen in *AO* v *Italy* (2001) 29 EHRR CD 92. In that case the Italian police were held to have violated the applicant's right to peaceful enjoyment of his property when they continually failed to send any officers to his flat, which he was trying to repossess from squatters. This case shows that this right can be violated even in circumstances where the police have no direct contact with an individual's property (and answer A is therefore incorrect).

Although the action for repossession in *AO* v *Italy* had been going on for over four years, the case also illustrates one way in which private law matters can become issues of liability for public authorities such as police services. Answer D is therefore incorrect.

Finally, this Protocol *does* cover premises and the term 'possessions' can be interpreted very widely and, under European case law, has extended to land, contractual rights and intellectual property. Answer C is therefore incorrect.

General Police Duties, paras 4.4.15, 4.17.7.4

5 Powers of Arrest (including Code G Codes of Practice) and Other Policing Powers

STUDY PREPARATION

The areas covered in this chapter could hardly be more important. In practical terms, this chapter contains the police officer's tool kit—and if it is relevant in practice, it is highly relevant in preparing for an examination or course of study.

In deciding what to do in any given situation, it is vital that you know what you are *empowered* to do. Following on from the previous chapter, it is also important to realise that each police power equals a reduction of, or interference with, someone's human rights. As holders of such powers, police officers are under a duty to exercise them properly—lawfully, proportionately and fairly.

An understanding of s. 24 of PACE and Code G of the PACE Codes of Practice is critical for operational officers, in respect of what constitutes a lawful arrest and when an arrest is 'necessary'.

QUESTIONS

Question 5.1

Constable HORNER was on patrol when she came across a large group of people outside a pub. The people were talking loudly and the officer approached them. Constable HORNER established that MINTON, who was standing amongst the group, had been arguing with another person and although no violence had been used, MINTON was in an agitated state. Constable HORNER turned away from the group to call for back-up and while she was waiting for colleagues to arrive, she was struck on the back of her head. Constable NEARY was first to arrive on the scene and found Constable HORNER on the floor, conscious, but with a head injury. The group of people was still present, but they refused to say who had assaulted Constable HORNER; the officer was unable to identify the person herself. Constable NEARY decided to arrest MINTON to prevent a breach of the peace, with a view to seeking CCTV evidence relating to the assault on Constable HORNER.

Was Constable NEARY's arrest of MINTON lawful in the circumstances?

A Yes, provided the officer had reasonable grounds for suspecting that MINTON had actually committed the substantive offence.

B Yes, while the officer sought reasonable grounds for suspecting that MINTON had committed the substantive offence.

C No, arresting a person for a 'holding' offence would be deemed unlawful.

D No, the officer should have arrested MINTON formally for the offence of assault, otherwise the case would fail in court.

Question 5.2

Constable SANTOS was on foot patrol in a busy town centre. The officer heard observations being passed on the radio for a vehicle and a description of the occupant who was wanted for an offence; however, because of the noise coming from nearby traffic, Constable SANTOS did not hear what the offence was. Immediately after hearing the radio message, Constable SANTOS saw GALE get out of a vehicle nearby; both GALE and the vehicle matched the description given. The officer approached GALE and fearing that he may run off, told him he was under arrest. However, at the time Constable SANTOS could not say what the offence was, or the grounds for the arrest.

Has Constable SANTOS acted unlawfully, by failing to inform GALE of the reason and grounds for the arrest?

A No, provided GALE is informed of the grounds for the arrest as soon as practicable.

B Yes, an arrest is unlawful unless the person is informed of the grounds at the time of the arrest.

C Yes, an arrest is unlawful unless the person is informed of the specific offence they are being arrested for, at the time of the arrest.

D No, a constable is not required to give this information if he/she reasonably believes that the person may try to escape before being arrested.

Question 5.3

Constable POTTER was called to a domestic disturbance at the home of HENDERSON and LeBOW. On the officer's arrival, HENDERSON was shouting loudly at LeBOW and making threats. Constable POTTER arrested HENDERSON for a breach of the peace and HENDERSON began struggling violently. Constable POTTER later recorded the facts in a pocket notebook, noting that HENDERSON had not been cautioned at the time of the arrest because of the violent struggle.

Which of the following statements is correct in relation to the requirement to caution a person, according to the PACE Codes of Practice?

A There was a requirement for Constable POTTER to caution HENDERSON because she was not cautioned immediately before the arrest.

B There was no requirement for Constable POTTER to caution HENDERSON at the time of arrest, because she was not being arrested for an offence.

C Constable POTTER was required to caution HENDERSON at the time of arrest, because she was not in the process of escaping from the officer.

D There was no requirement for Constable POTTER to caution HENDERSON at the time of arrest, because of her behaviour; however, the officer was required to caution her as soon as practicable afterwards.

Question 5.4

Constable HAYWOOD stopped JENNINGS for a motoring offence on a road. The officer conducted a PNC check on the vehicle and discovered it was not registered to JENNINGS. Constable HAYWOOD then tried to obtain personal details; however, JENNINGS was acting in a vague and evasive manner which led the officer to consider that an arrest may be necessary, under s. 24(5) of the Police and Criminal Evidence Act 1984.

What does Code C, para. 2.9 of the PACE Codes of Practice state about the steps Constable HAYWOOD should take to make sure JENNINGS understands why the arrest would be necessary?

A Constable HAYWOOD *must* warn JENNINGS that she will be arrested if she fails to give her name and address and, if practicable, tell her why the arrest is necessary.

B If practicable, Constable HAYWOOD should warn JENNINGS that she will be arrested if she fails to give her name and address; also, if it is practicable, the officer should tell her why the arrest is necessary.

C Constable HAYWOOD is not required to warn JENNINGS that she will be arrested if she fails to give her name and address; however, she should be told, if practicable, why the arrest is necessary.

D Constable HAYWOOD is only required to inform JENNINGS of the grounds for the arrest in these circumstances.

Question 5.5

DOWNEY worked as a security guard in a shopping centre and saw FENTON walking towards the public car park outside. It was clear to DOWNEY that FENTON was drunk from the way she was staggering. DOWNEY saw FENTON approach a car with the keys in her hand and decided to detain her, before she could drive the vehicle. DOWNEY made a 'citizen's arrest' on FENTON as she stood alongside the car and then contacted the police on his mobile phone.

Did DOWNEY have the power to arrest FENTON in these circumstances?

A Yes, provided it was not reasonably practicable for a constable to make the arrest instead.

B No, a member of the public only has the power to arrest a person to prevent a person from committing an indictable offence.

C Yes, regardless of whether there was a constable available to make the arrest instead.

D No, a member of the public only has the power to arrest a person when an indictable offence is being committed, or has been committed.

Question 5.6

THORPE was arrested for an assault and following a period of detention was charged, fingerprinted, photographed and had provided a sample of DNA. Following THORPE's conviction in court two months later, it was discovered that an administrative error had occurred and the DNA sample had been lost. This information was forwarded to Inspector MARDEN in the Custody Services Department, with a request that a further DNA sample be obtained from THORPE for the database.

Section 63A of the Police and Criminal Evidence Act 1984 provides a power of arrest without warrant to obtain samples from people in certain circumstances; would the use of this power be suitable in these circumstances?

A Yes, a DNA sample has been taken but it is no longer available.

B No, provided the sample THORPE gave was sufficient for analysis.

C Yes, because THORPE has now been convicted of a recordable offence.

D No, there is no power to take a second sample from someone, when they have previously provided one during the investigation.

Question 5.7

Constable FRENCH, an officer from Dumfries and Galloway Constabulary, was pursuing a vehicle which was stolen from the Dumfries and Galloway Constabulary area. The vehicle crossed the Scottish border into Cumbria Constabulary's area, in England, where it eventually stopped. Before officers from Cumbria Constabulary arrived at the scene, Constable FRENCH arrested the driver, KELLEY.

What action should now be taken, in respect of KELLEY?

A KELLEY must be taken to the nearest designated station in Scotland, where the original offence took place.

B KELLEY must be taken to the nearest designated station in England, where the arrest took place.

C KELLEY must be taken to the nearest designated station in Scotland or to the nearest designated police station in England.

D KELLEY should be further arrested by an officer from Cumbria Constabulary and be taken to the nearest designated station in England.

Question 5.8

BENTLEY was in police detention waiting to appear in court. He had been arrested for a warrant which had been issued by the court for failing to appear to answer a charge of burglary. BENTLEY asked to see the duty inspector to make a complaint against Constable MOORE, who had arrested him the previous evening. The foundation for BENTLEY's complaint was that Constable MOORE was not in possession of the warrant when she arrested him, and that she did not tell him he was under arrest.

If BENTLEY's case was genuine, has Constable MOORE acted unlawfully in these circumstances?

A Yes, Constable MOORE should have been in possession of the warrant at the time of the arrest and she should have informed BENTLEY that he was under arrest.

B No, there was no requirement for Constable MOORE to have been in possession of the warrant at the time of the arrest, or to have informed BENTLEY that he was under arrest.

C Yes, although there was no requirement for Constable MOORE to have been in possession of the warrant at the time of the arrest, she should have informed BENTLEY that he was under arrest.

D Yes, Constable MOORE should have been in possession of the warrant at the time of the arrest, although it was not necessary for her to inform BENTLEY that he was under arrest.

Question 5.9

DC SHARPE was interviewing HUNTER for a burglary. The officer suspected that HUNTER had committed more than one burglary, but only had reasonable grounds to arrest him for the one offence. In the interview, HUNTER provided DC SHARPE with reasonable grounds to suspect he should be arrested for two other offences. At that time, the officer made a decision that HUNTER would be further arrested for those offences, but not until after the interview. HUNTER was actually arrested for the further offences two hours after the interview concluded.

Considering s. 31 of the Police and Criminal Evidence Act 1984, which of the following statements is correct in relation to the timing of HUNTER's arrest?

A HUNTER should have been arrested when DC SHARPE had reasonable grounds to suspect him of further offences; the officer has acted unlawfully.

B HUNTER should have been arrested when DC SHARPE made the decision to arrest him for the further offences; the officer has acted unlawfully.

C HUNTER should have been arrested before the end of the interview; the officer has acted unlawfully.

D DC SHARPE has acted lawfully; there was no requirement to arrest HUNTER before the officer did so.

Question 5.10

MILLS had been detained by Constable GROVES for an offence of burglary which occurred an hour ago. MILLS matched the description of a person seen running away from the scene; the officer informed him he was under arrest and after caution, MILLS replied, 'it couldn't have been me, I was in my mate's house. Take me round there now and he'll tell you I was there'.

Section 30(1A) of the Police and Criminal Evidence Act 1984 requires a person to be taken by a constable to a police station as soon as practicable after the arrest. Would the information provided by MILLS allow Constable GROVES to deviate to his friend's address before taking him to the station?

A Yes, this may be a valid reason for not taking a person to a police station as soon as practicable after the arrest, provided the matter required immediate investigation.

B No, the only reason not to take a person to a police station as soon as practicable after the arrest is to recover evidence related to an indictable offence for which he/she has been arrested.

C No, a person must be taken to a police station as soon as practicable after the arrest on every occasion.

D No, there are circumstances in which a person may not be taken to a police station as soon as practicable after the arrest; however, checking an alibi would not amount to such an exception.

ANSWERS

Answer 5.1

Answer **A** — The practice of arresting someone on a 'holding' offence was accepted by the Court of Appeal in *R* v *Chalkley* [1998] QB 848 *provided the arresting officers had reasonable grounds for suspecting that the person had actually committed that offence*. If that suspicion is present then the fact that the officers making the arrest are doing so with the intention of investigating another, more serious offence does not render the arrest unlawful. If, however, there are no such grounds to suspect that the person had in fact committed the offence, or the officers know at the time of the arrest that there is no possibility of the person actually being charged with it, the arrest will be unlawful. Therefore, while Constable NEARY was entitled to arrest MINTON to prevent a breach of the peace, it would not be lawful to do so to allow the officer to *seek* reasonable grounds for suspecting the person: the reasonable grounds for suspicion must be present before the arrest takes place. Answers B and C are therefore incorrect.

The Divisional Court has held that, where officers who had arrested a man for a breach of the peace failed to arrest him formally for the further offence of assault on the police, their omission did not impact on the magistrates' decision that there was a case to answer in respect of the assault charge (*Blench* v *DPP* [2004] EWHC 2717 (Admin)). Answer D is therefore incorrect.

General Police Duties, paras 4.5.2, 4.5.10

Answer 5.2

Answer **A** — Section 28(1) and (3) of the Police and Criminal Evidence Act 1984 states:

(1) Subject to subsection (5) below, where a person is arrested, otherwise than by being informed that he is under arrest, the arrest is not lawful unless the person arrested is informed that he is under arrest as soon as is practicable after his arrest.

(2) ...

(3) Subject to subsection (5) below, no arrest is lawful unless the person arrested is informed of the ground for the arrest at the time of, or as soon as is practicable after, the arrest.

Nothing in s. 28 states that the person must be informed of the specific offence they are being arrested for; the section requires the person to be informed that they are under arrest and the *grounds* for that arrest and the court has held that it does not matter that the words describe more than one offence (e.g. 'burglary' or 'fraud'), provided that they adequately describe the offence for which the person has been arrested (*Abbassy* v *Metropolitan Police Commissioner* [1990] 1 WLR 385). Answer C is therefore incorrect.

The officer has complied with s. 28(1), in the previous extract, by informing the person he is under arrest; subs. (3), in the previous extract, allows for a person to be told the information as soon as is practicable after the arrest, which in this case could be when the officer manages to speak to a colleague or the control room over the radio. Answer B is therefore incorrect.

Finally, s. 28(5) states that nothing in this section is to be taken to require a person to be informed:

(a) that he is under arrest; or
(b) of the ground for the arrest,
if it was not reasonably practicable for him to be so informed by reason of his having escaped from arrest before the information could be given.

However, there is no provision for the officer to fail to give the information if he/she reasonably believes that the person may try to escape before being arrested and answer D is therefore incorrect.

General Police Duties, para. 4.5.2.1

Answer 5.3

Answer **B** — Code C, para. 10.4 of the PACE Codes of Practice requires that a person must be cautioned on arrest or further arrest. There are exceptions to the requirement to administer the caution and these are:

- where it is impracticable to do so by reason of the person's condition or behaviour at the time; or
- where he/she has already been cautioned immediately before the arrest in accordance with Code C, para. 10.1 (requirement to caution where there are grounds to suspect commission of an offence).

However, consideration also needs to be given to Code G, para. 4, Note for Guidance 1A, which states that the Code will not apply where a person is being arrested for a warrant or other matters, such as a breach of bail. It also states that the Code does not apply when a person is being arrested under a common law power to stop or prevent a breach of the peace. The caution should be given if it is intended to question a person about an 'offence' and since this is not a requirement for an arrest which is meant to simply place a person before the court, a caution is not required regardless of any other exceptions in Code C. Answers A and C are therefore incorrect.

Section 28(5) of PACE allows that a person need not be informed of the reason or grounds for their arrest if it was not reasonably practicable by reason of his/her having escaped from arrest before the information could be given. However, this exception is not listed in Code C, para. 10.4, which relates to cautions. Answer C is incorrect for this reason also.

There is nothing in Code C requiring a person to be cautioned as soon as practicable after their arrest, if they were not cautioned at the time, and therefore answer D is incorrect.

General Police Duties, paras 4.5.2.1, 4.5.2.2

Answer 5.4

Answer **B** — Code C, para. 2.9 of the PACE Codes of Practice states:

> When it is practicable to tell a person why their arrest is necessary (as required by paragraphs 2.2 and 3.3), the constable should outline the facts, information and other circumstances which provide the grounds for believing that their arrest is necessary and which the officer considers satisfy one or more of the statutory criteria in sub-paragraphs (a) to (f).

Answer D is therefore incorrect.

A warning is not expressly required by para. 2.9, but officers should, if practicable, consider whether to issue a warning which points out the person's offending behaviour, and explains why, if the person does not stop, the resulting consequences may make his/her arrest necessary. Such a warning might:

- if heeded, avoid the need to arrest; or
- if ignored, support the need to arrest and also help prove the mental element of certain offences, for example the person's intent or awareness, or help to rebut a defence that he/she was acting reasonably.

Answers A and C are incorrect for this reason.

General Police Duties, paras 4.5.4.4, 4.5.4.6

Answer 5.5

Answer **D** — Under s. 24A of the Police and Criminal Evidence Act 1984 certain powers of arrest are provided for any person. Section 24A states:

> (1) A person other than a constable may arrest without a warrant—
> (a) anyone who is in the act of committing an indictable offence;

(b) anyone whom he has reasonable grounds for suspecting to be committing an indictable offence.

(2) Where an indictable offence has been committed, a person other than a constable may arrest without a warrant—

(a) anyone who is guilty of the offence;

(b) anyone whom he has reasonable grounds for suspecting to be guilty of it.

(3) But the power of summary arrest conferred by subsection (1) or (2) is exercisable only if—

(a) the person making the arrest has reasonable grounds for believing that for any of the reasons mentioned in subsection (4) it is necessary to arrest the person in question; and

(b) it appears to the person making the arrest that it is not reasonably practicable for a constable to make it instead.

(4) The reasons are to prevent the person in question—

(a) causing physical injury to himself or any other person;

(b) suffering physical injury;

(c) causing loss of or damage to property; or

(d) making off before a constable can assume responsibility for him.

Section 24A(4)(d) of PACE does allow a member of the public to make a 'citizen's' arrest, where it is not reasonably practicable for a constable to make it instead; however, unlike the powers of arrest available to police officers (which apply to all offences), the 'citizen's' power of arrest only applies where the relevant offence is *indictable*. Answers A and C are therefore incorrect.

Under s. 24A, a person other than a constable may make such an arrest when an indictable offence *is* being committed, or *has* been committed; the power to make a preventative arrest (i.e. where an indictable offence is *about* to be committed) only applies to police officers. Answer B is therefore incorrect.

General Police Duties, para. 4.5.7

Answer 5.6

Answer **B** — Section 63A of the Police and Criminal Evidence Act 1984 provides a power of arrest without warrant in respect of people who:

- have been charged with/reported for a recordable offence and who have not had a sample taken or the sample was unsuitable/insufficient for analysis;
- have been convicted of a recordable offence and have not had a sample taken since conviction;
- have been so convicted and have had a sample taken before or since conviction but the sample was unsuitable/insufficient for analysis.

Whether the person has been charged or convicted, the only reason to arrest them to take samples is when the sample has not previously been taken or, if it has been taken, it was insufficient for analysis; however, a sample may not be taken simply because it has been lost by the police. Answers A and C are incorrect.

Answer D is incorrect because there *is* a power to take a second sample from someone, when they have previously provided one during the investigation, but it cannot be done in the circumstances described.

General Police Duties, para. 4.5.8.4

Answer 5.7

Answer **C** — The Criminal Justice and Public Order Act 1994 (ss. 136 to 140) makes provision for officers from one part of the United Kingdom to go into another part of the United Kingdom to arrest someone there in connection with an offence committed within their jurisdiction, and gives them powers to search on arrest.

An officer from a Scottish police force may arrest someone suspected of committing an offence in Scotland who is found in England, Wales or Northern Ireland if it would have been lawful to arrest that person had he/she been found in Scotland. Since this power is granted to Constable FRENCH, there is no requirement for an officer from an English police force to further arrest KELLEY and therefore answer D is incorrect.

Where an officer from a Scottish police force has arrested someone suspected of committing an offence in Scotland, who is found in England, the officer must take the person to the nearest convenient designated police station in Scotland *or* to the nearest convenient designated police station in England or Wales (see s. 137(7)).

Section 137(7) goes on to say that the person must be taken to the police station as soon as reasonably practicable. This would suggest that the arrested person should be taken to the nearest police station if the distance to one or another is too great. Since the arresting officer has a choice of police stations, answers A and B are incorrect.

General Police Duties, para. 4.5.8.5

Answer 5.8

Answer **C** — Warrants issued in connection with 'an offence' do not need to be in the possession of the officer executing them at the time. Answers A and D are therefore incorrect.

However, the requirement under s. 28 of the Police and Criminal Evidence Act 1984, to tell a person why he/she is being arrested, *does* apply to arrests under warrant. Answers B and D are incorrect for this reason also.

General Police Duties, para. 4.5.9

Answer 5.9

Answer **D** — Section 31 of the Police and Criminal Evidence Act 1984 states that where:

(a) a person—
  (i) has been arrested for an offence; and
  (ii) is at a police station in consequence of that arrest; and
(b) it appears to a constable that, if he were released from that arrest, he would be liable to arrest for some other offence, he shall be arrested for that other offence.

In *R* v *Samuel* [1988] QB 615, the Court of Appeal said that the purpose of the s. 31 requirement was to prevent the release and immediate re-arrest of an offender—therefore, the court noted, s. 31 did not prevent any further arrest from being delayed until the release of the prisoner for the initial arrest was imminent.

Therefore, there was no requirement to arrest HUNTER at any time before he was actually arrested. The only obligation under s. 31 is that the person should not be released from police detention and then rearrested, when there were sufficient grounds to arrest him/her before he/she was released. Answers A, B and C are therefore incorrect.

General Police Duties, para. 4.5.10

Answer 5.10

Answer **A** — Section 30 of the Police and Criminal Evidence Act 1984 states:

(1) Subsection (1A) applies where a person is, at any place other than a police station—
  (a) arrested by a constable for an offence, or
  (b) taken into custody by a constable after being arrested for an offence by a person other than a constable.

(1A) The person must be taken by a constable to a police station as soon as practicable after the arrest.

Section 30(1A) allows the officer to delay taking the arrested person to a police station where his/her presence elsewhere is necessary in order to carry out such investigations as it is reasonable to carry out immediately. Where there is such a delay, the reasons for it must be recorded when the person first arrives at the police station (s. 30(11)). Section 30(10) was confirmed in *R* v *Kerawalla* [1991] Crim LR 451, where the court held that if the matter can wait, the exception will not apply and the person must be taken straight to a police station. Answer C is therefore incorrect.

In *Dallison* v *Caffery* [1965] 1 QB 348, it was held that taking an arrested person to check out an alibi before going to a police station *may* be justified in some circumstances. Answer D is therefore incorrect.

Section 18(5)(a) of the Act allows a premises to be searched before the person is taken to a police station for evidence related to an indictable offence for which the person has been arrested or some other indictable offence which is connected with or similar to that offence. However, this is an *additional* power to the one under s. 30(10) and answer B is incorrect.

General Police Duties, paras 4.5.11, 4.7.5.3

6 Stop and Search

STUDY PREPARATION

One of the main functions of the police service is to prevent and detect crime. A key power given to police officers is the ability to stop and search individuals, or the vehicles they are in, to establish whether they are in possession of articles which are either stolen, or which may be used to commit crimes.

The police service has for years struggled to strike a balance between a pro-active approach to the use of these powers for these reasons, and a proportionate response to the needs of our diverse communities. As a result, police forces have signed up to the 'Best Use of Stop and Search Scheme' which is designed to enable forces to use stop and search strategically in an effort to improve confidence and trust.

The Police and Criminal Evidence Act 1984 (PACE) and the accompanying Codes of Practice provide the main legislative basis for police officers' use of stop and search powers; it is for line managers to ensure that they are used proportionately and in a non-discriminatory manner.

This chapter also covers the extended search powers available under the Criminal Justice and Public Order Act 1994 and the Terrorism Prevention and Investigation Measures Act 2011.

QUESTIONS

Question 6.1

Constable OVERTON was on patrol late at night and received a call concerning a person acting suspiciously. The officer attended immediately and found COSTA in the rear garden of a house. COSTA was extremely drunk and the officer could not establish why he was actually in the garden. Constable OVERTON spoke to the occupier of the house and she did not know COSTA and did not know why he was there. The officer decided to search COSTA to see if he had any identification, to establish who he was.

Did Constable OVERTON have the power to search COSTA under s. 1 of the Police and Criminal Evidence Act 1984, in these circumstances?

A No, searches in the garden of a dwelling are prohibited; this is not a public place.

B Yes, COSTA was not in his own garden and it would be lawful to search him for this reason.

C Yes, COSTA was not in his own garden and was not there with the occupier's permission; it would be lawful to search him for this reason.

D No, searches in the garden of a dwelling are not prohibited; however, there is no power to search COSTA for the reasons stated.

Question 6.2

Constable CORK attended a report of a theft in the High Street; a store detective had witnessed a female person removing two IPhones from a display and walking out of the shop. The female was now being tracked by the CCTV operator, who reported that she was accompanied by two girls; one was about 5 years of age and the other was about 2 years of age, in a pushchair. As Constable CORK approached the suspect, she was told that she had placed one of the IPhones in the older child's pocket and had hidden the other in the pushchair. Constable CORK detained the female and the two children.

Which of the following statements is correct, in relation to Constable CORK's power to search the two children, under s. 1 of the Police and Criminal Evidence Act 1984?

A Constable CORK could not search the children; because of their ages, they could not form the necessary criminal intent for this crime.

B Constable CORK could search the children, provided she had reasonable grounds to suspect she would find the stolen articles.

C Constable CORK could not search the children, because they are in innocent possession of stolen articles.

D Constable CORK could search the pushchair, because it is not a 'person'; however, she could not search the older child, because it could not form the necessary criminal intent for this crime.

Question 6.3

Constable HOLT was on patrol in a neighbourhood which is renowned for gangs of young people being involved in dealing drugs. As a member of the Neighbourhood Policing Team, Constable HOLT was aware that one of the main gangs in the area wore distinctive blue hoodies with a target on the rear of the garment as a means of their identification. The officer saw a group of young people outside a leisure centre, which was the usual location for dealing in the area, wearing clothing that identified them as part of the gang. Constable HOLT called for the assistance of other officers to approach the individuals and conduct a stop and search.

A stop and search under s. 1 of PACE generally requires the officer to have 'reasonable grounds' to stop and search a person. Would the distinctive clothing the gang is wearing provide such grounds?

A No, the reasonable grounds cannot be based on generalisations or stereotypical images of certain groups, such as wearing distinctive clothing.

B Yes, the distinctive clothing may provide Constable HOLT with the reasonable grounds for a search.

C Yes, the distinctive clothing would automatically provide Constable HOLT with the reasonable grounds to search all people wearing such clothing.

D No, the reasonable grounds can be based on personal factors, such as wearing distinctive clothing, but only if Constable HOLT anticipates discovering offensive weapons or other dangerous instruments.

Question 6.4

A football match is due to take place in Inspector CARTER's area, and she is the officer in charge of a support unit positioned outside the train station. Intelligence has suggested that approximately 200 away supporters will be arriving, and staff on the train have reported seeing several weapons being carried by fans. Inspector CARTER is considering searching all supporters before they leave the train station.

In relation to the powers to authorise searches under s. 60 of the Criminal Justice and Public Order Act 1994, which statement is correct?

A The inspector may authorise the searches, but only if she suspects there will be incidents involving serious violence.

B The inspector may authorise the searches, but only of those suspected of carrying weapons.

C The inspector may authorise the search of any of the fans, in these circumstances alone.

D The inspector may not authorise the searches; this power is restricted to superintendents.

Question 6.5

An authorisation is in place in the Eastshire Police area under s. 60 of the Criminal Justice and Public Order Act 1994. There were serious riots and looting on the Friday night when the authorisation was granted. On the Saturday night, intelligence suggests that further riots will take place over the whole weekend and into the following week, with gang members carrying knives and other weapons. Superintendent LEACH is the senior officer in charge of policing for the area and is considering whether or not the s. 60 authorisation should be extended.

In relation to such an extension, which of the following statements is correct?

A Superintendent LEACH may extend the authorisation period, for up to seven days, depending on the intelligence.

B Superintendent LEACH may extend the authorisation period once, for 24 hours; further use of the powers would require a new authorisation.

C Superintendent LEACH may extend the authorisation period for 24 hours; further extensions may take place for 24-hour periods, up to a maximum of seven days.

D Superintendent LEACH may extend the authorisation period twice, for two 24-hour periods; further use of the powers would require a new authorisation.

Question 6.6

Constable WILLIS was on patrol in uniform in the early hours of the morning in an area where there had recently been outbreaks of serious public disorder between two gangs, who were known to carry weapons. An order was in force, under s. 60 of the Criminal Justice and Public Order Act 1994, to stop and search persons in the locality. Constable WILLIS saw MOORE walking in the street wearing a ski mask, which was concealing his face.

In what circumstances could Constable WILLIS ask MOORE to remove his mask?

A If he reasonably believed that MOORE was likely to be involved in violence.

B No further circumstances are required, as an order is in force under s. 60.

C If he reasonably believed that MOORE was attempting to conceal his identity.

D If he reasonably believed that MOORE was carrying a dangerous instrument or an offensive weapon.

Question 6.7

Eastshire Constabulary control room received a report of a suspicious vehicle driving around at night. The informant stated that there were four male persons in the vehicle and that they were all wearing masks covering their faces. Constable BUNCE was on mobile patrol and heard the observations for the vehicle. Shortly afterwards, the officer spotted the vehicle and began following it. Constable BUNCE was aware that there had recently been incidents of serious public disorder in the locality and that there was an order in force, under s. 60 of the Criminal Justice and Public Order Act 1994, to stop and search persons for weapons. It was dark and Constable BUNCE could not tell whether the occupants were wearing masks or not, but the officer intended stopping the vehicle to establish if they were.

What powers would be available to Constable BUNCE under s. 60AA(1) of the Criminal Justice and Public Order Act 1994 (requirement to remove items worn for the purpose of concealing identity), in these circumstances?

A Constable BUNCE has the power to stop the vehicle under s. 60AA(1), in order to require the occupants to remove their masks.

B Constable BUNCE would have to use the general power under s. 163 of the Road Traffic Act 1988 to stop the vehicle; however, there is a power to search a vehicle for items used to conceal a person's identity under s. 60AA(1).

C Constable BUNCE has the power to stop the vehicle under s. 60AA(1), in order to require the occupants to remove their masks, or to search the vehicle for such items, if they are not wearing any.

D Constable BUNCE would have to use the general power under s. 163 of the Road Traffic Act 1988 to stop the vehicle; there is no power to search a vehicle for items used to conceal a person's identity under s. 60AA(1).

Question 6.8

Detective Constables SHELBY and MINTO have attended at KHAN's home address to serve a Terrorism Prevention and Investigation Measures (TPIM) notice on him under s. 2 of the Terrorism Prevention and Investigation Measures Act 2011, to restrict his movements because of his suspected links to terrorism. The officers are considering searching KHAN when the notice has been served to ascertain whether there is anything on him that contravenes the measures specified in the notice.

Which of the following statements is correct, in relation to any reasonable suspicion the officers must have, before such a search can take place?

A If they are in possession of a warrant accompanying the notice, they do not require any reasonable grounds to suspect that KHAN has anything on him that contravenes the measures specified in the notice.

B They do not require any reasonable grounds to suspect that KHAN has anything on him that contravenes the measures specified in the notice, regardless of whether or not they have a warrant.

C They require reasonable grounds to suspect that KHAN is in possession of articles connected with terrorism.

D They require reasonable grounds to suspect that KHAN is in possession of articles that could be used to threaten or harm any person.

Question 6.9

MIAH has previously been served with a Terrorism Prevention and Investigation Measures (TPIM) notice, under s. 2 of the Terrorism Prevention and Investigation Measures Act 2011. The police are in possession of intelligence that MIAH has obtained a smartphone and has been communicating with people abroad, over the Internet. This is contrary to the measures specified in the TPIM notice. The intelligence suggests he is using the phone whilst away from his home and the police have obtained a warrant to search MIAH for the phone.

Which of the following statements is correct, in relation to the measures that must be taken in order to conduct the search?

A The police may search MIAH on one occasion, within 28 days of the warrant being issued.

B There is no time limit in which the police have to perform the search, but they may only conduct it once.

C The police may search MIAH on more than one occasion if it is necessary to do so, but must do so within 28 days of the warrant being issued.

D The police may search MIAH on one occasion, within three months of the warrant being issued.

Question 6.10

DUNN was stopped in the street by Constables MEEK and PHELAN, both male officers. The officers had reasonable suspicion that DUNN was in possession of controlled drugs, as they had been conducting surveillance on him. They believed that the drugs were contained in a clear bag, hidden in his trousers, or possibly his underwear. While they were speaking to him, a police van pulled up to see if they needed assistance. The officers wish to search DUNN by requiring him to remove his trousers or if necessary his underwear.

To what extent could the officers search DUNN under s. 1 of the Police and Criminal Evidence Act 1984 (PACE), in these circumstances?

A They could require DUNN to remove these items of clothing in the rear of the van, provided it is out of public view.

B They would have to take DUNN to a nearby police station if they want to remove his underwear.

C They could take DUNN to a nearby police station, or another nearby location which is out of public view, if they want to remove his underwear.

D They could not remove DUNN's underwear anywhere; this would be an intimate search which may not be authorised under s. 1 of PACE.

Question 6.11

Constable DANIELLS, a male officer, and Constable NEVIN, a female officer, stopped BENTLEY in the car park of a shopping centre. The officers had reasonable suspicion that BENTLEY was in possession of stolen goods, having received information from a CCTV operator who had seen her shoplifting. The officers were in a police van at the time and had been told that BENTLEY was possibly hiding a stolen necklace in her coat pocket.

Which of the following statements is correct, according to the PACE Codes of Practice, in relation to searching BENTLEY?

A Only Constable NEVIN could search BENTLEY in these circumstances.

B Either officer could search BENTLEY, provided they were only searching her outer garments.

C Either officer could search BENTLEY, provided they were only searching her outer garments and the search took place out of public view.

D Only Constable NEVIN could search BENTLEY in these circumstances, although the search could take place in the presence of Constable DANIELLS.

Question 6.12

Constable LIPINSKI conducted a stop and search of GRANTHAM, who was driving a motor vehicle on a road, and the vehicle itself. The officer correctly provided GRANTHAM with a copy of the stop/search form. GRANTHAM was not the owner of the vehicle and indicated that MORLING, the actual owner, would probably wish to have a copy at some stage.

Which of the following statements is correct, in relation to MORLING being allowed a copy of the stop/search record?

A If MORLING requests a copy, one should be provided within three months of the date of the search.

B MORLING is not entitled to a copy; Constable LIPINSKI has correctly supplied GRANTHAM with one as the driver of the vehicle and the person searched.

C MORLING must be provided with a copy within three months of the date of the search.

D If MORLING requests a copy, one should be provided within 12 months of the date of the search.

Question 6.13

Constable BAIRD attended a suspicious incident reported by POOLE, a CCTV operator. POOLE saw two men acting suspiciously near a 4 × 4 vehicle, and saw one of the men hand the other a bag of white powder. He believed the bag was placed inside the cover of the spare wheel attached to the rear door of the vehicle. As a result of this information, Constable BAIRD searched the spare wheel, but found nothing inside.

Is Constable BAIRD required to supply a notice of this search, under s. 2 of the Police and Criminal Evidence Act 1984?

A Yes, it should be placed on the vehicle, and a copy sent to the registered owner.

B No, a notice is not required as the inside of the vehicle was not searched.

C Yes, it should be placed inside the vehicle, which may be entered by force to do so.

D Yes, a notice must be placed somewhere on the vehicle.

ANSWERS

Answer 6.1

Answer **D** — Under s. 1(2) of the Police and Criminal Evidence Act 1984, a constable:

(a) may search—
  (i) any person or vehicle;
  (ii) anything which is in or on a vehicle, for stolen or prohibited articles or any article to which subsection (8A) below applies or any firework to which subsection (8B) below applies; and
(b) may detain a person or vehicle for the purpose of such a search.

The authority under s. 1 of PACE may be used to search for *stolen or prohibited* articles; there is no specific power to search a person to establish their identity in these circumstances. Answers B and C are therefore incorrect.

Searches in gardens of dwellings are not prohibited altogether; under s. 1(4), where a person is in a garden or yard occupied with and used for the purposes of a dwelling or on other land so occupied and used, a constable may not search him/her in the exercise of the power conferred by this section unless the constable has reasonable grounds for believing:

(a) that he/she does not reside in the dwelling; and
(b) that he/she is not in the place in question with the express or implied permission of a person who resides in the dwelling.

The officer *could* have searched the suspect for stolen or prohibited articles, provided there were reasonable grounds to do so, but not for the reasons stated in the question.

General Police Duties, para. 4.6.4.1

Answer 6.2

Answer **B** — Under s. 1(2) of the Police and Criminal Evidence Act 1984, a constable:

(a) may search—
  (i) any person or vehicle;
  (ii) anything which is in or on a vehicle, for stolen or prohibited articles or any article to which subsection (8A) below applies or any firework to which subsection (8B) below applies; and
(b) may detain a person or vehicle for the purpose of such a search.

Paragraph 2.2A of Code A states that:

> The exercise of these stop and search powers depends on the likelihood that the person searched is in possession of an item for which they may be searched; it does not depend on the person concerned being suspected of committing an offence in relation to the object of the search.

Paragraph 2.2A further states that a police officer who has reasonable grounds to suspect that a person is in innocent possession of a stolen or prohibited article, controlled drug or other item for which the officer is empowered to search, may stop and search the person even though there would be no power of arrest. Answers C and D are therefore incorrect.

This would even apply when a child under the age of criminal responsibility (10 years) is suspected of carrying any such item, even if they knew they had it. Answers A and D are incorrect for this reason also.

General Police Duties, paras 4.6.4.1, 4.6.4.3

Answer 6.3

Answer **B** — Under s. 1(2) of PACE, a constable may search any person or vehicle, or anything which is in or on a vehicle, for stolen or prohibited articles, fireworks or any article to which subs. (8A) (articles in connection with burglary, theft, etc.) applies. Section 1(3) states that a constable does not have a power to search a person or vehicle or anything in or on a vehicle unless he/she has reasonable grounds for suspecting that he/she will find such articles.

Code A, para. 2.2 outlines the objective basis for that suspicion based on facts, information and/or intelligence which are relevant to the likelihood of finding an article of a certain kind and goes on to state that reasonable suspicion cannot be based on generalisations or stereotypical images of certain groups or categories of people as more likely to be involved in criminal activity. However, under para. 2.6 of the Code:

> where there is reliable information or intelligence that members of a group or gang habitually carry knives unlawfully or weapons or controlled drugs, and wear a distinctive item of clothing or other means of identification to indicate their membership of the group or gang, that distinctive item of clothing or other means of identification may provide reasonable grounds to stop and search a person.

Therefore, the distinctive clothing and the officer's prior knowledge of the group *may* provide the required reasonable grounds to conduct a stop and search for controlled drugs and for this reason answers A and D are incorrect.

However, para. 2.6 does not provide an *automatic power to search all people wearing such clothing*. There would have to be an objective basis for the search and therefore answer C is incorrect.

General Police Duties, para. 4.6.4.3

Answer 6.4

Answer **C** — Under s. 60 of the Criminal Justice and Public Order Act 1994, if an inspector reasonably believes that incidents of serious violence may take place in his/her area, or that people are carrying dangerous instruments or offensive weapons, he/she may give an authorisation to stop any pedestrian and search him/her for offensive weapons or dangerous instruments.

The power used to be restricted to superintendents, but may now be exercised by an inspector (which is why answer D is incorrect). However, when the power is exercised by an inspector, he/she must inform an officer of the rank of superintendent as soon as is reasonably practicable.

The authorisation may be given either for incidents of serious violence *or* to search for dangerous instruments or offensive weapons (making answer A incorrect). The power is to search any pedestrian, and is not restricted to those who may be carrying dangerous instruments or offensive weapons (which is why answer B is incorrect).

General Police Duties, para. 4.6.4.5

Answer 6.5

Answer **B** — Under s. 60 of the Criminal Justice and Public Order Act 1994, if an inspector reasonably believes that incidents of serious violence may take place in his/her area, or that people are carrying dangerous instruments or offensive weapons, he/she may give an authorisation to stop any pedestrian and search him/her for offensive weapons or dangerous instruments.

It is for the authorising officer, who must be a superintendent, to determine the period of time during which the power may be exercised and in any event this must not exceed 24 hours. The officer should set the minimum period he/she considers necessary to deal with the risk of violence, the carrying of knives or offensive weapons.

A direction to *extend* the period authorised under the power may be given only once. This extension is for a maximum period of 24 hours and thereafter further use of the powers requires a new authorisation. In the context of this question, the extension may be granted on the Saturday night, but if intelligence suggests further incidents will take place on the Sunday and Monday night, a new authorisation may be put in place on the Sunday, which can be extended to the Monday if necessary.

Answers A, C and D are incorrect for these reasons.

General Police Duties, paras 4.6.4.5, 4.6.4.6

Answer 6.6

Answer **C** — Under s. 60AA(1) of the Criminal Justice and Public Order Act 1994, where an authorisation under s. 60 is in force, a constable in uniform may require any person to remove any item which the constable reasonably believes that person is wearing wholly or mainly for the purpose of concealing his/her identity. The power is not absolute, as the constable has reasonably to believe that the person is wearing the item to conceal his/her identity (therefore answer B is incorrect). There is no need, however, for the constable reasonably to believe that the person is carrying a dangerous instrument or an offensive weapon, or that the person is likely to be involved in violence, in order to exercise the power under s. 60AA(1). Those matters would have been considered before the authorisation was granted under s. 60. Answers A and D are therefore incorrect.

General Police Duties, para. 4.6.4.9

Answer 6.7

Answer **D** — Under s. 60AA(1) of the Criminal Justice and Public Order Act 1994, where an authorisation under s. 60 is in force, a constable in uniform may require any person to remove any item which the constable reasonably believes that person is wearing wholly or mainly for the purpose of concealing his/her identity. However, unlike s. 60, there is no specific power under this section to stop vehicles and therefore answers A and C are incorrect.

There is also no power to search for face coverings etc. under s. 60AA(1). The Divisional Court has held that the predecessor to this power (the old s. 60(4A)) neither involved nor required a 'search' and that therefore the provisions of s. 2 of the Police and Criminal Evidence Act 1984 did not apply (*DPP* v *Avery* [2001] EWHC 748 (Admin)). The court went on to hold that, although the power amounted to a significant interference with a person's liberty, it was justified by the type of situation envisaged by the legislators, whereby the police may need to call upon the law. Clearly, if an item is found during a lawful search for other articles (say, under s. 60(4)) which does not require any 'reasonable belief' by the officer, face coverings and masks could then be seized under s. 60AA(2)(b). As there is no accompanying power of search under s. 60AA, answer B is incorrect.

Given that this is a power for police officers in uniform, the general power to stop vehicles under s. 163 of the Road Traffic Act 1988 could be used.

General Police Duties, paras 4.6.4.9, 4.6.4.13

Answer 6.8

Answer **B** — Paragraph 3 of sch. 5 to the Terrorism Prevention and Investigation Measures Act 2011 allows a constable to detain an individual to be searched under the following powers:

- para. 6(2)(a) when a TPIM notice is being, or has just been, served on the individual for the purpose of ascertaining whether there is anything on the individual that contravenes measures specified in the notice;
- para. 8(2)(a) in accordance with a warrant to search the individual if that search is necessary to determine whether an individual is complying with measures specified in the notice (see para. 2.20); and
- para. 10 to ascertain whether an individual in respect of whom a TPIM notice is in force is in possession of anything that could be used to threaten or harm any person.

The officers in the question are exercising their powers under para. 6(2)(a)—serving a TPIM notice without a warrant—which allows them to search KHAN.

Paragraph 2.19 of the PACE Code of Practice in relation to sch. 5 states that when exercising his/her powers of search, there is no requirement for the constable to have reasonable grounds to suspect that the individual has been, or is, contravening any of the measures specified in the TPIM notice; or is not complying with measures specified in the TPIM notice; or is in possession of anything that could be used to threaten or harm any person.

In summary, the officers can simply search KAHN because they are attending to serve the TPIM notice on him, and answers A, C and D are incorrect.

General Police Duties, para. 4.6.4.14

Answer 6.9

Answer **A** — Paragraph 8(2)(a) of sch. 5 to the Terrorism Prevention and Investigation Measures Act 2011 allows a constable to detain and search an individual in accordance with a warrant, if that search is necessary to determine whether an individual is complying with measures specified in the notice.

Paragraph 2.20 of the PACE Code of Practice in relation to sch. 5 states that a search of an individual on warrant under the power mentioned must be carried out within 28 days of the issue of the warrant and:

- the individual may be searched on one occasion only within that period;
- the search must take place at a reasonable hour unless it appears that this would frustrate the purposes of the search.

This means that answer A is correct, and answers B, C and D are incorrect.

General Police Duties, para. 4.6.4.14

Answer 6.10

Answer **C** — Code C, para. 3.5 of the PACE Codes of Practice states that there is no power to require a person to remove any clothing in public other than an outer coat, jacket or gloves (except under s. 60AA of the Criminal Justice and Public Order Act 1994, which empowers a constable to require a person to remove any item worn to conceal identity).

Paragraph 3.6 states that where, on reasonable grounds, it is considered necessary to conduct a more thorough search (e.g. by requiring a person to take off a T-shirt or trousers), this must be done out of public view, for example in a police van or police station if there is one nearby.

Paragraph 3.7 states that searches involving exposure of intimate parts of the body may be carried out only at a nearby police station *or other nearby location* which is out of public view (but not a police vehicle). Answers A and B are therefore incorrect.

This paragraph goes on to say that a search involving exposure of intimate parts of the body must be conducted in accordance with the requirements of Annex A to Code C (intimate searches), but that an intimate search may not be authorised or carried out under any stop and search powers. However, what the officers propose to do amounts to a strip search only (intimate searches involve searching body orifices other than the mouth) and this *may* be conducted under s. 1, at either of the locations described previously. Answer D is therefore incorrect.

General Police Duties, para. 4.6.5

Answer 6.11

Answer **B** — Code C, para. 3.5 of the PACE Codes of Practice states that there is no power to require a person to remove any clothing in public other than an outer coat, jacket or gloves (except under s. 60AA of the Criminal Justice and Public Order Act 1994, which empowers a constable to require a person to remove any item worn to conceal identity).

A search in public of a person's clothing which has not been removed must be restricted to superficial examination of outer garments. This does not, however, prevent an officer from placing his/her hand inside the pockets of the outer clothing, or feeling round the inside of collars, socks and shoes if this is reasonably necessary in the circumstances to look for the object of the search or to remove and examine any item reasonably suspected to be the object of the search. For the same reasons, subject to the restrictions on the removal of headgear, a person's hair may also be searched in public.

The only time the gender of the officer is mentioned in this Code is when it relates to conducting a more thorough search. Paragraph 3.6 states that where on reasonable grounds it is considered necessary to conduct a more thorough search (e.g. by requiring a person to take off a T-shirt), this must be done out of public view, for example in a police van or police station if there is one nearby.

This paragraph goes on to say that any search involving the removal of more than an outer coat, jacket, gloves, headgear or footwear, or any other item concealing identity, may only be made by an officer of the same sex as the person searched and may not be made in the presence of anyone of the opposite sex unless the person being searched specifically requests it.

This means that Constable DANIELLS *could* go through BENTLEY's pockets, according to Code C, but if the item is not found and a more thorough search is required, the male officer may not be present or conduct the search. Answers A and D are therefore incorrect.

There is no requirement to conduct a search of outer garments out of public view and answer C is incorrect.

Note that this question is simply a matter of what is written in Code C; it may be that some forces have a policy which prohibits officers searching people of the opposite sex and care would need to be taken not to breach the Equality Act 2010. However, in the circumstances, there would be nothing wrong with asking BENTLEY to take her coat off so that the pockets may be searched by either officer.

General Police Duties, para. 4.6.5

Answer 6.12

Answer **A** — Where a search record has been made, the person searched, the owner or the person who was in charge of any vehicle that was searched, will be entitled to a copy of the record. Answer B is therefore incorrect.

The person must be supplied with a copy *if he/she requests one*. Answer C is incorrect, as this will be supplied on request.

The Crime and Security Act 2010 reduced the entitlement from 12 months to three months; therefore, answer D is incorrect.

General Police Duties, para. 4.6.6.2

Answer 6.13

Answer **D** — Section 2(6) of the Police and Criminal Evidence Act 1984 states that 'on completing the search of an unattended vehicle, or anything in or on such a vehicle, a constable shall leave a notice'. Therefore, even though the spare tyre was not actually in the vehicle, a notice must be left, and for that reason answer B is incorrect.

There may be occasions when officers have to force entry into a vehicle in order to search it. On such an occasion, the officer must, if practicable, leave the vehicle secure (Code A, para. 4.10). However, where the vehicle has not been damaged during the search, s. 2(7) states that 'the constable shall leave the notice inside the vehicle unless it is not reasonably practicable to do so without damaging the vehicle'. Answer C is therefore incorrect.

There is no obligation on the officer to send a notice to the registered owner's address, and therefore answer A is incorrect.

General Police Duties, para. 4.6.6.2

7 Entry, Search and Seizure

STUDY PREPARATION

In the previous chapter, we examined the powers to search people and vehicles for evidence of an offence. This chapter deals with the powers to enter and search *premises* either to seize evidence of an offence, or to arrest a person. These powers generally fall into two categories:

1. search of premises under the authority of a warrant;
2. search of premises without the authority of a warrant.

Knowing and understanding these powers leads to confidence, not just as a student or exam candidate but as a police officer generally.

Changes were made to PACE procedures by the Serious Organised Crime and Police Act 2005, in respect of the application and execution of warrants and the extent to which some non-warranted police staff may enter and search premises to seize evidence of an offence.

Part 2 of the Criminal Justice and Police Act 2001 provides a power allowing officers searching premises to seize documents and sift through them at a different location.

QUESTIONS

Question 7.1

DC HALL is investigating an allegation that FRISK, who owns a building company, paid bribes to officers in a local authority planning department over a number of years, to push through planning applications. DC HALL has recovered evidence from a search of FRISK's offices and anticipates seizing numerous documents and computers at the local authority offices. DC HALL is seeking a multiple entry search warrant, but is uncertain how many visits will be required to complete the evidence-gathering process.

Which of the following statements is correct, in relation to the type of warrant DC HALL is seeking?

A DC HALL must state the maximum number of entries desired in the application for the warrant.

B DC HALL may apply for a warrant authorising unlimited entries in these circumstances, because the maximum number is unknown.

C DC HALL is not required to specify the number of entries desired; the warrant will automatically authorise unlimited entries.

D DC HALL is not required to specify the number of entries desired; an inspector may authorise further entries if necessary.

Question 7.2

DC GRANT is investigating a case involving a series of frauds. The officer has obtained an all premises warrant which authorises the search of PEDERSON's office and home address. DC GRANT has recovered documents that suggest PEDERSON owns two other premises where evidence may be found.

Will the warrant in DC GRANT's possession authorise the search of the other two premises?

A Yes, provided entry to those premises is authorised by an inspector in writing.

B Yes, provided entry to those premises is authorised by a superintendent in writing.

C No, DC GRANT will have to apply to a magistrate for another all premises warrant to search those premises.

D Yes, provided entry to those premises is authorised by an inspector in writing, or if one is not readily available, the senior officer on duty.

Question 7.3

DC GOMEZ was the officer in charge of a search which was conducted at MALONEY's home address. Officers entered the premises by force under the authority of a warrant to search for property stolen from a recent burglary at a jeweller's shop. The search team found several items of jewellery matching the description of the stolen goods and these were seized as evidence. MALONEY was not present when the search took place and DC GOMEZ established that there was no other person available who appeared to be in charge of the premises; however, the officer forgot to leave a copy of the warrant in a prominent place in the premises.

Given that DC GOMEZ has failed to follow the requirements of s. 16(7) of PACE by not leaving a copy of the warrant in a prominent place, which of the following statements is correct?

A The search was unlawful; this may result in the exclusion of any evidence obtained under the warrant and officers could be made to return the jewellery to MALONEY.

B This is a minor deviation from the terms of the warrant which would not render the search unlawful or result in the exclusion of any evidence obtained.

C The search was unlawful; this may result in the exclusion of any evidence obtained under the warrant, but officers could not be made to return the jewellery to MALONEY.

D The search was unlawful, but a failure to follow the requirements of s. 16 will not result in the exclusion of any evidence obtained under the warrant.

Question 7.4

A number of raves have been taking place on weekends and officers suspect that COOKSLEY is the organiser. The location of the events changes every week and intelligence suggests that COOKSLEY is dealing Class A drugs from a tent that is erected at each venue, which also contains the sound equipment for the rave. Officers have information that COOKSLEY transports the equipment and drugs to the venues in the back of a van. They are considering applying for a warrant under the Misuse of Drugs Act 1971 to search the vehicle and tent for drugs. However, COOKSLEY's address is unknown and officers will have to wait until the following weekend for intelligence on the next venue.

Which of the following statements is correct, in relation to the officers' intentions?

A Only the tent is a 'premises' in respect of a search warrant; there is no power to apply for a warrant to search a vehicle in this way.

B Both the tent and the vehicle are 'premises' and officers could apply for a search warrant in respect of both.

C Neither the tent (which is a moveable structure) nor the vehicle are 'premises' in respect of a search warrant; officers will have to use other powers to search them.

D Officers will have to use other powers to search both the tent and the vehicle; a search warrant requires a location to be specified in it before one can be issued.

Question 7.5

DC PRICE is investigating a fraud case and has uncovered evidence that a number of solicitors from a local firm may be involved. The officer has applied to a justice of the peace for a warrant under s. 8 of the Police and Criminal Evidence Act 1984, to enter and search the solicitors' offices for evidence relating to the offence. DC PRICE has reasonable cause to believe that there may be communications between solicitors and clients referring to the fraud. The officer is aware that there may be a substantial amount of paper and computer records on the premises and is anticipating having to use powers under s. 50 of the Criminal Justice and Police Act 2001 to seize and sift evidence.

Which of the following statements is correct, in relation to items subject to legal privilege which may be on the premises?

A Any communication between solicitors and clients is subject to legal privilege and cannot be searched for or seized under the terms of a warrant.

B Any items found that relate to criminal offences are not subject to legal privilege and may be searched for or seized.

C A warrant cannot authorise a search for legally privileged material and if such material is inadvertently seized, it would render the search unlawful.

D The possession of a warrant under s. 8 authorises any material found on the premises to be seized and sifted.

Question 7.6

Late at night, Constable CLYNE was in uniform following a motor vehicle on a road, which was not displaying any lights. The officer activated the sirens and blue lights to the police vehicle, attempting to get the other vehicle to stop. However, the other vehicle accelerated away from Constable CLYNE and was lost after a period of time. About an hour later, the officer attended the address of the registered owner of the vehicle, found outside, and knocked on the door; however, there was no reply. There were lights on at the premises and Constable CLYNE believed that the driver was inside the premises.

Given that Constable CLYNE may have had reasonable grounds for believing that the driver was on the premises, was there a power of entry in these circumstances?

A No, the driver had not been involved in an accident which involved injury to any person.

B Yes, the driver of the vehicle failed to stop when required to do so by a constable in uniform.

C No, Constable CLYNE was not in immediate pursuit of the driver of the vehicle.

D Yes, but only if Constable CLYNE had reason to believe that the driver was unfit to drive through drink or drugs.

Question 7.7

Constable LIU has attended the scene of a road traffic collision where a van had collided with a parked and unattended car at the side of the road. The parked car had sustained substantial damage and the driver of the van had made off from the collision. People at the scene stated that they had followed the van for some time and they believed the driver was drunk from the manner of driving they had witnessed. Also, they had seen the driver drinking from cans of lager while driving on the road and throwing empty cans out of the window. Constable LIU was considering searching the van for evidence that the driver had been drinking, under s. 32 of the Police and Criminal Evidence Act 1984.

Which of the following statements is correct in relation to any power Constable LIU may have to search the vehicle in these circumstances?

A Constable LIU may not search the vehicle under this section; it is restricted to searching for articles which may assist a person to escape from lawful custody.

B Constable LIU may search the vehicle under this section for anything which might be evidence relating to an offence.

C Constable LIU may not conduct a search under this section; it is restricted to searching people or premises and not vehicles.

D Constable LIU may not conduct a search under this section; the driver has not been arrested for an indictable offence.

Question 7.8

A burglary occurred in the early hours of the morning; a witness took the registration number of a vehicle driving away. Following intelligence checks, Constable JULIEN traced the vehicle to BARRY and attended his home with Constable RUSSELL. Entering the street, the officers saw BARRY stood next to the suspect vehicle, which was parked outside the relevant address. As the officers approached, BARRY was using a mobile phone and they heard him say, 'Get round the house now and get rid of the stuff; the police are here'. Constable RUSSELL immediately arrested BARRY for burglary and the officers debated whether they had a power to enter the premises immediately, to try to prevent any stolen property being disposed of.

Given that the officers were correct in assuming that BARRY lived at the address, could Constable JULIEN enter and search the premises without further authority?

A No, Constable JULIEN would require written authority from an inspector to enter and search the premises.

B No, Constable JULIEN would require authority from an inspector, but because of the urgency of the situation this may be verbal; the authority must be confirmed in writing as soon as is reasonably practicable.

C Yes, provided Constable JULIEN had reasonable grounds to believe BARRY was on the premises immediately prior to the arrest.

D Yes, provided Constable JULIEN informed an inspector as soon as practicable after the search was conducted.

Question 7.9

SHERWOOD has been arrested on suspicion of burglary and is detained at a police station. The officer in the case, DC FREDRICKS, intends seeking permission from the duty inspector to search SHERWOOD's home address, under s. 18 of the Police and Criminal Evidence Act 1984 (PACE); however, SHERWOOD has claimed to be of no fixed abode. DC FREDRICKS has found a recent address for SHERWOOD on the Force Intelligence System, which is believed to be his girlfriend's residence.

Could DC FREDRICKS receive authority to search SHERWOOD's girlfriend's address under s. 18(1) of PACE, in these circumstances?

A Yes, DC FREDRICKS has reasonable suspicion that SHERWOOD resides at the premises.

B Yes, DC FREDRICKS has reasonable cause to suspect that SHERWOOD occupies or controls the premises.

C No, DC FREDRICKS would need more than a reasonable cause to suspect that SHERWOOD occupies or controls the premises.

D No, even if SHERWOOD does live at his girlfriend's address, there is no reason to believe that he occupies *and* controls the premises.

Question 7.10

Constable ELLIS attended a dwelling burglary in progress at 2 am. On arrival, the officer was told that the householders had disturbed the suspect, who had escaped through the back door into the rear garden. They had seen the suspect carrying a bag, believed to have contained items stolen from their house. The victims' rear garden was enclosed and was adjacent to several other houses; it was believed that the suspect had climbed over fences and escaped through the other gardens, on to the main street nearby. Whilst making a search of the area, Constable ELLIS received a message that GRAFF had been arrested in a street nearby, by other officers, and that he matched the suspect's description. However, this person was not carrying a bag as described by the witnesses. Constable ELLIS intended returning to the crime scene to search the neighbours' gardens for the bag, to try to link it to GRAFF.

What authority would Constable ELLIS require, in order to search neighbours' gardens, in these circumstances?

A Constable ELLIS would require the occupiers' permission, unless she was in immediate pursuit of a suspect.

B Constable ELLIS would *not* require the occupiers' permission, as this may cause disproportionate inconvenience to the person concerned.

C Constable ELLIS would *not* require the occupiers' permission, as this may cause disproportionate inconvenience to the investigation.

D Constable ELLIS would require the statutory authority of a warrant or through PACE (s. 17, 18 or 32). Otherwise she would require the occupiers' permission.

Question 7.11

Constable ALLEN has attended SAYEED's home address to serve him with a Terrorism Prevention and Investigation Measures (TPIM) notice, under s. 2 of the Terrorism Prevention and Investigation Measures Act 2011, to restrict his movements because of his suspected links to terrorism. The TPIM requires SAYEED to reside at the address on the notice and prohibits him from travelling overseas. The notice also contains a list of people that SAYEED is not to contact. On serving the notice, Constable ALLEN decided that SAYEED's address should be searched to discover anything that might breach any measures specified in the TPIM notice.

Which of the following statements is correct, in relation to whether Constable ALLEN may search SAYEED's address?

A A search of premises in connection with a TPIM notice may only be made under warrant.

B A search of premises may only be made in connection with a TPIM notice without a warrant, where the person has absconded.

C A search of premises may only be made in connection with a TPIM notice without a warrant, if it is conducted for the purposes of finding the individual on whom the notice is to be served.

D A search of premises may be made without a warrant at the time of serving a TPIM notice, to ascertain whether there is anything in the premises that contravenes measures specified in the notice.

ANSWERS

Answer 7.1

Answer **B** — Section 15(2)(iii) of the Police and Criminal Evidence Act 1984 states:

> if the application is for a warrant authorising entry and search on more than one occasion, the ground on which he applies for such a warrant, and whether he seeks a warrant authorising an unlimited number of entries, or (if not) the maximum number of entries desired.

Therefore, an officer will normally be required to specify the number of entries desired and the warrant will *not* automatically authorise unlimited entries. Answer C is therefore incorrect.

On the other hand, s. 15(2)(iii) does provide some flexibility in case the number of entries is unknown (answer A is therefore incorrect).

Section 16(3B) of the Act deals with the authority required from an inspector in relation to multiple entry warrants. Under this section, premises may not be entered or searched for the second or any subsequent time under a warrant which authorises multiple entries, unless a police officer of at least the rank of inspector has authorised that in writing. The section does not give an inspector the power to authorise multiple entries; on the contrary, it places a restriction on such warrants so that each entry must be authorised by an inspector, even when multiple entries have been authorised by a magistrate. Answer D is therefore incorrect.

General Police Duties, paras 4.7.3.2, 4.7.3.3

Answer 7.2

Answer **A** — Section 16 of the Police and Criminal Evidence Act 1984 states:

> (3A) If the warrant is an all premises warrant, no premises which are not specified in it may be entered or searched unless a police officer of at least the rank of inspector has in writing authorised them to be entered.

There is no provision under this section for a senior officer on duty to authorise entry to new premises if an inspector is not readily available and there is no requirement for a superintendent to sign the authorisation. Answers B and D are therefore incorrect.

Also, there will be no requirement for the officer to apply to a magistrate for another all premises warrant to search those premises. Answer C is therefore incorrect.

General Police Duties, para. 4.7.3.3

Answer 7.3

Answer **A** — Section 16(7) of PACE states that if there is no person present who appears to the constable to be in charge of the premises, he/she shall leave a copy of the warrant in a prominent place on the premises. There was a clear breach of the terms of the warrant by DC GOMEZ in this case, which means that any entry and search made under a warrant will be unlawful. Further, a failure to follow the requirements of ss. 15 and 16 of PACE may result in the exclusion of any evidence obtained under the warrant. Answer D is therefore incorrect.

Where officers failed to provide the occupier of the searched premises with a copy of the warrant, they were obliged to return the property seized during the search (*R* v *Chief Constable of Lancashire, ex parte Parker* [1993] QB 577). As this is a possibility, answer C is incorrect.

Very minor departures from the letter of the warrant will not render any search unlawful (*Attorney General of Jamaica* v *Williams* [1998] AC 351); however, *Parker* suggests that failing to provide a copy of the warrant would not be considered a *minor* departure from the requirement to do so under s. 16.

General Police Duties, paras 4.7.3.3, 4.7.3.6

Answer 7.4

Answer **B** — Section 23 of PACE states that 'premises' include any place, and in particular:

(a) any vehicle, vessel, aircraft or hovercraft;
(b) any offshore installation;
(c) any renewable energy installation;
(d) any tent or moveable structure.

Answers A and C are therefore incorrect.

Since 'premises' includes any place, officers are not restricted by the fact that they are not yet aware of the location of the rave and therefore answer D is incorrect.

General Police Duties, para. 4.7.3.4

Answer 7.5

Answer **B** — Section 10(1) of the Police and Criminal Evidence Act 1984 states that subject to subs. (2), 'items subject to legal privilege' means:

(a) communications between a professional legal adviser and his client or any person representing his client made in connection with the giving of legal advice to the client;
(b) communications between a professional legal adviser and his client or any person representing his client or between such an adviser or his client or any such representative and any other person made in connection with or in contemplation of legal proceedings and for the purposes of such proceedings; and
(c) items enclosed with or referred to in such communications and made—
  (i) in connection with the giving of legal advice; or
  (ii) in connection with or in contemplation of legal proceedings and for the purposes of such proceedings,

when they are in the possession of a person who is entitled to possession of them.

Generally, material which falls within the definition in s. 10(1) is subject to legal privilege, which means that it cannot be searched for or seized. However, items held with the intention of furthering a criminal purpose are no longer subject to this privilege (s. 10(2)). Occasions where this will happen are very rare, but could include instances where a solicitor's firm is the subject of a criminal investigation (see *R* v *Leeds Crown Court, ex parte Switalski* [1991] Crim LR 559). Answer A is therefore incorrect.

Although a warrant cannot authorise a search for legally privileged material, the fact that such material is inadvertently seized in the course of a search authorised by a proper warrant does not render the search unlawful (*HM Customs* & *Excise, ex parte Popely* [2000] Crim LR 388). Answer C is therefore incorrect.

Possession of a warrant under s. 8 does not authorise police officers to seize *all* material found on the relevant premises to be taken away and 'sifted' somewhere else (*R* v *Chesterfield Justices, ex parte Bramley* [2000] QB 576). Officers using seize and sift powers will have to be able to show that it was essential (rather than simply convenient or preferable) to do so. Answer D is incorrect.

General Police Duties, paras 4.7.3.7, 4.7.3.8, 4.7.8.7

Answer 7.6

Answer **B** — There are several powers to enter premises under s.17 of the Police and Criminal Evidence Act 1984, including circumstances when the constable has reason to believe that the driver was unfit to drive through drink or drugs. However, under s. 17(1)(c)(iiia), provided the constable has reasonable grounds for believing that the person whom he/she is seeking is on the premises, the constable may enter for the purposes of arresting a person for an offence under s. 163 of the Road Traffic Act 1988 (failure to stop when required to do so by constable in uniform). Answer D is therefore incorrect.

There are powers to enter premises, under s. 6E of the Road Traffic Act 1988, to deal with breathalyser offences, where there are reasonable grounds to believe that the driver had been involved in an accident which involved injury to any person; however, this is not the only power of entry and answer A is incorrect.

Finally, there are further powers under s. 17(d) to recapture a person who is unlawfully at large and whom the officer is pursuing; however, the power to enter premises under s. 17(iiia) does not require the constable to be in 'immediate pursuit' and answer C is incorrect.

General Police Duties, para. 4.7.5.1

Answer 7.7

Answer **D** — Under s. 32(2)(a) of the Police and Criminal Evidence Act 1984, a constable may search an arrested person for anything:

(a) which he might use to assist him to escape from lawful custody; or
(b) which might be evidence relating to an offence.

Under s. 32(2)(b), if the offence for which he/she has been arrested is an indictable offence, there is a further power to enter and search any premises in which the person was when arrested or immediately before he/she was arrested for evidence relating to the offence.

The section is not restricted to conducting a search for articles which may assist a person to escape from lawful custody; it may also be used to search for evidence of an offence, so answer A is incorrect.

Section 23 of PACE states that for the purpose of the Act, premises includes any vehicle, vessel, aircraft or hovercraft. Answer C is therefore incorrect.

The use of this power is restricted to searching a person or premises *after* they have been arrested for an indictable offence, which means that answer B is incorrect. It is worth noting that because the offence suspected is a summary offence, the officer would not have been able to utilise this search power even if the driver had remained at the scene.

General Police Duties, para. 4.7.5.2

Answer 7.8

Answer **D** — Under s. 18 of the Police and Criminal Evidence Act 1984, a constable may enter and search any premises occupied or controlled by a person who is under arrest for an indictable offence, if he/she has reasonable grounds for suspecting that there is on the premises evidence, other than items subject to legal privilege, that relates:

(a) to that offence; or
(b) to some other indictable offence which is connected with or similar to that offence.

Generally, the power may not be exercised unless an officer of the rank of inspector or above has authorised it in writing.

However, under s. 18(5), a constable may conduct a search under this subsection *before* the person is taken to a police station, without obtaining an authorisation, if the presence of the person at a place (other than a police station) is necessary for the effective investigation of the offence.

The circumstances described in this question would be covered by the exception in s. 18(5) and answers A and B are incorrect.

There is no requirement to show that the defendant was on the premises intended to be searched immediately prior to the arrest. This is a requirement for a search conducted under s. 32 of the Act and does not apply in these circumstances. Answer C is therefore incorrect.

General Police Duties, para. 4.7.5.3

Answer 7.9

Answer **C** — Section 18(1) of the Police and Criminal Evidence Act 1984 states that:

> a constable may enter and search any premises occupied or controlled by a person who is under arrest for an indictable offence, if he has reasonable grounds for suspecting that there is on the premises evidence, other than items subject to legal privilege, that relates—
> (a) to that offence; or
> (b) to some other indictable offence which is connected with or similar to that offence.

The premises that may be searched is one which is occupied *or* controlled by the person and is not restricted to where the person resides. Answers A and D are therefore incorrect.

The power under s. 18 only applies to premises which *are* occupied and controlled by a person under arrest for an indictable offence; reasonable *suspicion* that the person occupies or controls the premises is *not sufficient*. Answer B is therefore incorrect.

General Police Duties, para. 4.7.5.3

Answer 7.10

Answer **B** — Generally, Code B of the PACE Codes of Practice deals with the search of premises through the statutory authority of a warrant or through PACE (s. 17, 18 or 32). However, para. 5 of this Code deals with searches with the consent of the occupier, or the person 'entitled to grant consent'.

Paragraphs 5.1 to 5.3 deal with how such consent should be obtained, however, para. 5.4 states that it is unnecessary to seek consent if this would cause disproportionate inconvenience *to the person concerned*. Answer C is incorrect, as it is the inconvenience to the occupier that matters.

Note for Guidance 5C outlines that para. 5.4 is intended to apply when it is reasonable to assume innocent occupiers would agree to, and expect, police to take the proposed action, e.g. if:

- a suspect has fled the scene of a crime or to evade arrest and it is necessary quickly to check surrounding gardens and readily accessible places to see if the suspect is hiding;
- police have arrested someone in the night after a pursuit and it is necessary to make a brief check of gardens along the pursuit route to see if stolen or incriminating articles have been discarded.

Therefore, it would be reasonable for Constable ELLIS to search the gardens without the occupiers' permission, even though she was not in immediate pursuit of a suspect, because to have woken the entire street in the middle of the night to search for a bag may have seemed disproportionate in these circumstances. This search could have been conducted *without* the statutory authority of a warrant, or other powers derived from PACE. Answers A and D are therefore incorrect.

General Police Duties, paras 4.7.6, 4.7.6.1

Answer 7.11

Answer **D** — Terrorism Prevention and Investigation Measures (TPIMs) are a civil preventative measure, issued under s. 2 of the Terrorism Prevention and Investigation Measures Act 2011, which are intended to protect the public from the risk posed by suspected terrorists who can be neither prosecuted nor, in the case of foreign nationals, deported, by imposing restrictions intended to prevent or disrupt their engagement in terrorism-related activity.

Section 24 gives effect to sch. 5. The schedule provides for powers of entry, search, seizure and retention in a number of scenarios relating to TPIM notices. These include:

Without a warrant:

- the power to search *without a search warrant in para. 5* (for purposes of serving TPIM notice), finding the individual on whom the notice is to be served;
- the power to search *without a search warrant in para. 6* (at time of serving TPIM notice), ascertaining whether there is anything in the premises that contravenes measures specified in the notice;
- the power to search *without a search warrant under para. 7* (suspected absconding), ascertaining whether a person has absconded or if there is anything on the premises which will assist in the pursuit or arrest of an individual in respect of whom a TPIM notice is in force who is reasonably suspected of having absconded.

With a warrant:

- in relation to the power to search *under a search warrant issued under para. 8* (for compliance purposes), determining whether an individual in respect of whom a TPIM notice is in force is complying with measures specified in the notice.

Therefore, searches *may* take place without a warrant for several reasons and answers A, B and C are incorrect.

General Police Duties, para. 4.7.11

8 Hatred and Harassment Offences

STUDY PREPARATION

The law in relation to offences involving hatred and harassment has been subject to considerable development in recent times. The result is a wide-ranging set of offences and powers that enable appropriate action to be taken in relation to such activity and, in certain circumstances, to protect against such activity occurring in the first place.

Covered in this chapter are the powers given to the police and the courts to deal with *personal* harassment and stalking, which are covered in various pieces of legislation such as the Protection from Harassment Act 1997 and the Public Order Act 1986.

QUESTIONS

Question 8.1

MEREDITH is a racist. One day he was at home with several friends who share his beliefs, when COWANS, who is black, knocked on his door collecting money on behalf of charity. MEREDITH invited COWANS into his house on the pretext of looking for money. When they were in the living room of the house, MEREDITH began racially abusing COWANS in front of his friends. His intention all along was to stir up racial hatred. When COWANS eventually left the house, he contacted the police to report the incident.

Considering offences under s. 18 of the Public Order Act 1986 (using words or behaviour or displaying written material stirring up racial hatred), does the fact that the incident took place in a dwelling affect whether or not the police can take any action?

A No, the offence may be committed anywhere.
B Yes, the offence may only be committed in a public place.
C No, the offence may be committed in a public or private place.
D Yes, the offence may not be committed when both persons are in a dwelling.

Question 8.2

HAWKINS was walking through a city centre after a lunchtime drink one afternoon. At the time, a religious Hindu festival was taking place, involving people in traditional dress, who were walking to a place of worship nearby. HAWKINS began shouting, 'If these people want to live in our country, they should adopt a proper religion' and, 'Look at those stupid costumes they've got on, they're ridiculous.' HAWKINS's words were heard by pedestrians standing nearby, but not by the people in the procession. HAWKINS's intention was to insult the people taking part in the procession, because of their religious beliefs, and to stir up hatred amongst passers-by who did not share the same beliefs.

Would HAWKINS's behaviour amount to an offence under s. 29B of the Public Order Act 1986 (use of words or behaviour intended to stir up religious hatred)?

A Yes, as HAWKINS's intention was to stir up religious hatred.
B Yes, whether or not HAWKINS intended stirring up religious hatred.
C No, as HAWKINS's words were not threatening.
D No, as the people in the procession did not hear the comments.

Question 8.3

WADE lives in a small cul-de-sac and is openly homophobic. WADE became aware that two people of the same sex had bought a house in the street and the rumours amongst the neighbours were that the people were in a homosexual relationship. One day, neighbours noticed several posters in the front windows of WADE's house, on which were written, 'Sign my petition to get rid of sexual deviants from this street'. WADE's intention was to make the new neighbours uncomfortable about living in the area, so that they would move out.

Could WADE be guilty of an offence under s. 29AB of the Public Order Act 1986, of stirring up hatred against the neighbours, on the grounds of sexual orientation?

A No, WADE has not made threats to the neighbours, intending to stir up hatred on the grounds of their sexual orientation.

B Yes, WADE has used threatening, abusive or insulting words or behaviour, intending to stir up hatred on the grounds of their sexual orientation.

C No, this offence can only be committed where a person uses words or behaviour, and does not include the use of written materials.

D Yes, WADE has used threatening, abusive or insulting words or behaviour, intending to stir up hatred on the grounds of sexual orientation, or where hatred was likely to be stirred up.

Question 8.4

CRUTCHER and BOYCE are members of an animal rights extremist group and were targeting two companies, which CRUTCHER and BOYCE believed were suppliers to a third company which tested its products on animals. Following a discussion between the two, CRUTCHER sent a threatening letter to the chief executive of one company and BOYCE sent a threatening email to the chief executive of the other. Their intention was to persuade both companies to stop supplying the third company with their products.

Given that the recipients are likely to be caused alarm and distress by the communications, would CRUTCHER and BOYCE's actions amount to a 'course of conduct' in respect of an offence under s. 1(1A) of the Protection from Harassment Act 1997?

A Yes, their conduct would be sufficient to amount to a 'course of conduct' in these circumstances.

B No, each person would have to send communications to at least two people.

C No, each person would have to send communications to at least two people from each company.

D No, because the communication they sent to each person was in a different form.

Question 8.5

BARON has sent two threatening letters to his probation officer. However, the second letter was not received until four-and-a-half months after the first.

Could BARON be guilty of harassment contrary to ss. 1 and 2 of the Protection from Harassment Act 1997?

A No, as probation officers are unlikely to feel distress.

B No, owing to the length of time between the letters.

C Yes, but only if the probation officer is likely to feel alarmed and distressed.

D Yes, but only if the probation officer is likely to feel alarmed or distressed.

Question 8.6

Following the break-up of a long-term relationship with FRAMPTON, CLARKSON moved away to live with friends in Scotland. Before leaving, CLARKSON was convicted of harassment against FRAMPTON, contrary to s. 2 of the Protection from Harassment Act 1997. FRAMPTON has heard that CLARKSON intends returning to live nearby and has also been told by friends that CLARKSON is still angry about the break-up and will try to resume contact. FRAMPTON intends seeking a county court injunction against CLARKSON, to avoid being subjected to further harassment.

Could a county court issue an injunction in such circumstances, when there has been no evidence that CLARKSON has actually committed a further offence contrary to the Protection from Harassment Act 1997?

A No, only the High Court may issue an injunction in respect of an apprehended breach of the 1997 Act.

B No, an injunction may not be issued in respect of an apprehended breach of the 1997 Act.

C No, an injunction could only be issued in these circumstances if CLARKSON had previously been convicted of an offence contrary to s. 4 of the 1997 Act.

D Yes, the county court could issue an injunction even for an apprehended breach of the 1997 Act.

Question 8.7

MURRAY had been involved in a long-standing dispute with her neighbour, WALTON, and had been made subject to a restraining order under s. 5(1) of the Protection from Harassment Act 1997. The order prohibited MURRAY from 'using abusive words or actions' towards WALTON. While the order was still in force, WALTON was visited by friends, who parked their car in the street outside the house. A short while later, WALTON observed MURRAY move her own car, which was also parked in the street, into such a position that it effectively blocked in WALTON's friends' car. WALTON contacted the police, claiming that MURRAY had breached the restraining order. When the officers arrived, MURRAY claimed that she was not aware that her behaviour amounted to a breach of the order.

Which of the following statements is correct, in respect of whether MURRAY could be found guilty of breaching the restraining order?

A MURRAY's behaviour was not serious enough to amount to harassment; therefore, the restraining order has not been breached.

B MURRAY's behaviour *may* have amounted to harassment, but she may have a defence if she could show that she honestly believed that her conduct did not breach the terms of the restraining order.

C MURRAY's belief is irrelevant; once the prosecution demonstrates that the restraining order was in place and the behaviour amounted to harassment, the court should find that the order has been breached.

D MURRAY's behaviour was not directed at WALTON; therefore, the restraining order has not been breached.

Question 8.8

HENLEY has been arrested for an offence of harassment, under s. 4 of the Protection from Harassment Act 1997, over a dispute about money owed to him by CAURTI. It is alleged that HENLEY made three phone calls to CAURTI, during which he threatened to injure his family if the money was not paid within a week. HENLEY intended CAURTI to fear that he would carry out the threat and was prepared to do so.

Given that HENLEY has engaged in a course of conduct, what would have to be shown in relation to CAURTI's state of mind, in order for the offence to be complete?

A That HENLEY's course of conduct caused CAURTI to fear that violence would be used against him.

B That HENLEY's course of conduct caused CAURTI to fear that violence may be used against him.

C That HENLEY's course of conduct caused CAURTI to fear that violence would be used against him or his family.

D That HENLEY's course of conduct caused CAURTI to fear that immediate violence would be used against him.

Question 8.9

BERTRAND worked in the Information Department of Eastshire Police and specialised in computer programming. BERTRAND had previously been in a relationship with ROSS, a work colleague, which had ended recently. BERTRAND was upset at the break-up and became convinced that ROSS was now in a relationship with another colleague. BERTRAND managed to access ROSS's emails and monitored them remotely every day for about a month, to obtain information about the new relationship. ROSS suspected this was happening and asked BERTRAND to stop. BERTRAND was aware that ROSS was upset, but carried on accessing the emails.

Would BERTRAND's behaviour amount to stalking, under s. 2A(1) of the Protection from Harassment Act 1997?

A Yes, provided a course of conduct can be proved.

B No, this offence requires some positive action by the defendant and BERTRAND has not actually used the information for anything.

C Yes, regardless of whether a course of conduct can be proved.

D No, this offence requires some form of act or omission by the defendant, which has not occurred in these circumstances.

Question 8.10

When BERRY split up from her boyfriend, TROTT, he began posting abusive messages on his Facebook account, calling her a 'slut' and 'whore'. The abuse got worse and TROTT posted a number of photographs on his account of BERRY with no clothes on. Eventually, TROTT posted explicit photographs of the pair having sex. After each Facebook message or photograph, TROTT sent BERRY a message telling her to look at this account. BERRY was not concerned about her safety and initially ignored the abuse and photographs of her with no clothes on; however, she became extremely distressed because of the explicit photographs. Eventually, BERRY moved away from the area and changed her telephone number to avoid receiving messages from TROTT. She also stopped all contact with her family and friends because of the Facebook account.

Would TROTT's behaviour amount to stalking, under s. 4A of the Protection from Harassment Act 1997?

A No, TROTT has not threatened BERRY with violence.

B No, BERRY was not in fear that TROTT would use violence against her.

C No, BERRY only became extremely distressed when TROTT posted the explicit photographs; this was a single act and did not amount to a course of conduct.

D Yes, TROTT has pursued a course of conduct which has had a substantial adverse effect on BERRY's day-to-day activities.

ANSWERS

Answer 8.1

Answer **D** — An offence is committed contrary to s. 18(1) of the Public Order Act 1986, where a person uses threatening, abusive or insulting words or behaviour, intending to stir up racial hatred (or where it is likely to be stirred up). Certainly, the behaviour of the person in the question would meet these criteria. However, s. 18(2) states that the offence may be committed in a public or private place, but not when the words or behaviour used are not heard by persons other than those in that or another dwelling. The requirement is similar to those under ss. 4 and 5 of the same Act, and since both persons were in the same dwelling, no offence is committed, whatever MEREDITH's intentions! Answers A, B and C are incorrect for this reason.

General Police Duties, para. 4.8.2.1

Answer 8.2

Answer **C** — Section 29B(1) of the Public Order Act 1986 states that:

> A person who uses threatening words or behaviour, or displays any written material which is threatening, is guilty of an offence if he/she intends thereby to stir up religious hatred or hatred on the grounds of sexual orientation.

This offence is similar to the one contained in s. 18 of the Act, where a person may be guilty of stirring up racial hatred by using threatening, abusive or insulting words or behaviour (or displays any written material) with intent to stir up racial hatred or where it is likely to be stirred up. One of the key differences between these offences is that under s. 29B, the words or behaviour must amount to some sort of threat. To reinforce this, s. 29J of the Act provides that the offences of stirring up religious hatred are not intended to limit or restrict discussion, criticism or expressions of antipathy, dislike, ridicule or insult or abuse of a particular religion or belief.

Therefore, even though HAWKINS's words were insulting and intended to stir up religious hatred, this particular offence would not be made out. (There may of course be a case to prosecute HAWKINS for an offence under s. 18 or even s. 4A of the Public Order Act 1986.) Answers A and B are therefore incorrect.

Since it is the defendant's intent that is relevant under this section, it is immaterial whether or not religious hatred was actually stirred up, or whether the people who were the subject of the behaviour were actually concerned by it. Answer D is therefore incorrect.

General Police Duties, para. 4.8.2.5

Answer 8.3

Answer **A** — Section 29AB of the 1986 Act defines 'hatred on the grounds of sexual orientation'. The definition covers hatred against a group of persons defined by reference to their sexual orientation, be they heterosexual, homosexual or bisexual. The new ss. 29B to 29G of the 1986 Act have extended the various religious hatred offences in those sections to cover hatred on the grounds of sexual orientation. The offence may involve the use of words or behaviour or *display of written material* (s. 29B). Therefore, answer C is incorrect.

However, the offences differ from the offences of stirring up racial hatred in two respects. First, the offences apply only to 'threatening' words or behaviour, rather than 'threatening, abusive or insulting' words or behaviour. Answers B and D are incorrect, because the behaviour exhibited, whilst being very insulting, did not contain threats. The second difference is that in this section, the offences apply only to words or behaviour if the accused 'intends' to stir up hatred on grounds of sexual orientation. They do not apply in circumstances which are 'likely' to stir up hatred and answer D is incorrect for this reason also.

General Police Duties, para. 4.8.2.5

Answer 8.4

Answer **A** — Under s. 1(1A) of the Protection from Harassment Act 1997, a person commits an offence if he/she pursues a course of conduct which involves harassment of two or more persons and which he/she knows or ought to know involves harassment of those persons and by which he/she intends to persuade any person not to do something which he/she is entitled or required to do, or to do something that he/she is not under any obligation to do.

Under s. 7(3)(b) of the Act, a course of conduct for this offence must involve, in the case of conduct in relation to two or more people, conduct on at least one occasion to each of those people. The fact that the letters were sent by two different people is irrelevant, because under s. 7(3A), a person's conduct may be aided and abetted by another, and both would commit this offence provided it can be shown they were acting together. Answer B is therefore incorrect.

Home Office Circular 34/2005 provides examples of offences which might be committed under s. 1(1A). In this guidance, it cites the example of an animal rights extremist sending a threatening email to an individual on one occasion working for one company and another similar letter to a different individual working for another company, with the intention of persuading them to stop supplying a third company with their products (similar to the circumstances in this question). Since the offence may be committed by sending different forms of communication to only one person from each company, answers C and D are incorrect (this is true even though the communications were sent by two different people).

General Police Duties, para. 4.8.4.4

Answer 8.5

Answer **D** — Section 1 of the Protection from Harassment Act 1997 states that a person must not pursue a course of conduct:

(a) which amounts to harassment of another, and
(b) which he knows or ought to know amounts to harassment of the other.

Course of conduct has been considered by the courts. In *Lau* v *DPP* [2000] 1 FLR 799, the Divisional Court held that although only two incidents are necessary, the fewer the number of incidents and the further apart they are, the less likely it is that there will be a finding of harassment. In *Baron* v *CPS* (2000) 13 June, unreported, the court accepted that the more spread out and limited in number the incidents and the more indirect their means of delivery (in this case by letter), the less likely it is that a course of conduct amounting to harassment will be found. However, there is no rule and it will depend upon the facts of each individual case. In *Baron*, two letters sent some four-and-a-half months apart could be a course of conduct amounting to harassment, and therefore answer B is incorrect.

Note it is alarm *or* distress; the court need only be satisfied that the behaviour involved one or the other (*DPP* v *Ramsdale* [2001] EWHC 106 (Admin)), and therefore answer C is incorrect.

Finally, the court in *Baron* refused to endorse the view that public service employees are less likely to be caused distress by threatening letters, and therefore answer A is incorrect.

General Police Duties, paras 4.8.4.3, 4.8.4.5

Answer 8.6

Answer **D** — Under ss. 3 and 3A of the Protection from Harassment Act 1997, the High Court *or* a county court may issue an injunction in respect of civil proceedings brought in respect of an actual *or* apprehended breach of s. 1(1) and (1A). Answers A and B are therefore incorrect.

The effect of this is that a defendant may be made the subject of an injunction even though their behaviour has not amounted to an offence under the 1997 Act, or regardless of whether they were previously convicted of a s. 4 offence. Answer C is therefore incorrect.

General Police Duties, para. 4.8.4.10

Answer 8.7

Answer **B** — Section 5(5) of the Protection from Harassment Act 1997 states that if without reasonable excuse the defendant does anything which he/she is prohibited from doing by an order under this section, he/she is guilty of an offence.

The circumstances in this question are similar to those in *R* v *Evans (Dorothy)* [2004] EWCA Crim 3102. In that case the appellant had been convicted of harassing her neighbours and a restraining order had been made by the court. Among other things, the order prohibited the appellant from 'using abusive words or actions' towards her neighbours. Some time into the life of the order, the neighbour called a plumber out to her house and he parked his van in the street. It was alleged that the appellant then moved her own car, which was also parked in the street, into such a position that it effectively blocked the plumber's van. The appellant was convicted of the offence of breaching the order and appealed, partly on the basis that her conduct could not properly be said to have amounted to 'abusive action'.

The Court of Appeal held that such matters should be approached in the same way as specific legislation which outlaws abusive conduct, and that a jury was entitled to conclude that, as she had been motivated by spite, the appellant's actions *could* be 'abusive' for this purpose. This was regardless of whether MURRAY's behaviour was directed at WALTON, or a third party. Answers A and D are therefore incorrect.

However, in the *Evans* case, the Court of Appeal also considered the issue of 'reasonable excuse', when it came to the defendant's understanding of the terms of the order. The court held that harassment takes many forms and therefore the courts need to be able to prohibit conduct in fairly wide terms (e.g. in the wording of the order). It is, however, unclear just how far the defendant's subjective understanding of the terms of the order will be relevant. *If a defendant honestly believed that his/her conduct did not breach the terms of the order, this would certainly be relevant when considering whether or not he/she had a 'reasonable excuse'.* MURRAY's belief is therefore relevant, which makes answer B correct, and answer C incorrect.

General Police Duties, paras 4.8.4.13, 4.8.4.14

Answer 8.8

Answer **A** — Under s. 4(1) of the Protection from Harassment Act 1997:

> A person whose course of conduct causes another to fear, on at least two occasions, that violence will be used against him is guilty of an offence if he knows or ought to know that his course of conduct will cause the other so to fear on each of those occasions.

The course of conduct is proved because threats were made by HENLEY on three occasions; however, the defendant's course of conduct must cause the victim to fear that violence *will* be used against him/her, rather than *might*. This is a strict requirement and showing that the conduct caused the victim to be seriously frightened of what might happen in the future is not enough (*R* v *Henley* [2000] Crim LR 582). Answer B is therefore incorrect.

On the other hand, s. 4 does not state that the victim must fear that *immediate* violence would be used against him/her. Answer D is therefore incorrect.

Finally, answer A is correct and answer C is incorrect, because the course of conduct for the purpose of s. 4 has to cause a person to fear, on at least two occasions, that violence would be used against *him/her*, rather than against a member of their family (*Mohammed Ali Caurti* v *DPP* [2001] EWHC Admin 867).

General Police Duties, para. 4.8.5

Answer 8.9

Answer **A** — Under section 2A(1) of the Protection from Harassment Act 1997, a person is guilty of an offence if:

- the person pursues a course of conduct in breach of s. 1(1) of the 1997 Act (i.e. a course of conduct which amounts to harassment); and
- the course of conduct amounts to stalking.

There are two matters, therefore, which need to be proved. Has the person pursued a course of conduct which amounts to harassment? Does the conduct amount to stalking? Answer C is incorrect because a course of conduct must be proved.

Section 2A(2) states that a course of conduct amounts to stalking of another person if it amounts to harassment and the person knows or ought to know that the course of conduct amounts to harassment of the other person. This section also states that the acts or omissions involved must be those that are associated with stalking; therefore, answer B is incorrect.

Section 2A(3) lists examples of behaviours associated with stalking, which include:

(a) following a person,
(b) contacting, or attempting to contact, a person by any means,
(c) publishing any statement or other material—
  (i) relating or purporting to relate to a person, or
  (ii) purporting to originate from a person,
(d) monitoring the use by a person of the internet, email or any other form of electronic communication,
(e) loitering in any place (whether public or private),
(f) interfering with any property in the possession of a person,
(g) watching or spying on a person.

Since simply monitoring a person's email amounts to an offence, answers B and D are incorrect.

General Police Duties, para. 4.8.6.1

Answer 8.10

Answer **D** — Section 4A of the Protection from Harassment Act 1997 prohibits a course of conduct relating to the offence of stalking involving fear of violence or serious alarm or distress. The first arm of the offence prohibits a course of conduct that causes the victim to fear, on at least two occasions, that violence will be used against them (which is similar to the existing s. 4 offence).

The second arm of the offence prohibits a course of conduct which causes 'serious alarm or distress' which has a 'substantial adverse effect on the day-to-day activities of the victim', which will include the victim moving home and changing the way they socialise. This is designed to recognise the serious impact that stalking may have on victims, even where an explicit fear of violence is not created by each incident of stalking behaviour. Answers A and B are incorrect as the offence may be committed when *either* of these outcomes is present and BERRY has most certainly changed her lifestyle as a result of TROTT's behaviour.

The issue of a 'course of conduct' relating to the s. 4 offence was addressed in *R (On the application of A)* v *DPP* [2004] EWHC 2454 (Admin). In this case, the defendant's conduct on the first occasion (e.g. a threat to burn the victim's house down) did not cause the victim undue concern, but a second threat some time later to do the same thing *did* put the victim in fear of violence, partly because this was the second time the threat had been made. The defendant argued that the victim had only been put in fear of violence by his threats to burn her house down on the second occasion and therefore there had been no course of conduct (i.e. the victim had only feared violence on one occasion, as opposed to the two occasions that were required by the section). The Divisional Court disagreed and held that the magistrates were entitled to find as a matter of fact that the two incidents had put the victim in fear of violence, notwithstanding her admission that, on the first occasion, she had not been too concerned. While this case relates to a different offence, the elements for a course of conduct will be the same for s. 4 and s. 4A and therefore answer C is incorrect.

General Police Duties, paras 4.8.5, 4.8.6.2

9 Anti-social Behaviour

STUDY PREPARATION

The focus on community safety within the whole criminal justice process has been sharply defined since the Crime and Disorder Act 1998. A range of statutory measures exist, giving the police (and other agencies) duties in relation to community safety and powers to help them take positive action and work together to deal with harassment and intimidation.

The Anti-social Behaviour Act 2003 provided the police and statutory partners with further tools in the tool kit to protect the community from fear, intimidation and anti-social behaviour (ASB); however, the Anti-social Behaviour, Crime and Policing Act 2014 completely overhauled the previous ASBO system and simplified powers to deal with ASB.

The main legislation is supported by other enactments, such as the Fireworks Regulations 2004, the Noise Act 1996 and the Environmental Protection Act 1990 (litter). Taken together, these measures feature highly in regional and local policing strategies to tackle crime and the fear of crime. This makes them important, not only to police officers but also, as a result, to those training and examining police law.

QUESTIONS

Question 9.1

The police and local authority are holding a strategy meeting to discuss McCANN, who is 10 years of age. Numerous referrals have been made to the anti-social behaviour coordinator over several months, showing evidence that McCANN has been acting in an anti-social manner towards PATEL, an elderly next-door neighbour who lives alone.

Given that McCANN has acted in an anti-social manner against PATEL, could a civil injunction under Part 1 of the Anti-social Behaviour, Crime and Policing Act 2014 be applied for in these circumstances?

A Yes, provided McCANN's conduct amounts to anti-social behaviour, an injunction may be granted.

B No, even if the conduct amounts to anti-social behaviour, an injunction cannot be granted because of McCANN's age.

C Yes, if the conduct amounts to anti-social behaviour an injunction may be granted; McCANN's age is not relevant in an application for a civil injunction.

D No, because only one person in another household has been affected by McCANN's behaviour.

Question 9.2

The court has granted a civil injunction against KANE, aged 19, for conduct which amounted to anti-social behaviour. The court has decided that because drug misuse had been a major cause of the behaviour that led to the injunction being made, it would be appropriate for KANE to comply with a drug rehabilitation programme.

What is the maximum period of time the court can specify for KANE to comply with the injunction?

A A maximum period of six months.

B A minimum period of 12 months.

C A maximum period of two years.

D There is no maximum period.

Question 9.3

PENGELLI is 13 years of age and is appearing before the court for failing to comply with a civil injunction. An injunction was previously issued requiring PENGELLI not to drink alcohol in public places; however, the court has heard that she has continued a pattern of persistent behaviour, which involves her regularly drinking in public places and behaving in an anti-social manner. An application is now being made for a supervision order against PENGELLI and the prosecutor is considering applying for her to be placed on a curfew, with an electronic monitoring requirement to be attached to it.

Would an application by the prosecutor for these restrictions be likely to succeed?

A No, PENGELLI is under 14 and cannot be made subject to a curfew as part of the supervision order.

B Yes, PENGELLI can be made subject to a curfew, with an electronic monitoring requirement to be attached to it in these circumstances.

C No, PENGELLI may be made subject to a curfew as part of the supervision order, but the court cannot make an electronic monitoring requirement part of the order.

D No, PENGELLI is under 16 and cannot be made subject to a curfew or an electronic monitoring requirement as part of the order.

Question 9.4

MURRAY, aged 21, was convicted by the magistrates' court for an offence contrary to s. 5 of the Public Order Act 1986, following abusive behaviour towards an elderly neighbour, and was given a conditional discharge for the offence. Prior to sentence, the court heard that MURRAY was alcohol-dependent and was regularly involved in abusing people in the street when drunk. Several intervention initiatives had been attempted, but had failed because of MURRAY's continuous drinking.

In these circumstances, would it be suitable for the prosecutor to ask the court to make a Criminal Behaviour Order (CBO) in relation to MURRAY?

A No, MURRAY has only been given a conditional discharge for the offence.

B Yes, provided the police and local authority have consulted before the case and that one of these partners supports the application.

C Yes, provided either the police or the local authority supports the application.

D Yes, a prosecutor can make such a request regardless of the wishes of the police or local authority.

Question 9.5

The court has granted a Criminal Behaviour Order (CBO) against SHAW, aged 16, for conduct which amounted to anti-social behaviour. The court has decided that because drunkenness had been a significant contributing factor to the behaviour that led to the CBO being made, it would be appropriate for the order to require SHAW not to consume alcohol in a public place.

Which of the following statements is correct in relation to the time period the court can specify for SHAW to comply with the order?

A The order should be set for a minimum period of six months.

B The order should be set for a minimum period of 12 months.

C The order should be set for a minimum period of two years.

D There is no minimum period for the order to be set.

Question 9.6

Constable DONAHUE is the community beat officer on a housing estate, which has been suffering an ongoing youth annoyance problem outside a small shopping centre. One bank holiday weekend, the police were called to the location to deal with intimidation and annoyance towards shopkeepers and customers, on average 20 times a day. Constable DONAHUE was on duty on the bank holiday Monday and visited the shopping centre during the afternoon. There were two youths present who the officer knew were the main instigators. After speaking to the shopkeepers, Constable DONAHUE formed the opinion that there would be further harassment that afternoon and evening. Constable DONAHUE was considering whether an order should be given under s. 34(1) of the Anti-social Behaviour, Crime and Policing Act 2014, to disperse the two youths before the problem escalated again.

Would an order under s. 34(1) be appropriate in these circumstances?

A No, because there are only two people present.

B Yes, because there are two or more people present.

C No, this power may not be used at such short notice.

D Yes, a direction may be necessary to prevent anti-social behaviour regardless of how many people are present.

Question 9.7

A dispersal notice under s. 34(1) of the Anti-social Behaviour, Crime and Policing Act 2014 is in place in a shopping centre, because of anti-social behaviour that had been caused by youths drinking excessively, intimidating shoppers and committing a number of robberies. One Saturday, a group of 20 people attended the shopping centre to stage a protest against several American-owned fast-food outlets. They intended preventing people from entering the shops and persuading them not to buy food there. They began shouting at shoppers who were entering the food hall and many people felt harassed and intimidated by their actions. The police were called to deal with the incident.

Would officers attending the scene be able to use powers under s. 34(1) of the Anti-social Behaviour, Crime and Policing Act 2014 to disperse the protesters, by virtue of the notice already in place?

A No, this would be an abuse of power; the notice was in place for unrelated incidents of anti-social behaviour.

B Yes, but they would need an authorising officer to extend the criteria in the notice to include the protest.

C No, a fresh dispersal notice will need to be applied for to take in the behaviour by the protesters.

D Yes, the attending officers would have the power to vary the notice if the circumstances require them to do so.

Question 9.8

Constable DARCH was on patrol at 7.30 pm in a housing estate where, following incidents of significant and persistent anti-social behaviour, a dispersal notice had been issued. Constable DARCH saw PURSE, aged 15, and CHALMERS, aged 16, staggering around shouting loudly and clearly drunk. Constable DARCH was concerned that they would continue to act in an anti-social manner if left at the location.

Would Constable DARCH have the power to take PURSE and CHALMERS home in these circumstances, utilising powers under s. 3 of the Anti-social Behaviour, Crime and Policing Act 2014 (power to remove people to their place of residence)?

A No, this power would only be available in relation to PURSE.

B No, these powers only apply between the hours of 9 pm and 6 am.

C Yes, as they are likely to commit anti-social behaviour.

D Yes, provided they have been instructed to leave the area and have refused.

Question 9.9

PCSO McLEAN works on a Neighbourhood Policing Team and has been consulting with the local authority about a shop on a housing estate which has been the subject of numerous complaints in recent neighbourhood meetings. The shop is open late every night and young people congregate outside depositing litter in the street. PCSO McLEAN has spoken to the shop owner several times, who has stated that the local authority is tasked with clearing up litter, not business owners. Consideration is being given to issuing the owner with a Community Protection Notice (CPN).

Which of the following statements is correct in relation to the issuing of such a notice?

A The notice may only be issued by the local authority as this is an environmental issue.

B The notice may be issued by the local authority or any police constable.

C The notice may be issued by the local authority or any police constable, provided it has been authorised by an inspector.

D The notice may be issued by the local authority or the police, including designated PCSOs.

Question 9.10

A house in a neighbourhood has been the source of numerous complaints by residents because of weekend all-night parties and the significant disorder they attract. The premises are owned by RAWLINGS, who rents them out to a tenant, who only uses them on weekends to hold the parties. The police have been unsuccessful in trying to speak to RAWLINGS or the tenant and they have decided to issue a closure notice. Inspector MEDINA wishes to enter the premises and post notices before the next party and has been in discussion with the manager of the local authority housing department about the best way to secure the premises after the notice has been posted.

Who is authorised to enter the premises to secure them in these circumstances—the police or the local authority?

A Only the police, because the premises are privately owned.

B Either organisation, provided they have consulted with each other about the notice.

C Only the police, because the notice is being issued by them.

D Either organisation, but if force is to be used, a member of the local authority must be accompanied by a police officer.

Question 9.11

Constable ELSOM is part of a Neighbourhood Policing Team and has been liaising with the local authority about premises that have been subject to a number of complaints at public meetings because of persistent anti-social behaviour problems. A closure notice has been issued in respect of the premises and an application is being prepared for a closure order to be issued by the court.

When must the application for a closure order be taken before the court?

A The application must be heard by the court not later than 24 hours after service of the closure notice.

B The application must be heard by the court not later than 48 hours after service of the closure notice.
C The application must be heard by the court not later than one week after service of the closure notice.
D The application must be heard by the court not later than one month after service of the closure notice.

Question 9.12

The police were concerned with the increasing number of calls they were receiving relating to loose horses on a main road. The horses were escaping from a field adjacent to the road and the problem was responsible for significant disruption, especially in the mornings and afternoons when people were on their way to work or taking children to school. The police have sought advice from the CPS as to whether the owner of the horses, PRICE, could be guilty of causing a public nuisance.

If PRICE were to be prosecuted for causing a public nuisance, what evidence would the court require in relation to the disruption caused to the community?

A It must be demonstrated that a representative cross-section of the community was affected by the problem.
B It must be demonstrated that the whole community was affected by the problem.
C Provided it can be shown there was danger to the public, the number of people affected by the problem is irrelevant.
D There is no requirement to demonstrate that disruption was actually caused to anyone; it must be shown that there was *potential* for a large part of the community to be affected by the problem.

Question 9.13

MULLER owns a company which organises large firework displays, for which he is authorised. He has several employees working for him, who help in his warehouse, accepting delivery of fireworks from the manufacturer and loading them into his van prior to displays. One such person is PLATT, who is 17 years of age. PLATT does not accompany MULLER to the displays; however, on a daily basis in the warehouse he handles large fireworks, which are specified as category 4 fireworks under the Fireworks Regulations 2004.

Does PLATT commit an offence under reg. 4(1) of the Fireworks Regulations 2004, by being in possession of fireworks that fall under category 4?

A Yes, as he is under the age of 18.
B No, as he is handling the fireworks as part of his work.
C Yes, regardless of his age.
D No, as he is not in a public place.

Question 9.14

COURT was hosting a party at his house on the evening of his son's wedding, on a warm evening in August. At midnight, COURT set off a series of fireworks in his garden to celebrate the wedding. The fireworks were of a standard type that he had bought in a supermarket the previous November and had kept aside for the occasion. COURT finished setting off the fireworks at about 30 minutes past midnight.

Regulation 7 of the Fireworks Regulations 2004 deals with the prohibition of use of fireworks at night time. In relation to these regulations, which of the following is correct?

A COURT has committed an offence because of the hour that he set the fireworks off.
B COURT has committed no offence because of the type of fireworks he set off.
C COURT may have committed an offence if local residents were disrupted or annoyed by the noise.
D COURT has committed an offence because of the hour that he set the fireworks off, but he could have avoided this by seeking permission from the local authority to do so.

Question 9.15

Whilst out on patrol at 2 am, Constable CLEAREY was approached by BERGEN, who was complaining about a noisy party being held at a house in the street. When standing outside BERGEN's house, Constable CLEAREY could hear very loud music coming from another house five doors away. The officer radioed the control room, asking them to contact the local authority's on-duty environmental health officers, however, no one was available and on duty.

Given that the music emanating from the house may amount to 'excessive noise', which of the following statements is correct?

A The test for 'excessive' noise is whether or not it may be heard in a public place; however, evidence of acoustic measurements of the level of noise will always be required.

B The test for 'excessive' noise is whether or not it may be heard in another dwelling and evidence of acoustic measurements of the level of noise will always be required.

C The test for 'excessive' noise is whether or not it may be heard in another dwelling and while evidence of acoustic measurements of the level of noise is desirable, it is not essential.

D The test for 'excessive' noise is whether or not it may be heard in a public place and while evidence of acoustic measurements of the level of noise is desirable, it is not essential.

Question 9.16

Constable WHEELER was called to a local shopping centre because of a person causing annoyance. On arrival, Constable WHEELER saw GRAY sitting in a shop doorway, playing a guitar, busking for money. There were coins on a blanket in front of GRAY. At the officer's request, GRAY packed away the guitar and moved away from the doorway. However, the officer then observed GRAY approach a pedestrian and ask them for money.

Would GRAY's behaviour, as observed by Constable WHEELER, amount to an offence of begging, contrary to s. 3 of the Vagrancy Act 1824?

A No, GRAY's behaviour would not amount to begging in these circumstances.

B Yes, but only when GRAY asked for money; busking would not amount to begging.

C Yes, GRAY committed offences both when asking for money and whilst busking.

D Yes, but only when GRAY was busking; approaching one person to ask for money would not amount to begging.

ANSWERS

Answer 9.1

Answer **A** — Part 1 of the Anti-social Behaviour, Crime and Policing Act 2014 creates the power for a civil court to grant injunctions if it is satisfied, on the balance of probabilities, that the respondent has engaged or threatened to engage in anti-social behaviour and it is just and convenient to grant the injunction for the purpose of preventing the respondent from engaging in anti-social behaviour.

Section 2(1) of the 2014 Act defines 'anti-social behaviour' as:

(a) conduct that has caused, or is likely to cause, harassment, alarm or distress to any person, or
(b) conduct capable of causing nuisance or annoyance to a person in relation to that person's occupation of residential premises, or
(c) conduct capable of causing housing-related nuisance or annoyance to any person.

Previously, s. 1 of the Crime and Disorder Act 1998 required the person to have acted in an anti-social manner to one or more persons not of the same household as himself/herself. However, the 2014 Act requires the person to have engaged in conduct that has caused, or is likely to cause, harassment, alarm or distress to *any person* regardless of where they live. Answer D is therefore incorrect.

A court may only grant an injunction against a person aged 10 or over (s. 1(1)); therefore answers B and C are incorrect.

General Police Duties, para. 4.9.2

Answer 9.2

Answer **D** — Part 1 of the Anti-social Behaviour, Crime and Policing Act 2014 creates the power for a civil court to grant injunctions if it is satisfied, on the balance of probabilities, that the respondent has engaged or threatened to engage in anti-social behaviour and it is just and convenient to grant the injunction for the purpose of preventing the respondent from engaging in anti-social behaviour.

The court may attach conditions to the injunction (such as attending a drug rehabilitation programme) and specify the person (an individual or an organisation) who is responsible for supervising compliance.

There is no minimum or maximum term for the injunction for adults, so the court may decide that the injunction should be for a specified period or an indefinite period (however, in the case of injunctions against under-18s, the maximum term is 12 months).

Answers A, B and C are therefore incorrect.

General Police Duties, para. 4.9.2.4

Answer 9.3

Answer **B** — A breach of an injunction by someone aged under 18 could result in the youth court imposing a supervision order or a detention order; however, a detention order can only be imposed when the court considers that the severity or extent of the behaviour warrants it and that no other sanction available to it is appropriate. In this case, an application for a supervision order is appropriate and the court must be satisfied beyond reasonable doubt that the under-18 has, without reasonable excuse, breached the injunction.

There are certain restrictions in respect of a young person's age; for example, a detention order cannot be imposed on a person under the age of 14. However, there are no such restrictions in relation to a supervision order, which may be made against any person appearing before the court (provided they are over the age of 10).

A supervision order may contain one or more of the following requirements: a supervision requirement, an activity requirement or a curfew requirement. An electronic monitoring requirement may be attached to a curfew requirement in order to monitor compliance. Since this applies to all persons over the age of 10, answers A, C and D are incorrect.

General Police Duties, para. 4.9.2.7

Answer 9.4

Answer **C** — Part 2 of the Anti-social Behaviour, Crime and Policing Act 2014 creates the Criminal Behaviour Order (CBO). An order may only be made against an offender when he/she has been sentenced for the offence or given a conditional discharge (s. 22(6)) (however, no order may be made where the offender has been given an absolute discharge or has only been bound over to keep the peace). Answer A is therefore incorrect.

The legislation has deliberately kept formal consultation requirements to a minimum, to enable agencies to act quickly where needed to protect victims and communities. The previous requirement (under the Crime and Disorder Act 1998) for the police and local authority to consult before the application is made no longer exists (unless the offender is under 18, when the prosecution must find out the views of the local youth offending team (YOT) before applying for the CBO). Although it is accepted that in most cases the statutory partners will probably have consulted as part of their strategies for dealing with anti-social behaviour, under the 2014 Act either of the statutory partners may make the request of their own volition and answer B is incorrect.

On the other hand, a court will only be able to make a CBO against an offender if the prosecutor applies for it following advice from either the police or the local authority. Answer D is therefore incorrect.

General Police Duties, para. 4.9.3.1

Answer 9.5

Answer **B** — Part 2 of the Anti-social Behaviour, Crime and Policing Act 2014 creates the Criminal Behaviour Order (CBO). Unlike civil injunctions (granted under Part 1), there are set periods and the terms of the CBO must include the duration of the order. For adults, there is a minimum of two years up to an indefinite period.

For orders given to people under the age of 18, there is a minimum period of 12 months and a maximum period of three years.

Answers A, C and D are therefore incorrect.

General Police Duties, para. 4.9.3.5

Answer 9.6

Answer **D** — Part 3 of the Anti-social Behaviour, Crime and Policing Act 2014 established a dispersal power that enables officers (constables in uniform and PCSOs) to direct a person who has committed, or is likely to commit, anti-social behaviour to leave a specified area and not return for a specified period of up to 48 hours.

The dispersal power can only be used where an officer of at least the rank of inspector has authorised its use in a specified locality (s. 34(1)) and the inspector reasonably believes that the exercise of the dispersal powers may be required in order to remove or reduce the likelihood of the anti-social behaviour occurring. Unlike the previous power (under s. 30 of the Anti-social Behaviour Act 2003), there is no requirement to consult with the local authority or publicise the dispersal notice in advance; the notice under the 2014 Act may be used spontaneously, provided the appropriate authorisation is given in writing. Answer C is therefore incorrect.

Again, unlike the 2003 Act, there is no requirement for at least two people to be present before the power may be used to disperse people. A direction may be given to 'a person' to leave the area and not return.

Answers A and B are therefore incorrect.

General Police Duties, para. 4.9.4

Answer 9.7

Answer **D** — Part 3 of the Anti-social Behaviour, Crime and Policing Act 2014 contains a dispersal power that enables officers (constables in uniform and PCSOs) to direct a person who has committed, or is likely to commit, anti-social behaviour to leave a specified area and not return for a specified period of up to 48 hours.

The dispersal power can only be used where an officer of at least the rank of inspector has authorised its use in a specified locality (s. 34(1)) and the inspector reasonably believes that the exercise of the dispersal powers may be required in order to remove or reduce the likelihood of the anti-social behaviour occurring.

In *R (On the application of Singh)* v *Chief Constable of West Midlands* [2005] EWHC 2840 (Admin), the court considered a case with similar circumstances where a dispersal order was in place under s. 30 of the Anti-social Behaviour Act 2003. It was held that the use of s. 30(4) powers to disperse a group of protesters who were causing harassment, alarm or distress to members of the public was lawful even though the order which was already in force related to quite different anticipated anti-social behaviour. In addition to this, the 2014 Act allows any constable to vary or withdraw a previously authorised notice; they must do this in writing to the person originally issued with the order unless not reasonably practicable (s. 35(8) and (9)).

Therefore, the police in this question may use their powers to disperse the group, without applying for a new order.

Answers A, B and C are incorrect for this reason.

General Police Duties, para. 4.9.4.1

Answer 9.8

Answer **A** — Part 3 of the Anti-social Behaviour, Crime and Policing Act 2014 contains a dispersal power that enables officers (constables in uniform and PCSOs) to direct a person who has committed, or is likely to commit, anti-social behaviour to leave a specified area and not return for a specified period of up to 48 hours.

The dispersal power can only be used where an officer of at least the rank of inspector has authorised its use in a specified locality (s. 34(1)) and the inspector reasonably believes that the exercise of the dispersal powers may be required in order to remove or reduce the likelihood of the anti-social behaviour occurring.

The officer must specify the area from which the person is excluded, and may specify when and by which route they must leave the area (s. 35(5)(b) and (c)). Where the officer believes that an individual is under the age of 16, an officer can remove that individual to a place where he/she lives or to a place of safety (s. 35(7)). There is no requirement to have warned an individual before utilising the power to take them home and since this power only applies to those under the age of 16, answers C and D are incorrect.

There was a similar power to take a person home under s. 30(6) of the Anti-social Behaviour Act 2003, if a constable found someone in a public place who was under the age of 16 and not under the effective control of a parent or a responsible person aged 18 or over. Under *that* section, the power could only be exercised between the hours of 9 pm and 6 am; however, no such restrictions apply under the 2014 Act, so answer B is incorrect.

Note that in *R (W)* v *Metropolitan Police Commissioner* [2006] EWCA Civ 458, a case dealing with the use of powers under the 2003 Act, it was held that the word 'remove' in s. 30(6) naturally and compellingly means 'take away using reasonable force if necessary'.

General Police Duties, para. 4.9.4.2

Answer 9.9

Answer **D** — Part 4 of the Anti-social, Crime and Policing Act 2014 deals with Community Protection Notices (CPNs). The notice is intended to deal with unreasonable, ongoing problems or nuisances which negatively affect the community's quality of life by targeting the person responsible (s. 43(1)). The notice can direct any individual over the age of 16, business or organisation responsible to stop causing the problem and it could also require the person responsible to take reasonable steps to ensure that it does not occur again (s. 43(3)).

Generally, local authorities are likely to take the lead in dealing with these kinds of issues and they will continue to be able to issue the new notice. However, the power to issue a notice will also be available to the police and PCSOs, if designated by the chief constable (s. 53(5)). Answers A and B are incorrect.

There is no requirement for an officer of the rank of inspector to authorise notices under this section; therefore answer C is incorrect.

General Police Duties, paras 4.9.5, 4.9.5.1

Answer 9.10

Answer **B** — A closure notice may be issued either by the police or the local authority, under s. 76 of the Anti-social Behaviour, Crime and Policing Act 2014. Before issuing the notice, the police or local authority must consult any person or agency they consider appropriate, and must also make reasonable efforts to inform the owner, landlord, licensee and anyone who appears to be residing in the premises (s. 76(6) and (7)).

Section 79(4) provides an authorised person with a power of entry to the premises, using reasonable force if necessary, to secure the notice to the premises. The authorised person may be a police officer or a member of the local authority, regardless of the organisation issuing the notice; answer C is therefore incorrect.

There is no requirement under s. 76 for a member of either organisation to be accompanied by the other to enter premises by force—they are only required to consult with the appropriate person or agency. Answer D is incorrect.

The fact that the premises are privately owned will not bar the local authority from becoming involved, therefore answer A is incorrect.

General Police Duties, para. 4.9.5.2

Answer 9.11

Answer **B** — When a closure notice is issued, the police or local authority must apply to the magistrates' court for a closure order (s. 80(1)). The magistrates' court must hear the application for the closure order within 48 hours of the closure notice being issued (excluding Christmas Day) unless the closure notice has been cancelled by a cancellation notice (s. 80(3)).

Answers A, C and D are therefore incorrect.

General Police Duties, para. 4.9.5.3

Answer 9.12

Answer **A** — The behaviour of the defendant must interfere with the material rights enjoyed by a class of Her Majesty's subjects (*R* v *Johnson* [1997] 1 WLR 367). Answer D is therefore incorrect.

Although there is no 'magic number' of people who must suffer from the annoyance or obstruction in order for it to amount to a *public nuisance*, you must show that the act or omission affected the public in general as opposed to a small group of people (such as the employees of a firm). Therefore, in *R* v *Madden* [1975] 1 WLR

1379, where a person made a hoax bomb call to an organisation, it was held that such behaviour could in theory amount to a public nuisance, although in *Madden* it did not, as the annoyance/obstruction was limited in its effect.

Further, in Lord Denning's view (*Attorney General* v *PYA Quarries Ltd* (*No. 2*) [1957] 2 QB 169), a nuisance would need to be 'so widespread in its range or so indiscriminate in its effect' that it would not be reasonable to expect one person to bring proceedings on his/her own to put a stop to it. Therefore, the number of people affected by the problem *is* relevant, and the number must be significant, regardless of how much danger is caused to the community. Answer C is therefore incorrect.

On the other hand, it was also held in the *PYA Quarries Ltd* case that it is *not* necessary to prove that every member within a class of people in the community has been affected by the defendant's behaviour; simply that a representative cross-section has been so affected. Answer B is therefore incorrect.

General Police Duties, paras 4.9.6.1, 4.9.6.2

Answer 9.13

Answer **B** — There are two offences covering *possession* of fireworks under the Fireworks Regulations 2004. First, an offence is committed by a person under the age of 18, who is in possession of an adult firework in a public place (reg. 4(1)). Adult fireworks are ordinary fireworks, which may be purchased by people over the age of 18, and will usually be used by families at their own homes on Bonfire Night. The second offence is committed where any person is in possession of a category 4 firework anywhere (reg. 5). Fireworks listed under category 4 are those which are more powerful than the ordinary ones referred to previously, and are used in large displays.

However, both of these offences are subject to the exception listed in reg. 6, which states that possession will not be unlawful if a person is in possession of fireworks in the course of his/her work or business, or where he/she has been properly authorised to conduct displays. Therefore, even though PLATT may not be authorised to conduct displays, he will be in possession of the fireworks as part of his work and does not commit the offence. Answer C is therefore incorrect. Also, because of this exception, it is irrelevant that he is under 18 (and answer A is therefore incorrect). Answer D is incorrect, as PLATT has a defence not because he is not in a public place, but because of the exception noted earlier.

General Police Duties, para. 4.9.7.4

Answer 9.14

Answer **B** — Regulation 7(1) of the Fireworks Regulations 2004 states that subject to para. (2), no person shall use an adult firework during night hours (11 pm–7 am).

Paragraph (2) lists the exceptions to this offence, which include setting fireworks off on 'permitted fireworks nights', such as Bonfire Night, during Diwali and on New Year's Eve; however, reg. 7 prohibits the setting off of *adult* fireworks, in other words, category 4 fireworks, which are generally only for sale to fireworks (or pyrotechnic) professionals. The type of fireworks bought by COURT in the supermarket are not affected by reg. 7, which is why answers A, C and D are incorrect.

General Police Duties, para. 4.9.7.4

Answer 9.15

Answer **C** — The Noise Act 1996 provides powers for local authorities to tackle the problems of noise within their community. Sections 2 and 3 of the Act allow for the serving of warning notices in relation to 'excessive noise' emanating from one house which can be heard in another at night (which is defined as being between 11 pm and 7 am). Since the test is that noise is emanating from one house which can be heard in another, answers A and D are incorrect.

The noise level should be measured using an 'approved device' (s. 6) and any warning must be served on the person who appears to be responsible for the noise or by leaving the warning notice at the 'offending premises' (s. 3(3)). However, under the Environmental Protection Act 1990 there is no requirement for evidence of acoustic measurements and a court may convict on other evidence, for example evidence from an environmental enforcement officer of excessively loud music being played (see *Lewisham Borough Council* v *Hall* [2002] EWHC 960 (Admin)). Answers A and B are also incorrect for this reason.

Note that s. 2(2)(b) of the 1996 Act includes noise emitted from any premises in respect of which a premises licence or a temporary event notice has been issued under the Licensing Act 2003, that can be heard in a dwelling.

General Police Duties, para. 4.9.8

Answer 9.16

Answer **A** — Section 3 of the Vagrancy Act 1824 creates the ancient offence of begging or gathering alms in streets and public places. A single act of approaching one person and asking for money is not, without more, enough to raise a *prima facie* case of begging (*R* v *Dalton* [1982] Crim LR 375). Answers B and C are therefore incorrect.

Where the person seeking money is doing something in exchange, such as singing as a busker, it has been held that this conduct does not amount to begging either (see *Gray* v *Chief Constable of Greater Manchester Police* [1983] Crim LR 45). Answers C and D are incorrect for this reason.

General Police Duties, para. 4.9.10

10 Offences Involving Communications

STUDY PREPARATION

In the previous chapter, we studied the effects of more direct forms of harassment and anti-social behaviour. This chapter deals with perhaps more subtle communications, forming a more personal type of abuse, which can be equally distressing for the victim. The legislation covering these offences is varied, encompassing the Postal Services Act 2000 and the Malicious Communications Act 1988, and deals with harassment by letter, telephone call, text and email.

The chapter also covers offences of communicating false information, under the Anti-terrorism, Crime and Security Act 2001 and the Criminal Law Act 1977, with the intention of inducing fear that people's lives are at risk.

QUESTIONS

Question 10.1

CORTEZ belonged to a hard-line group, which was protesting against the occupation of Middle Eastern countries by Western governments. At a pre-arranged time during a demonstration, CORTEZ along with some other demonstrators sprayed liquid in the faces of officers policing the demonstration, shouting that the substance was acid. In fact, the substance was a mild irritant, which produced no long-term effects.

What would the prosecution have to show in relation to CORTEZ and the others' states of mind, in order to convict them of an offence under s. 114 of the Anti-terrorism, Crime and Security Act 2001 (noxious substances etc.)?

A They intended that any person would fear either that his/her life was endangered, or that there would be a serious risk to human health.

B Only that they intended any person to fear that his/her life was endangered.

C They intended either to endanger life, or to create a serious risk to human health.

D They intended a particular person, or a particular group of people, to fear that their life/lives would be endangered.

Question 10.2

Until recently, MELLOR worked for a company that owned five night clubs and was the manager of one of the clubs; however, MELLOR was sacked after falling out with the owner, BOYD. On a busy Saturday night, between midnight and 12.30 am, MELLOR rang the receptionist at each of the five clubs stating that there was a bomb at one of the premises. MELLOR then texted BOYD with the same message. MELLOR was deliberately unspecific about the location, intending to cause maximum disruption, hoping that each premises would be evacuated.

Which of the following statements is correct in relation to MELLOR's liability under s. 51(2) of the Criminal Law Act 1977 (communicating false information)?

A Provided the intention was to cause the receptionist at each premises to fear that a bomb was likely to explode, MELLOR could be guilty of this offence.

B Provided the intention was to cause any person to fear that a bomb was likely to explode, MELLOR could be guilty of this offence.

C Provided the intention was to cause BOYD to fear that a bomb was likely to explode, MELLOR could be guilty of this offence.

D This section requires the offender to be specific about the location of the alleged threat; MELLOR could not be guilty of this offence as the message was too vague.

Question 10.3

FENWICK was due to go on a skiing holiday; however, leading up to the holiday, significant snowfall caused the airport to close down and flights were delayed. Three days before FENWICK was due to go on holiday, he posted a tweet on his Twitter account which stated, 'Airport still closed! They've got three days to get their act together or I'm blowing the airport sky high!!' The tweet was posted as a joke and was read by several hundred people; the comment received several replies, all of which were of a humorous nature. However, a week after it was posted, the tweet was read by a member of staff who worked at the airport, YOUNG, who considered that the matter was serious enough to make a report to the police.

Could FENWICK be liable for an offence in these circumstances, under s. 127 of the Communications Act 2003 (improper use of public electronic communications network)?

A Yes, even though the message was posted as a joke, it was menacing in its nature.

B Yes, although the message was not menacing in its nature, FENWICK sent a message which he knew to be false, causing needless anxiety to another (YOUNG).

C No, the message was not of a menacing character and FENWICK had no intention of causing needless anxiety to another.

D No, but FENWICK could be guilty of an offence under s. 51(2) of the Criminal Law Act 1977 (hoax bomb calls).

Question 10.4

Leading up to Christmas, HULL had ordered a number of items on Amazon and eBay and was expecting the packages to be delivered by post. HULL received one parcel addressed to a neighbour, WILLIS, which was delivered by mistake. HULL opened the package.

Section 84(3) of the Postal Services Act 2000 outlines an offence committed by a person who opens a postal package that was incorrectly delivered to him/her. What must be shown in relation to HULL's state of mind, if this offence were to be proved?

A That HULL acted to the neighbour's detriment and knew, or reasonably suspected, that the package had been incorrectly delivered.

B That intending to act to another person's detriment and without reasonable excuse, HULL opened the package knowing, or reasonably suspecting, that the package had been incorrectly delivered.

C That intending to make a gain and without reasonable excuse, HULL opened the package knowing that the package had been incorrectly delivered.

D That HULL knew, or reasonably suspected, that by opening the package it would be delayed in arriving with the neighbour.

Question 10.5

ANDREWS runs a general store on a housing estate. The shop contains a counter within the premises that acts as an agent for the Post Office, providing a general postal service. LIMOUTH is a local resident whom ANDREWS had previously banned from the premises for shoplifting. LIMOUTH entered the store one day to use the post office counter to pay a bill. ANDREWS threatened to call the police if LIMOUTH did not leave immediately.

Which of the following statements is correct in relation to the power to remove a person from premises, under s. 88(4) of the Postal Services Act 2000?

A ANDREWS has the power to remove LIMOUTH under s. 88(4) at this point, before the arrival of the police.

B Section 88(4) does not create a power for members of the public to remove people from premises; however, the police may do so when they arrive.

C ANDREWS does not have the power to remove LIMOUTH under s. 88(4), because these premises are not covered by the Postal Services Act 2000.

D ANDREWS does not have the power to remove him under s. 88(4), without any further adverse behaviour by LIMOUTH.

Question 10.6

BOLIN was expecting an important parcel, but was out of the house when it arrived. BOLIN drove into the street as a van belonging to a national parcel delivery service was being driven away. BOLIN followed the van to the next delivery address and approached the driver, QUINLAN, asking whether she had a parcel for him. QUINLAN stated that parcels could only be delivered to an address and that if BOLIN's was on the van, it would be delivered the next day. BOLIN became angry and blocked in QUINLAN's van, refusing to move until she handed over his parcel. QUINLAN called the police and Constable NORTON arrived a short while later.

Considering offences and powers under s. 88 of the Postal Services Act 2000, which of the following statements is correct?

A Constable NORTON is required under this section to remove BOLIN from the scene, or assist QUINLAN to do so.

B Constable NORTON is required under this section to remove BOLIN, or assist QUINLAN; however, QUINLAN had the power to do so herself.

C BOLIN has committed an offence under this section by obstructing QUINLAN; however, the power to remove people only applies in a post office or related premises.

D BOLIN has committed no offence under this section; the offence only relates to an obstruction caused in a post office or related premises.

Question 10.7

BURTON was undergoing an acrimonious separation from his partner, HASTINGS, who had started seeing another person, GRANT. BURTON managed to find out where GRANT was working and left a message with a colleague. BURTON asked the person answering the phone to pass an urgent message to GRANT, stating that HASTINGS was in hospital after a car crash and had suffered life-threatening injuries. The story was completely false.

Considering the offence under s. 1 of the Malicious Communications Act 1988, which of the following statements is correct?

A This was not a threatening or indecent message, therefore, this offence is incomplete.

B The offence would only be complete if it was BURTON's intention to cause GRANT anxiety or distress.

C The offence would be complete if it was BURTON's intention to cause GRANT or any other person anxiety or distress.

D The offence would only be complete if BURTON intended causing anxiety or distress to the person he actually spoke to, which in these circumstances was unlikely.

Question 10.8

POOLE owns a property which he is renting out privately to REECE. REECE has failed to pay the rent for the last three months and despite calling at the premises several times in the last month, POOLE has been unable to collect the money owed to him. In desperation, POOLE sent a text message to REECE which said, 'I'm coming to reclaim my property Monday and if you are there, I'm going to personally throw you into the street'. REECE was fearful because of the contents of the text and contacted the police.

Section 1(2) of the Malicious Communications Act 1988 outlines a defence for someone who sends a message which amounts to a threat. In respect of this defence, what would POOLE have to show in order to avoid prosecution for this offence?

A POOLE would have to show that he did not intend the message to be threatening.

B POOLE would have to show that an ordinary person would think the demands were reasonable.

C POOLE would have to show that he reasonably believed that the threat was a proper means of enforcing the demand.

D POOLE would have to show that there were reasonable grounds for making the demand, that he believed the threat was a proper means of enforcing the demand and that reasonable grounds existed for that belief.

Question 10.9

HEALD was infatuated with his neighbour, FARR, and continually asked her out on dates. FARR was flattered and not at all threatened by this, but refused to go out with him. HEALD then made an indecent phone call to FARR in an effort to 'turn her on'. HEALD did not, however, intend FARR to be distressed by these calls. She was not threatened and found it all mildly amusing.

Consider the offence outlined in s. 127 of the Communications Act 2003 of improper use of a public electronic communications network. Has HEALD committed this offence?

A Yes, but only if it can be proved the phone call was grossly offensive.

B Yes, even though HEALD did not intend to cause distress and FARR was not distressed by the call.

C No, HEALD did not make persistent use of a public electronic communications network.

D No, FARR was not caused annoyance, inconvenience or needless anxiety by the call.

ANSWERS

Answer 10.1

Answer **A** — Under s. 114(1) of the Anti-terrorism, Crime and Security Act 2001, a person is guilty of an offence if he/she:

(a) places any substance or other thing in any place; or
(b) sends any substance or other thing from one place to another (by post, rail or any other means whatever);

with the intention of inducing in a person anywhere in the world a belief that it is likely to be (or contain) a noxious substance or other noxious thing and thereby endanger human life *or* create a serious risk to human health.

Answer B is therefore incorrect.

You do not have to show that the defendant had any particular person in mind in whom he/she intended to induce the belief in question (see the Anti-terrorism, Crime and Security Act 2001, s. 115(2) and the Criminal Law Act 1977, s. 51(3)). Answer D is therefore incorrect.

The key element to this offence is *not* any actual endangering of life or risk to human health, or an intention to do so; it is committing an act with the intention that someone else would believe such a thing would happen. Answer C is therefore incorrect.

General Police Duties, para. 4.10.2

Answer 10.2

Answer **B** — Under s. 51(2) of the Criminal Law Act 1977, a person who communicates any information which he/she knows or believes to be false to another person with the intention of inducing in him/her or any other person a false belief that a bomb or other thing liable to explode or ignite is present in any place or location whatever is guilty of an offence.

There is no need for the person making the communication to have any particular person in mind at the time the threat is made (s. 51(3)); therefore, answers A and C are incorrect.

It has been held that while the information communicated need not be specific, a message saying that there is a bomb somewhere has been held to be enough, even though no location was given (*R* v *Webb* (1995) 92(27) LSG 31). Answer D is therefore incorrect.

General Police Duties, para. 4.10.3

Answer 10.3

Answer **C** — The Communications Act 2003, s. 127 states:

(1) A person is guilty of an offence if he—
  (a) sends by means of a public electronic communications network a message or other matter that is grossly offensive or of an indecent, obscene or menacing character; or
  (b) causes any such message or matter to be so sent.

(2) A person is guilty of an offence if, for the purpose of causing annoyance, inconvenience or needless anxiety to another, he—
  (a) sends by means of a public electronic communications network, a message that he knows to be false;
  (b) causes such a message to be sent; or
  (c) persistently makes use of a public electronic communications network.

Communications under this Act take in public social media systems such as Twitter (see *Chambers* v *DPP* [2012] EWHC 2157 (Admin)). This case involved a man posting a joke on his Twitter account about a bomb hoax at an airport, who was arrested and charged under s. 127. *However*, while the Divisional Court confirmed that a message posted on Twitter would fall within the remit of s. 127, it overturned Chambers's conviction on the grounds that the message itself was not menacing in its nature in the context in which it was posted—the circumstances were similar to those in this question. Answer A is therefore incorrect.

If an offence under s. 127(1) is ruled out, has an offence been committed under s. 127(2)? While the member of staff who worked at the airport, YOUNG, was caused anxiety, s. 127(2) requires that the offender sent the message 'for the *purpose* of causing annoyance, inconvenience or needless anxiety to another'. This intent is not present in the circumstances outlined; therefore, answer B is incorrect.

Finally, under s. 51(2) of the Criminal Law Act 1977, a person who communicates any information which he/she knows or believes to be false to another person with the intention of inducing in him/her or any other person a false belief that a bomb or other thing liable to explode or ignite is present in any place or location whatever is guilty of an offence. However, the wording of the 1977 Act offence is in the present tense, which suggests that a message threatening to place a bomb etc. some time in the future would not suffice. Answer D is therefore incorrect.

General Police Duties, paras 4.10.3, 4.10.6

Answer 10.4

Answer **B** — Under s. 84(3) of the Postal Services Act 2000, a person commits an offence if, intending to act to a person's detriment and without reasonable excuse, he/she opens a postal packet which he/she knows or reasonably suspects has been incorrectly delivered to him/her.

The 'intent' element of this offence is important; it must be shown that the person:

- opened the package;
- knowing or reasonably suspecting that it had been incorrectly delivered to him/her; and that
- he/she did so intending 'to act to another person's detriment' (this can be any other person's detriment, not simply the addressee's).

Answer B contains the only correct combination; therefore, answers A, C and D are incorrect.

(Note that there is a separate offence under s. 84(1) of delaying a package, but this offence would not apply in these circumstances because the person must be shown to have intentionally delayed or opened a postal packet in the course of its transmission by post.)

General Police Duties, para. 4.10.4

Answer 10.5

Answer **D** — Under s. 88(1) of the Postal Services Act 2000, a person commits an offence if, without reasonable excuse, he/she obstructs a person engaged in the business in connection with the provision of a universal postal service, or obstructs the course of business of any universal postal service post office or related premises.

Under s. 88(3), a person commits a further offence if without reasonable excuse, he/she fails to leave a universal postal service post office or related premises when required to do so by a person who is engaged in the business of a universal service provider, and reasonably suspects him of committing an offence under subs. (1).

Section 88(4) provides that a person who commits an offence under subs. (3) may be removed by any person engaged in the business of a universal service provider.

This needs to be viewed as a step-by-step process; a person may be removed from premises using the power under s. 88(3) when he/she has first committed an offence under s. 88(1) *and* then refused to leave the relevant premises having committed an offence under s. 88(3). Returning to the scenario in this question, LIMOUTH has neither caused an obstruction nor has he failed to leave at this stage. Therefore, without any further adverse behaviour by him, there is no power to remove him from the premises at this stage. Answer A is therefore incorrect.

Anyone failing to leave when properly required to do so under subs. (3) may be removed by the post office staff but also, subs. (5) provides that '*any constable shall on demand remove, or assist in removing, any such person'*. Whilst this places a clear duty on individual police officers to help in removing offenders under these circumstances, post office staff may do so independently of the police and answer B is therefore incorrect.

Finally, 'related premises' are any premises belonging to a universal postal service post office *or* used together with any such post office (s. 88(6)), which would cover the type of premises in this scenario. Answer C is therefore incorrect.

General Police Duties, para. 4.10.4.2

Answer 10.6

Answer **C** — Under s. 88(1) of the Postal Services Act 2000, a person commits an offence if he/she obstructs a person engaged in the business of a universal service provider in the execution of his/her duty in connection with the provision of a universal postal service, *or* obstructs, while in any universal postal service post office or related premises, the course of business of a universal service provider. Since the obstruction offence may be committed in either of these circumstances, answer D is incorrect.

Under s. 88(5), a constable *shall* on demand remove, or assist in removing, any person who has committed an obstruction under this section and has without reasonable excuse failed to leave when required to do so by someone engaged in the postal provider's business. However, the power to remove a person only applies when he/she has committed an obstruction in a post office or related premises, and has refused to leave there. Answer A is therefore incorrect (although, of course, there may be offences committed under other Acts of Parliament).

Finally, under s. 88(4), a person who commits an offence under subs. (3) *may* be removed by any person engaged in the business of a universal service provider. Again, this power only relates to an offence committed on post office or related premises and therefore answer B is incorrect.

General Police Duties, para. 4.10.4.2

Answer 10.7

Answer **C** — Under s. 1(1)(a) of the Malicious Communications Act 1988, a person commits an offence if he or she sends to another person a letter, electronic communication or article of any description which conveys:

(i) a message which is indecent or grossly offensive;
(ii) a threat; or
(iii) information which is false and known or believed to be false by the sender;...

The offence is not restricted to threatening or indecent communications and can include giving false information and answer A is incorrect.

It must be shown that one of the sender's purposes in so doing is to cause distress or anxiety, which may be intended towards the recipient or *any other person*. Answer B is therefore incorrect.

The offence can be committed by using someone else unconnected to the situation to send, deliver or transmit a message. It is not necessary to show that the defendant intended to cause *that* person anxiety or distress and answer D is incorrect.

General Police Duties, para. 4.10.5

Answer 10.8

Answer **D** — The wording of the statutory defence has been changed (by the Criminal Justice and Police Act 2001) to make the relevant test objective. It will no longer be enough that the person claiming the defence under s. 1(2) believed that he/she had reasonable grounds; the defendant will have to show that:

- there were in fact reasonable grounds for making the demand;
- he/she believed that the accompanying threat was a proper means of enforcing the demand; and
- reasonable grounds existed for that belief.

Answer D contains the only correct combination; therefore, answers A, B and C are incorrect.

General Police Duties, para. 4.10.5.1

Answer 10.9

Answer **B** — Section 127 of the Communications Act 2003 contains two separate offences. Under s. 127(1), a person is guilty of an offence if he/she:

(a) sends by means of a public electronic communications network a message or other matter that is grossly offensive or of an indecent, obscene or menacing character; or
(b) causes any such message or matter to be so sent.

Since the offence may be committed by sending a message that is grossly offensive *or* of an indecent character, answer A is incorrect.

The offence under subs. (1) is designed to deal with nuisance calls, and the offence is complete when the defendant sends the relevant message or other matter that is, as a matter of fact, indecent, obscene or menacing. There is no need to show intention on the part of the defendant, nor any resultant distress caused (answer D is therefore incorrect). The offence is complete by simply making an indecent phone call.

The separate offence under s. 127(2) of the Act *does* deal with causing annoyance, inconvenience or needless anxiety to another. Under this section, a person is guilty of an offence when they send or cause a message by means of a public electronic communications network that he/she knows to be false, or persistently makes use of such a network. However, since the behaviour of the person in this scenario is covered by s. 127(1), the offence is complete and answer C is incorrect.

General Police Duties, para. 4.10.6

11 Terrorism and Associated Offences

STUDY PREPARATION

The law on terrorism contained in this chapter relates to the Terrorism Act 2000, the Terrorism Act 2006, the Counter-Terrorism Act 2008, the Terrorism Prevention and Investigation Measures Act 2011 and the Counter-Terrorism and Security Act 2015.

In addition, offences under the Explosive Substances Act 1883 are still relevant.

Areas covered in this chapter include the greatly extended definition of 'terrorism' and a 'terrorist' and police powers to deal with someone suspected of being one, as well as the obligations placed on members of the public to assist the authorities in identifying and dealing with terrorism.

Finally, the chapter deals with the policing powers derived from the Serious Organised Crime and Police Act 2005 to deal with campaigners opposed to experiments with animals.

QUESTIONS

Question 11.1

The police are investigating MARTINEZ, a member of an extreme animal rights group which, because of its suspected terrorist connections, has recently become a proscribed organisation in the United Kingdom.

Under s. 11 of the Terrorism Act 2000, a person commits an offence if they belong to a proscribed organisation; however, are there any circumstances under which MARTINEZ may claim a defence to this offence?

A Yes, MARTINEZ could claim that the organisation was not proscribed when she became a member.

B Yes, MARTINEZ would have to demonstrate visible evidence that she ceased to become a member of the organisation as soon as it was proscribed.

C Yes, MARTINEZ could claim that the organisation was not proscribed when she became a member *or* she has not taken part in the activities of the organisation at any time since it was proscribed.

D Yes, MARTINEZ could claim that the organisation was not proscribed when she became a member *and* she has not taken part in the activities of the organisation at any time since it was proscribed.

Question 11.2

GIRVAN is an employee of a well-known high street bank. Over the last few months she has become increasingly suspicious of a customer's account and has started to collect information which she suspects demonstrates links between the customer's account and an animal rights group. She suspects, but has no evidence, that the customer is providing money that will be used for acts of terrorism. However, she has collected information relating to his personal bank account that she suspects to be important.

In relation to disclosing her suspicions to the police, which of the following statements is correct?

A She should disclose the information as soon as it amounts to admissible evidence.

B She must disclose the information now even if it does not amount to admissible evidence.

C She should disclose only her suspicions now: the information she collected is confidential.

D There is no obligation to disclose: it is a matter of choice.

Question 11.3

CHARTERIS lived in a flat in London and believed that the person living in the opposite flat was a wanted terrorist. CHARTERIS's suspicions were based on a picture released by the police of a person who escaped after attempting to blow up a bus. CHARTERIS is too scared to contact the authorities.

Could CHARTERIS commit an offence under s. 38B(2) of the Terrorism Act 2000, by failing to disclose information about the person living in the opposite flat?

A Yes, CHARTERIS must disclose this information to a police officer as soon as reasonably practicable.

B Yes, CHARTERIS must disclose this information to a police officer or a member of Her Majesty's forces as soon as reasonably practicable.

C No, CHARTERIS did not come into possession of the information through work or employment.

D No, this offence is only committed if a person fails to disclose information about an offence involving the commission, preparation or instigation of an act of terrorism.

Question 11.4

The police received information about a person who is suspected to be assisting in the commission of a terrorist act. The informant stated that a person had been seen covertly photographing a crowded shopping centre and that their behaviour was extremely suspicious. A surveillance operation took place and ZAFAR was identified and detained in the shopping centre. Officers confiscated a laptop and a camera, which contained hundreds of photographs of crowded areas and iconic sites.

The Terrorism Act 2000 creates a number of different offences. Which of the following statements is true in relation to s. 58 of the Act (collecting or making a record of information relating to terrorism)?

A It must be shown that the photographs were in ZAFAR's possession to encourage the commission of terrorist acts by any person.

B It must be shown that the photographs were in ZAFAR's possession to provide practical assistance to any person in relation to terrorist acts.

C There is no requirement to prove any intent on ZAFAR's behalf; simply being in possession of the photographs in these circumstances is an offence.

D It must be shown that the photographs were in ZAFAR's possession to provide practical assistance to himself in relation to terrorist acts.

Question 11.5

GUL is appearing in the Divisional Court, having appealed against a conviction for encouraging acts of terrorism under s. 1(2) of the Terrorism Act 2006. The circumstances of the case were that GUL was accused of uploading videos on YouTube of scenes showing attacks on soldiers of the Coalition forces in Iraq and Afghanistan by insurgents. GUL did not deny posting the videos, but argued that there had been no 'encouragement' in the form of words or a statement and that the videos were not depicting scenes of terrorism, since they were showing scenes of a war.

Which of the following statements is correct, in relation to the term 'encouragement', in regard to an offence under s. 1(2) of the Terrorism Act 2006?

A Communication without words or any other statement (such as posting a video) would amount to 'encouragement' under the Act and the conviction should be upheld.

B Communication without words or any other statement would amount to 'encouragement'; however, the scenes shown were not depicting scenes of terrorism.

C The defendant has not made an oral 'statement', therefore, this does not amount to 'encouragement'.

D The defendant has not made a 'statement', whether written or otherwise, therefore, this does not amount to 'encouragement'.

Question 11.6

FARR has become associated with people who are in the process of being radicalised by a terrorist group. Some of the people have been sent to a training camp in the United Kingdom and FARR has been invited. Although FARR has not been directly involved in preparing for acts of terrorism, he suspects that the purpose of the training camp may be for his friends to receive instructions on bomb-making equipment and that he has been invited as a test of his loyalty.

If FARR does attend the training camp, what more would need to be shown regarding his intent, in order for him to be guilty of an offence under s. 8(1) of the Terrorism Act 2006 (attending a place used for terrorist training)?

A That FARR knew that at least one other person was present to receive training for the commission or preparation of acts of terrorism.

B That FARR knew the training was being delivered for the commission or preparation of acts of terrorism.

C That it would have been obvious to a reasonable person that the training was being delivered for the commission or preparation of acts of terrorism.

D That FARR knew or believed the training was being delivered for the commission or preparation of acts of terrorism, or that he could not reasonably have failed to understand the purpose of the training.

Question 11.7

An authorisation is in place under s. 47A of the Terrorism Act 2000. Specific intelligence has been received that a terrorist suspect is going to leave an explosive package in a busy shopping area some time today. The police have decided to evacuate the centre, but an instruction has been given to search every person on their way out of the building.

Which of the following statements is correct in relation to the utilisation of this search power by the police?

A A constable may only use this power for the purpose of discovering whether the person concerned is a terrorist.

B A constable may only use this power if he/she reasonably suspects the person concerned is a terrorist.

C A constable may only use this power if he/she reasonably suspects the search will identify evidence that the person concerned is a terrorist.

D The purpose of the search is irrelevant; once an authorisation is in place under this section, the constable may simply search any person in the area.

Question 11.8

The police have been investigating five individuals suspected of preparing for acts of terrorism, and intelligence has been received that they are in possession of bomb-making equipment. In the early hours of the morning, their address is cordoned off, following a designation under s. 33 of the Terrorism Act 2000. Officers entered the address and arrested four of the five suspects. Intelligence is received that the fifth suspect is at an address—a nearby block of four flats—which was previously unknown to the investigation team. While an arrest team is en route to the address, further intelligence is received that the fifth person is in possession of the equipment. The Bronze Commander, Inspector BENSON, has contacted the Operational Commander, Chief Inspector CAWLEY, and asked for authorisation to cordon off the new location immediately. Inspector BENSON has asked that the block of flats be included in the authorisation, so that other residents may be removed from any danger presented by the bomb-making equipment.

Which of the following statements is correct, in relation to an urgent authorisation under s. 33 of the Terrorism Act 2000?

A Chief Inspector CAWLEY does not have the power to make such a designation urgently, only a superintendent may do so in these circumstances.

B Inspector BENSON could make such a designation if it is required as a matter of urgency.

C The designation must be made by a superintendent, unless there are reasonable grounds to suspect that an act of terrorism is about to take place in the locality.

D Inspector BENSON could make such a designation if it is required as a matter of urgency. However, the power relates to the removal of vehicles or pedestrians and not to people in dwellings.

Question 11.9

MALIK was arrested along with ten other suspects during an operation which identified a terrorist cell, believed to be preparing for acts of terrorism in the City of London. Following an extensive investigation, nine of the suspected terrorists were charged with offences under the Terrorism Act 2000; however, there was insufficient evidence to charge MALIK. The Assistant Commissioner responsible for SO15, Counter Terrorism Command, has been meeting with the Secretary of State to provide an update on the operation. The Assistant Commissioner has expressed concerns about MALIK being released without charge, because he presents a significant risk to the public due to his suspected terrorism-related activities. They discussed whether or not it would be suitable to serve a Terrorism Prevention and Investigation Measures (TPIM) notice on MALIK, to restrict his movements.

Which of the following statements is correct, in relation to the service of such a notice on MALIK in these circumstances?

A The Secretary of State may authorise a TPIM notice to be served on MALIK if the matter is urgent; otherwise, the permission of the court must be sought.

B The Secretary of State must seek permission of the court in every case, before a TPIM notice can be served on MALIK.

C The Assistant Commissioner may authorise a TPIM notice to be served on MALIK if the matter is urgent; otherwise, the permission of the Secretary of State must be sought.

D The Secretary of State may authorise a TPIM notice to be served on MALIK, without reference to the court.

Question 11.10

TELLER created a home-made pipe bomb, using explosives drained from a number of fireworks, having found out how to do so on the Internet. TELLER boasted about making the pipe bomb on a social networking site and the police were informed. A warrant was executed at TELLER's house and the bomb was found. TELLER was subsequently prosecuted for an offence under s. 4 of the Explosive Substances Act 1883, but pleaded not guilty on the grounds that the bomb was made out of mere curiosity and there was no criminal intent.

What might the court take account of, when deciding whether or not TELLER was guilty of this offence?

A That the bomb was capable of being detonated.

B That the bomb was in TELLER's possession for a criminal purpose.

C That the bomb was in TELLER's possession unlawfully.

D That TELLER or some other person intended that the bomb should be detonated in some way.

Question 11.11

HIGGINS is a campaigner opposed to the exploitation of animals. HIGGINS has managed to arrange a meeting with O'SULLIVAN, the CEO of Eastshire Holdings, a company which HIGGINS believes is about to supply products to Westshire Sciences Institute (WSI). WSI is known to conduct experimentation work with animals. At the meeting, HIGGINS intends to peacefully persuade O'SULLIVAN not to enter into a contract with WSI on moral grounds.

Would HIGGINS commit an offence under s. 145(1) of the Serious Organised Crime and Police Act 2005, in these circumstances?

A Yes, HIGGINS has tried to induce O'SULLIVAN into not entering a contract.

B No, this offence does not apply to contractual issues between companies.

C No, the offence would only be complete if HIGGINS had tried to persuade O'SULLIVAN to break a contract already in place.

D No, HIGGINS's peaceful behaviour would mean that no offence has been committed in these circumstances.

ANSWERS

Answer 11.1

Answer **D** — Under s. 11(1) of the Terrorism Act 2000, a person commits an offence if they belong to a proscribed organisation. It is a defence for a person charged with an offence under subsection (1) to prove:

(a) that the organisation was not proscribed on the last (or only) occasion on which he became a member or began to profess to be a member, *and*

(b) that he has not taken part in the activities of the organisation at any time while it was proscribed.

The defence is available for a person who can demonstrate *both* elements; therefore, answers A, B and C are incorrect.

General Police Duties, para. 4.11.2.1

Answer 11.2

Answer **B** — There are a number of offences contained in the Terrorism Act 2000, and some relate to money and its use for the purposes of terrorism. GIRVAN's suspicions about the customer's activities, if proved to be true, would amount to such an offence. Section 19 of the 2000 Act places a statutory duty on people who form a suspicion about activities they believe amount to the offences outlined here, if that belief/suspicion is based on information that comes to their attention in the course of their employment. The duty is to inform the police without delay of those suspicions, and answers A and D are therefore incorrect. They must also disclose the information on which it is based, and therefore answer C is also incorrect. Failure to comply with this duty is an offence, punishable with five years' imprisonment.

General Police Duties, para. 4.11.4.1

Answer 11.3

Answer **A** — Section 38B of the Terrorism Act 2000 states:

(1) This section applies where a person has information which he knows or believes might be of material assistance—

(a) in preventing the commission by another person of an act of terrorism, or

(b) in securing the apprehension, prosecution or conviction of another person, in the United Kingdom, for an offence involving the commission, preparation or instigation of an act of terrorism.

A person commits an offence if he/she does not disclose the information as soon as reasonably practicable (s. 38B(2)). This would include disclosing information which would lead to the arrest of a person for an offence involving the commission, preparation or instigation of an act of terrorism and therefore answer D is incorrect.

In England, Wales or Scotland, disclosure must be made to a constable, whereas in Northern Ireland, disclosure must be made to a constable or a member of Her Majesty's forces (s. 38B(3)). Answer B is therefore incorrect.

Section 19 of the Act places a statutory duty on people who form a suspicion about terrorism offences, based on information that comes to their attention in the course of their employment. However, this is not the case for disclosure under s. 38B. Answer C is therefore incorrect.

Note that it is a defence for a person charged with an offence under s. 38B(2) to prove that they had a reasonable excuse for not making the disclosure (s. 38B(4)).

General Police Duties, para. 4.11.4.3

Answer 11.4

Answer **B** — Section 58 of the Terrorism Act 2000 creates an offence of collecting or making a record of information (including photographs and electronic records) of a kind likely to be useful to a person committing or preparing an act of terrorism, or possessing a document or record containing information of that kind (s. 58). Since the offence relates to the collection etc. of documents for any person, answer D is incorrect.

The document etc. concerned must be of a kind that is likely to provide practical assistance to a person, rather than simply encouraging the commission of terrorist acts (*R* v *K* [2008] EWCA Crim 185 and *R* v *Muhammed* [2010] EWCA Crim 227). Answer A is therefore incorrect.

Finally, simply possessing such documents etc. will not amount to an offence in itself and answer C is for that reason incorrect.

Note that in *R* v *Brown* [2011] EWCA Crim 2751, it was held that s. 58 did not infringe the appellant's right to free speech under ECHR, Art. 10.

General Police Duties, para. 4.11.5

Answer 11.5

Answer **A** — An offence may be committed under s. 1(2) of the Terrorism Act 2006 when a person publishes a statement to encourage the commission, preparation or instigation of acts of terrorism or Convention offences ('Convention offences' include those in relation to explosives, biological weapons, chemical weapons, nuclear weapons, hostage-taking, hijacking, terrorist funds, etc.).

Section 3(1) provides that the offence can be committed by publishing a statement electronically, i.e. via the Internet and 'statement' includes a communication of any description, including a communication without words consisting of sounds or images or both (s. 20(6)). Answers C and D are therefore incorrect.

In *R* v *Gul* [2013] UKSC 64, the defendant's conviction was upheld by the Divisional Court after he had uploaded videos on to the Internet of scenes showing attacks on soldiers of the Coalition forces in Iraq and Afghanistan by insurgents. The court held that the videos *were* depicting scenes of terrorism within the definition of s. 1 of the Terrorism Act 2000 and therefore answer B is incorrect.

General Police Duties, para. 4.11.6.1

Answer 11.6

Answer **D** — For the purposes of the Terrorism Act 2006, offences are grouped into three specific areas: encouragement etc. of terrorism, preparation of terrorist acts and terrorist training, and offences involving radioactive devices and materials and nuclear facilities and sites. The offences within the *preparation of terrorist acts and terrorist training* group are:

- preparation for terrorist acts (s. 5(1));
- providing instruction or training in any of the skills mentioned for the commission or preparation of acts of terrorism or Convention offences (s. 6(1));
- receiving instruction or training in any of the skills mentioned for the commission or preparation of acts of terrorism or Convention offences (s. 6(2));
- attendance at a place used for terrorist training (s. 8(1)).

In relation to the offences of providing or receiving instruction or training under s. 6, the skills mentioned include the making, handling or use of a noxious substance; the use of any method or technique for doing anything capable of being done for the purposes of terrorism; and the design or adaptation for the purposes of terrorism of any method or technique for doing anything.

In *R* v *Da Costa* [2009] EWCA Crim 482, it was held that the person delivering the training had to know that one or more of those receiving it intended to use it for a terrorist purpose. However, this was the *mens rea* required to prove an offence by the person delivering training and not the person receiving it and therefore answer A is incorrect.

In order to prove an offence under s. 8(1), it must be shown that the person *either knew or believed that the instruction or training was wholly or partly for purposes connected with the commission or preparation of acts of terrorism, or that the person could not reasonably have failed to understand the purpose of such instruction or training* (s. 8(2)). This is wider than simply 'knowing' the purpose of the training, and therefore answer B is incorrect.

There is no mention of what would have been obvious to a reasonable person; therefore, answer C is incorrect.

General Police Duties, para. 4.11.6.2

Answer 11.7

Answer **A** — Under s. 47A of the Terrorism Act 2000, a senior police officer may give an authorisation for searches to take place in a specified area or place. An authorisation under this section authorises any constable in uniform to stop and search vehicles and pedestrians.

A constable in uniform may exercise the power conferred by an authorisation only for the purpose of discovering whether there is anything which may constitute evidence that the vehicle concerned is being used for the purposes of terrorism or (as the case may be) that the person concerned is a terrorist within the meaning of s. 40 (s. 47A(4)). Answer D is incorrect—the purpose of the search *is* relevant, it must be to discover if the person is a terrorist, or the vehicle is being used for terrorist activities.

However, the power conferred by such an authorisation may be exercised whether or not the constable reasonably suspects that there is such evidence on the person (s. 47A(5)). Answers B and C are therefore incorrect.

General Police Duties, para. 4.11.7.4

Answer 11.8

Answer **B** — Section 33 of the Terrorism Act 2000 provides the power to cordon off areas. Generally, the power to make such a designation is limited to a police officer who is of at least the rank of superintendent (s. 34(1)). However, s. 34(2) states that a constable who is not of the rank required by subs. (1) may make a designation if he considers it necessary by reason of urgency. Answer A is therefore incorrect.

Section 33(2) states that a designation may be made only if the person making it considers it expedient for the purposes of a terrorist investigation. Neither of these sections requires the authorising officer to have reasonable grounds to believe that an act of terrorism is about to take place in the locality, even if the matter is urgent, and therefore answer C is incorrect.

Section 36(1) of the Act outlines the actions a constable in uniform (or PCSO) may take in a cordoned area. They may order a person in a cordoned area to leave it immediately, order the driver or person in charge of a vehicle to move it from the area immediately, remove a vehicle in such an area or prohibit or restrict access to a cordoned area by pedestrians or vehicles. Under s. 36(1)(b) a power is given to order a person *immediately to leave premises which are wholly or partly in or adjacent to a cordoned area*. Answer D is therefore incorrect.

General Police Duties, paras 4.11.7.5, 4.11.7.6, 4.11.7.7

Answer 11.9

Answer **A** — Terrorism Prevention and Investigation Measures (TPIM) are a civil preventative measure, issued under s. 2 of the Terrorism Prevention and Investigation Measures Act 2011, which are intended to protect the public from the risk posed by suspected terrorists who can be neither prosecuted nor, in the case of foreign nationals, deported, by imposing restrictions intended to prevent or disrupt their engagement in terrorism-related activity.

The Secretary of State may impose requirements, restrictions and other provisions which may be made in relation to an individual by serving a TPIM notice on him/her if certain conditions are met (s. 2(1)). There are five conditions listed in s. 3, which must be met before a notice may be served. The first four, conditions A to D, generally relate to the reasonable belief of the Secretary of State that the notice is necessary to prevent or restrict the individual's involvement in terrorism-related activity.

Condition E states that a TPIM notice may be served if:

(a) the court gives the Secretary of State permission under section 6, *or*
(b) the Secretary of State reasonably considers that the urgency of the case requires terrorism prevention and investigation measures to be imposed without obtaining such permission.

Therefore, the Secretary of State *may* impose requirements, restrictions and other provisions which may be made in relation to an individual by authorising a TPIM notice to be served on him/her, provided the matter is urgent; and answer B is therefore incorrect. However, unless the circumstances are urgent, the permission of the court must be sought. Answer D is therefore incorrect.

There is no facility under s. 3 for a TPIM notice to be authorised by an Assistant Commissioner and for that reason answer C is incorrect.

General Police Duties, para. 4.11.8

Answer 11.10

Answer **C** — Section 4(1) of the Explosive Substances Act 1883 states:

> Any person who makes or knowingly has in his possession or under his control any explosive substance under such circumstances as to give rise to a reasonable suspicion that he is not making it or does not have it in his possession or under his control for a lawful object, shall, unless he can show that he made it or had it in his possession or under his control for a lawful object, be guilty of a felony...

Whether a person's purpose in having the items prohibited by these offences is a 'lawful object' will need to be determined in each case (see *R* v *Fegan* (1971) 78 Cr App R 189 and *R* v *G* [2009] UKHL 13).

In *R* v *Riding* [2009] EWCA Crim 892, a person alleged they had made a pipe bomb out of mere curiosity, using explosives drained from a number of fireworks. The defence contended that 'lawful object' meant the absence of a criminal purpose rather than a positive object that was lawful. However, the court was satisfied it meant the latter and mere curiosity could not be a 'lawful object' in making a lethal pipe bomb.

There is no requirement to show that the bomb was capable of being detonated, that it was in a person's possession for a criminal purpose, or that the defendant or some other person intended that the bomb should be detonated in some way. Answers A, B and D are therefore incorrect.

General Police Duties, para. 4.11.9

Answer 11.11

Answer **D** — A person commits an offence under s. 145(1) of the Serious Organised Crime and Police Act 2005 if, with the intention of harming an animal research organisation, he/she:

(a) does a relevant act, or
(b) threatens that he/she or somebody else will do a relevant act,

in circumstances in which that act or threat is intended or likely to cause a second person to take any of the steps in subsection (2).

A 'relevant act' is an act amounting to a criminal offence, or a tortious act causing the other party to suffer loss or damage of any description.

The steps referred to in subs. (2) are:

(a) not to perform any contractual obligation owed to a third person (whether or not such non-performance amounts to a breach of contract); or
(b) to terminate any contract; or
(c) not to enter into a contract with a third person.

Since the circumstances in the question are covered by s. 145(2)(c), answers B and C are incorrect.

Under s. 145(3)(b), no offence is committed if the only relevant tortious act is an inducement to break a contract. This means that no offence is committed by people peacefully arguing, or representing, that one person should cease doing business with another on the basis of the other's involvement with an animal research organisation. Answer A is therefore incorrect.

General Police Duties, para. 4.11.11.1

12 Public Order, Processions and Assemblies

STUDY PREPARATION

This chapter addresses the maintenance of public order using the increasingly wide range of offences and powers that are available to the police. In tackling that law, it is important to know the elements of the main offences and also the features that distinguish one event from another, whether the offence is committed by an individual or by more than one person.

The police have further powers under the Criminal Justice and Immigration Act 2008 to remove a person who is causing nuisance or disturbance on NHS premises.

The long-established legislation dealing with public meetings, assemblies, demonstrations and processions is also dealt with here.

QUESTIONS

Question 12.1

DENNIS owns an off-licence and had just closed the premises late at night, locking the door. HUDSON arrived at the premises in a drunken state demanding to be let in to buy a bottle of wine. DENNIS refused to allow HUDSON in and HUDSON began shouting, 'If you don't let me in, I'll smash all these windows.' HUDSON then sat on the wall waiting for DENNIS to open the shop door.

Assuming that an arrest may be necessary in these circumstances, does DENNIS have the power to arrest HUDSON for a breach of the peace, contrary to common law?

A No, the threats were made towards DENNIS's property, not DENNIS.
B Yes, provided DENNIS reasonably believed HUDSON would carry out the threat.
C Yes, provided DENNIS reasonably believed HUDSON was capable of carrying out the threat.
D No, only a police officer has the power of arrest to prevent a breach of the peace that has not yet occurred.

Question 12.2

Constable CAREY attended a report of a domestic dispute taking place in a home. On arrival, the officer could hear sounds of a disturbance coming from inside the premises. The front door was locked and despite Constable CAREY knocking loudly several times, there was no reply.

Considering Constable CAREY's powers of entry, which of the following statements is correct?

A Constable CAREY may enter the premises to prevent a breach of the peace and to remain there in order to do so.
B Constable CAREY may enter the premises only if s. 17 of the Police and Criminal Evidence Act 1984 applies; there are no additional powers to enter to prevent a breach of the peace.
C Constable CAREY may enter the premises, provided the disturbance affected members of the public outside the property.
D Constable CAREY may enter the premises, provided the disturbance could be heard by members of the public outside the property.

Question 12.3

A demonstration was taking place in a city centre and an authorisation was in place under s. 60 of the Criminal Justice and Public Order Act 1994. At one point, a group of approximately 100 individuals were 'penned' in one location to separate them from another more violent group, allowing the police to deal efficiently with both sets of protesters. As the violent protestors began to move away, the group that had been contained were released in small numbers. The police required these people to provide their personal details and submit to being filmed as they left. Some of this group have complained that they were deprived of their right to liberty under Art. 5 of the European Convention on Human Rights, because they had been peaceful protesters who were not about to commit a breach of the peace.

Which of the following statements is correct, in respect of the police's actions relating to the peaceful protesters who were contained in this way?

A The police acted unlawfully; they did not have reasonable grounds to apprehend an imminent breach of the peace from the peaceful protesters.

B The police did not act unlawfully, provided they could show that the peaceful protesters could potentially become violent in the circumstances.

C The police did not act unlawfully in containing the group; however, by detaining them further to take their personal details and submit them to being filmed, they have breached Art. 5.

D The police did not act unlawfully; the containment tactics were legitimate and they were entitled to film the group and take their details because of the s. 60 authorisation that was in place.

Question 12.4

A group of 20 people have been charged with the offence of riot, following a serious incident of disorder on a housing estate. The Crown Prosecution Service intends introducing evidence that at least 15 of the defendants were threatening violence towards people from a minority ethnic group, while five defendants actually used violence towards them. Other evidence shows that at least ten other people were gathered near those charged. These people did not take part in the threats or violence, but their presence added to the intimidation.

According to s. 1 of the Public Order Act 1986, who can be found guilty of riot in these circumstances?

A Any of the people present who were not victims of the incident.

B Any of the defendants who used or threatened to use unlawful violence.

C The five defendants who actually used unlawful violence.

D None of the people present, as only five defendants actually used violence.

Question 12.5

HOWLEY has been charged along with a number of other people, with an offence of violent disorder, under s. 2 of the Public Order Act 1986. HOWLEY intends to use the defence that he was intoxicated at the time of the incident, and that he was not aware of his actions.

What does s. 6 of the Public Order Act 1986 state in relation to the defence of intoxication?

A It cannot be used as a defence in relation to this offence, or an offence under s. 1.

B HOWLEY *may* use this defence if he can show either that his intoxication was not self-induced, or it was caused solely by taking a substance in the course of medical treatment.

C HOWLEY *may* use this defence, but only if he can show that his intoxication was not self-induced.

D HOWLEY *may* use this defence, but only if he can show that his intoxication was caused solely by taking a substance in the course of medical treatment.

Question 12.6

WORTON, CAMERON and MAHROOF appeared in Crown Court for violent disorder, contrary to s. 2 of the Public Order Act 1986, following a large fight outside a pub, which was captured on CCTV. After hearing the evidence, the jury acquitted WORTON of the offence.

Could CAMERON and MAHROOF still be convicted of the offence in these circumstances?

A Yes, only two people are required to have used or threatened unlawful violence during the incident for this offence to be complete.

B No, when there are three defendants and one is acquitted of this offence, the other two defendants *must* also be acquitted.

C Yes, the other two defendants *may* still be convicted of the offence, provided it can be shown that there were three or more people using or threatening unlawful violence during the incident.

D Yes, but only if it can be shown that CAMERON and MAHROOF actually used unlawful violence (as opposed to threatening unlawful violence) during the incident.

Question 12.7

Constable CARLISLE attended a report of a stolen vehicle being driven around a housing estate. On arrival, the officer saw SALTER getting out of the stolen vehicle. Constable CARLISLE arrested SALTER, who began violently to resist arrest. While the officer was waiting for back-up, a crowd of about eight people gathered around and each of them threatened violence towards Constable CARLISLE. Some of the people then started to punch and kick the officer to aid SALTER's escape.

Has an offence of violent disorder, under s. 2 of the Public Order Act 1986, been committed in these circumstances?

A Yes, if it can be shown that the people were present together, using or threatening unlawful violence.

B Yes, but only in respect of the people who were present together, using unlawful violence.

C Yes, if it can be shown that the people were present together, using or threatening unlawful violence simultaneously.

D Yes, if it can be shown that SALTER and the other people were deliberately acting together, to use or threaten unlawful violence.

Question 12.8

WEBB and CAHILL were in dispute about a boundary between their gardens. One day, CAHILL returned from work as WEBB was about to cut down a tree, which was in the disputed boundary area. CAHILL, who owned an Alsatian dog that lived in a kennel in the rear garden, saw what was happening and shouted at WEBB, 'Stop that or I'll set the dog on you and it will cause you serious injury.' The dog was still in the kennel, but WEBB was genuinely in fear that CAHILL would carry out the threat. At the time, WEBB was alone in one enclosed garden, and CAHILL was alone in the other. There were no other people present at the scene.

Could CAHILL be guilty of an offence under s. 3 of the Public Order Act 1986 (causing an affray) in these circumstances?

A No, there was no likelihood of another person being present at the scene, who would fear for their safety.

B Yes, CAHILL threatened WEBB with immediate personal violence.

C No, CAHILL would have to threaten or use personal violence towards WEBB, rather than making a threat with the dog.

D Yes, had a person of reasonable firmness been at the scene, they would have feared for their safety.

Question 12.9

HAWKER was drunk and was standing at the bar in a busy pub waiting to be served when HUGHES appeared alongside him. A bar staff member served HUGHES before HAWKER and he became very angry, shouting at HUGHES for pushing in. HUGHES made a sarcastic comment before moving away with his drinks. HAWKER continued drinking at the bar, brooding about the incident with HUGHES. Eventually, HAWKER saw HUGHES leaving the pub and followed him outside. HAWKER came up behind HUGHES and threw a punch, which completely missed, but would have caused serious injury had it connected. HAWKER was so drunk that he fell over before being able to follow up the punch. Constable DEANS was outside the pub and witnessed the incident. Because HUGHES was uninjured, the officer arrested HAWKER for an offence under s. 4 of the Public Order Act 1986.

Has Constable DEANS correctly arrested HAWKER for an offence contrary to s. 4 of the Public Order Act 1986 in these circumstances?

A No, HAWKER intended to take HUGHES by surprise, so that HUGHES would not have been aware of the assault until the act had occurred.

B No, because HUGHES did not believe that immediate and unlawful violence would be used against him.

C No, because HUGHES was not in fear that immediate and unlawful violence would be used against him.

D Yes, HAWKER intended to use immediate and unlawful violence against HUGHES.

Question 12.10

CONROY is appearing in court accused of using threatening behaviour towards Constable MERRECK, contrary to s. 4(1) of the Public Order Act 1986. CONROY has not denied using threatening behaviour, but is pleading not guilty on the grounds that the incident took place when both of them were inside a dwelling. The prosecution's solicitor has described the location of the alleged offence to the court: the incident took place in the hallway of a communal house that CONROY shares with seven other people. The hallway is accessed via a common front door, which has a digital keypad with the number restricted to the occupants. The residents have their own separate bedrooms with lockable doors and share other parts of the house, such as the lounge, kitchen and bathroom.

Would the location of the incident, as described by the prosecution's solicitor, qualify as a 'dwelling', under s. 8 of the Public Order Act 1986?

A No, where premises are shared by more than one person, no part of the structure can be classed as a dwelling as defined in s. 8.

B Yes, any part of a structure that is shared by more than one person will be classed as a dwelling as defined in s. 8.

C Yes, because the hallway could only be entered by way of a digital keypad and is restricted to the occupants, it will be classed as a dwelling as defined in s. 8.

D No, because this part of the premises is not occupied as a person's home it will not be classed as a dwelling as defined in s. 8.

Question 12.11

SADIQUE, who is Asian but from Uganda, has bought a product which has failed to work. He returns it to the shop and is dealt with by AKANJI, a shop assistant who is Nigerian by birth. Less than happy with the service, SADIQUE calls AKANJI 'an African twat' and 'an African bitch'. AKANJI is very distressed by this and contacts the police.

Has SADIQUE committed an offence contrary to s. 31(1)(b) of the Crime and Disorder Act 1998 (racially aggravated intentional harassment, alarm or distress)?

A No, as 'African' does not describe a racial group.

B No, as SADIQUE is from the same racial group as AKANJI.

C Yes, provided SADIQUE intended to distress AKANJI.

D Yes, there is no need to prove intent, provided distress is caused.

Question 12.12

Constable KELLEY stopped MAHER and his friend NEWTON, who were in a motor vehicle at night. Constable KELLEY had reasonable grounds to suspect they were in possession of stolen property and informed MAHER and NEWTON of his intention to search them and the vehicle. At the end of the search, which was negative, MAHER said to Constable KELLEY, 'I told you you wouldn't fucking find anything.'

Considering the requirements of s. 5 of the Public Order Act 1986 (using threatening or abusive words or behaviour), is MAHER likely to have committed this offence?

A Yes, provided it can be shown that NEWTON heard MAHER's bad language.

B Yes, Constable KELLEY heard MAHER's bad language, which is sufficient to prove the offence.

C No, as it is unlikely that those present would have been caused any harassment, alarm or distress.

D Yes, if an innocent bystander had heard MAHER's bad language, that person may have been caused harassment, alarm or distress.

Question 12.13

Constable ROBINSON was on patrol in a shopping centre, when she saw INCE walking along, shouting and swearing in a loud voice. There were a number of shoppers in the area and Constable ROBINSON approached INCE and advised him to stop swearing and annoying people. INCE ignored Constable ROBINSON and walked away, continuing to swear loudly at passers-by. Constable ROBINSON decided that it was necessary to issue INCE with a Disorder Penalty Notice for an offence contrary to s. 5 of the Public Order Act 1986.

What would have to be proved in relation to INCE's state of mind, for the offence under s. 5 to be made out?

A That he intended his behaviour to be threatening or abusive, or was aware that it was.

B That he actually intended his behaviour to be threatening or abusive.

C That he was aware that his behaviour was threatening or abusive, whether he intended it to be so or not.

D That he ought to have been aware that his behaviour was threatening or abusive.

Question 12.14

IRWIN was treated in the casualty department of a hospital, after falling and spraining a wrist. Although the injuries were not serious, IRWIN was convinced that the arm was broken. IRWIN returned to the hospital about four hours after being discharged and insisted on receiving further treatment. IRWIN began causing a disturbance and because the hospital staff were worried about their safety, they called the police. POWELL, the on-duty security guard, became aware of the disturbance and decided to deal with IRWIN before the police arrived. POWELL was a duly authorised NHS staff member.

Would POWELL have the authority to remove IRWIN from the premises before the arrival of the police?

A No, only a constable could do so, because IRWIN was a patient, waiting for medical advice.

B Yes, either POWELL, a constable or any NHS staff member could do so, because IRWIN was not a patient, waiting for medical advice.

C Yes, either POWELL or a constable could do so, because IRWIN was not a patient, waiting for medical advice.

D No, having received treatment less than eight hours ago, IRWIN may not be ejected from the premises.

Question 12.15

A public assembly was taking place in a main thoroughfare in a city centre to demonstrate against student fees. The chief constable of the force had placed conditions in advance, as to the location and the number of people who should be present. On the day of the event, road closures were in place and the demonstration went on for 10 hours. The length of the assembly was not included in the original conditions and although the demonstration was peaceful, the police had genuine concerns over the disproportionate disruption being caused to traffic and pedestrians. As a result, the chief constable issued a further notice, authorising the demonstration to be terminated.

Were the chief constable's actions lawful in these circumstances?

A Yes, provided the chief constable was present at the assembly.

B Yes, regardless of whether the chief constable was present at the assembly.

C No, there were no conditions set as to the length of the demonstration in the original notice and the police should have allowed it to continue.

D No, there was no evidence that it was necessary to terminate the demonstration to prevent disorder, damage or intimidation.

Question 12.16

Constable JEFFERS, who is in full uniform, has been deployed to deal with a trespassory assembly, in respect of which an order under s. 14A of the Public Order Act 1986 has been obtained prohibiting it taking place. The officer is four-and-a-half miles from the monument where the assembly was due to take place, and is carrying out powers granted by s. 14C of the 1986 Act, preventing access to the site. The officer has stopped a vehicle, and has directed the occupants not to proceed in the direction of the assembly.

Are the officer's actions lawful?

A Yes, as the officer was in uniform the actions are lawful.

B Yes, the actions are lawful; it is immaterial that the officer was in uniform.

C No, the officer is outside the radius set by the Act at four miles.

D No, the officer has no power to stop vehicles under this section.

Question 12.17

Sergeant FOULKES attended an appointment with the chair of the local town council. A public meeting is due to be held to discuss an application to build a new housing estate on a greenfield site on the outskirts of the town. The chair had heard that a number of people were attending to protest against the application and wanted to discuss the support the council could expect from the police during the meeting if people attending became disorderly.

An offence may be committed under s. 1(1) of the Public Meeting Act 1908, if a person is disorderly at such a meeting. What powers would Sergeant FOULKES have to deal with such an offence at the meeting?

A Sergeant FOULKES may use the statutory power provided by the Act, to arrest any person reasonably suspected of committing this offence.

B Sergeant FOULKES *may*, if requested by the chair, remove any person reasonably suspected of committing this offence.

C Sergeant FOULKES may, if requested by the chair, require any person reasonably suspected of committing this offence to declare his/her name and address.

D Sergeant FOULKES *must*, if requested by the chair, remove any person reasonably suspected of committing this offence.

ANSWERS

Answer 12.1

Answer **B** — A breach of the peace was defined specifically in *R* v *Howell* [1982] QB 416. A breach of the peace generally occurs when an act is done, or threatened to be done:

- which harms a person or, in his/her presence, his/her property; or
- which is likely to cause such harm; or
- which puts someone in fear of such harm.

Since DENNIS was in fear that harm would be done to the shop, answer A is incorrect.

A constable or any other person may arrest without warrant any person:

- who is committing a breach of the peace;
- whom he/she reasonably believes will commit a breach of the peace in the immediate future; or
- who has committed a breach of the peace, where it is reasonably believed that a recurrence of the breach of the peace is threatened.

The power of arrest is given to a constable or any other person (answer D is therefore incorrect). There is no requirement for the person to reasonably believe that the other person is capable of carrying out the threat, merely that the threat may be carried out. Answer C is incorrect.

General Police Duties, paras 4.12.2, 4.12.2.4

Answer 12.2

Answer **A** — A breach of the peace may take place on private premises as well as in public places (*R* v *Chief Constable of Devon and Cornwall, ex parte Central Electricity Generating Board* [1982] QB 458) and the police are entitled to enter premises to prevent a breach of the peace and to remain there in order to do so (*Thomas* v *Sawkins* [1935] 2 KB 249).This power is not affected by the general powers of entry provided by s. 17 of the Police and Criminal Evidence Act 1984—it is an additional power and answer B is incorrect.

Although the courts have declared that the presence of a member (or members) of the public is a highly relevant factor when dealing with a breach of the peace (*McConnell* v *Chief Constable of Greater Manchester Police* [1990] 1 WLR 364), it has also been held that if a breach of the peace takes place on private property, there is no requirement to show that the resulting disturbance affected members of the public outside that property (see *McQuade* v *Chief Constable of Humberside Police* [2001] EWCA Civ 1330). Answers C and D are therefore incorrect.

General Police Duties, para. 4.12.2.1

Answer 12.3

Answer **C** — The common law powers of the police allow them, where appropriate, to prevent people from travelling to certain locations; such exceptional powers to impose anticipatory restrictions on the movement of individuals, falling short of arrest, only arise if there is an imminent threat to public order.

When exercising these discretionary powers to prevent disorder, police officers will generally be expected to focus their attention on those who are likely to present the actual threat of violence or disorder (see *Redmond-Bate* v *DPP* [1999] Crim LR 998). However, where demonstrators were contained in a police pen, in a demonstration against Israel and its Head of State, it was held that the police may deploy reasonable force to prevent a breach of the peace that they reasonably apprehend as imminent (*Wright* v *Commissioner of Police for the Metropolis* [2013] EWHC 2739 (QB)). Such containment would be lawful in extreme and exceptional circumstances, even though the people contained did not appear to be about to commit a breach of the peace (see *Austin* v *United Kingdom* (2012) 55 EHRR 14 and *R (On the application of Moos)* v *Commissioner of Police of the Metropolis* [2011] EWHC 957 (Admin)). Answers A and B are therefore incorrect.

On the other hand, in *Mengesha* v *Commissioner of Police of the Metropolis* [2013] EWHC 1695 (Admin), it was held to be unlawful for the police to require people to provide their personal details and submit to being filmed as the price of release from a containment, notwithstanding that a s. 60 authorisation was in force allowing the lawful search of those present.

This means that the containment tactics used were lawful, but the delay in releasing them to take their personal details and submit them to being filmed was not, and Art. 5 was breached. Answer D is therefore incorrect.

General Police Duties, paras 4.12.2.2, 4.12.2.3

Answer 12.4

Answer **C** — Under s. 1(1) of the Public Order Act 1986:

> Where 12 or more persons who are present together use or threaten unlawful violence for a common purpose and the conduct of them (taken together) is such as would cause a person of reasonable firmness present at the scene to fear for his personal safety, each of the persons using unlawful violence for the common purpose is guilty of riot.

The offence of riot may be made out in these circumstances against the five defendants who actually used violence (answer D is therefore incorrect). However, only those defendants who actually used violence will be guilty and therefore answers A and B are incorrect. Of course, other defendants present may also be guilty of other serious Public Order Act offences.

General Police Duties, para. 4.12.3

Answer 12.5

Answer **B** — Section 6(5) of the Public Order Act 1986 states:

> For the purposes of this section a person whose awareness is impaired by intoxication shall be taken to be aware of that of which he would be aware if not intoxicated, unless he shows either that his intoxication was not self-induced or that it was caused solely by the taking or administration of a substance in the course of medical treatment.

The defence under s. 6(5) applies to all of the general Public Order Act offences; therefore, answer A is incorrect.

The defence may be raised either when the defendant claims intoxication was not self-induced or that it was caused solely by the taking or administration of a substance in the course of medical treatment. Answers C and D are therefore incorrect.

General Police Duties, para. 4.12.3.2

Answer 12.6

Answer **C** — Section 2(1) of the Public Order Act 1986 states:

> Where 3 or more persons who are present together use or threaten unlawful violence and the conduct of them (taken together) is such as would cause a person of reasonable firmness present at the scene to fear for his personal safety, each of the persons using or threatening unlawful violence is guilty of violent disorder.

Section 2(1) requires that *three* or more persons were present together who used or threatened unlawful violence and therefore answer A is incorrect.

In order to convict any defendant of this offence, it must be shown that there were three or more people using or threatening violence. However, where two of the defendants are acquitted, the remaining defendant can still be convicted (see *R* v *Mahroof* (1989) 88 Cr App R 317) as long as it can be proved that there *were* three or more people using or threatening violence (perhaps from CCTV evidence of the incident). If it cannot be proved that there were three or more people using or threatening unlawful violence, the court should acquit each defendant (*R* v *McGuigan* [1991] Crim LR 719). Therefore, answer B is incorrect.

For an offence of riot, under s. 1 of the Act, only the persons who actually used violence may be convicted. This is not the case for an offence under s. 2; therefore, answer D is incorrect.

General Police Duties, para. 4.12.4

Answer 12.7

Answer **A** — Under s. 2(1) of the Public Order Act 1986, where three or more persons who are present together use or threaten unlawful violence and the conduct of them (taken together) is such as would cause a person of reasonable firmness present at the scene to fear for their personal safety, each of the persons using or threatening unlawful violence is guilty of violent disorder. Unlike the offence of riot (under s. 1 of the Act), for this offence each of the persons using *or* threatening unlawful violence may be guilty of the offence; therefore, answer B is incorrect.

Under s. 2, there is no requirement to show that the persons using or threatening unlawful violence did so simultaneously (unlike the offence under s. 1) and therefore answer C is incorrect.

The circumstances in this question are similar to the case of *R* v *NW* [2010] EWCA Crim 404. In that case, a person was violently resisting arrest by a police officer, during which time a crowd gathered and various members of the crowd used or threatened violence. The Court of Appeal held that for the purposes of this section, it was not necessary for a person to deliberately act in combination with at least two other people present at the scene, but that it is sufficient that at least three people be present, each separately using or threatening unlawful violence. Answer D is therefore incorrect.

General Police Duties, para. 4.12.4

Answer 12.8

Answer **A** — Under s. 3(1) of the Public Order Act 1986, a person is guilty of affray if he/she uses or threatens unlawful violence towards another and his/her conduct is such as would cause a person of reasonable firmness present at the scene to fear for his/her personal safety.

However, in order to prove this offence, the threat cannot be made by words alone (s. 3(3)). CAHILL has not committed an act of violence towards WEBB (either personally or with the dog) in these circumstances as the behaviour merely amounted to a verbal threat. Answer B is therefore incorrect.

The 'action' by the defendant *may* consist of utilising something else such as a dog to threaten the violence (*R* v *Dixon* [1993] Crim LR 579). Answer C is therefore incorrect.

Finally, for this offence to be complete, the House of Lords has held that, in order to prove the offence of affray, the threat of unlawful violence has to be towards a person (or persons) present at the scene (*I* v *DPP* [2001] UKHL 10). This means that there does have to be *someone* other than the defendant at the scene.

Once this element has been proved, it will be necessary to prove the second element, namely whether the defendant's conduct would have caused a hypothetical person present at the scene to fear for his/her personal safety (see *R* v *Sanchez* (1996) 160 JP 321 and *R* v *Carey* [2006] EWCA Crim 17).

However, where the likelihood of a hypothetical person of reasonable firmness being present was low this element of the offence was not satisfied. In *R (On the application of Leeson)* v *DPP* [2010] EWHC 994 (Admin), a woman had issued a drunken threat to kill her long-term partner whilst holding a knife, in a bathroom, in an otherwise unoccupied house. In these circumstances the court held that there was no possibility of a hypothetical bystander fearing for their safety.

The most recent case (*Leeson* noted previously) places a different perspective on the 'hypothetical' third person, and in the example given in this question, the two parties were in separate enclosed gardens, with very little likelihood of another person being affected by the behaviour (as opposed to a situation in a pub, for example, where several people could be injured). This makes answer A correct, and answer D incorrect.

General Police Duties, para. 4.12.5

Answer 12.9

Answer **A** — Under s. 4(1) of the Public Order Act 1986: A person is guilty of an offence if he/she—

(a) uses towards another person threatening, abusive or insulting words or behaviour, or

> (b) distributes or displays to another person any writing, sign or other visible representation which is threatening, abusive or insulting,
>
> with intent to cause that person to believe that immediate unlawful violence will be used against him or another by any person, or to provoke the immediate use of unlawful violence by that person or another, or whereby that person is likely to believe that such violence will be used or it is likely that such violence will be provoked.

Under s. 6(3) of the Act, a person is guilty of an offence only if he/she *intends* his/her words or behaviour to be threatening, abusive or insulting, or is aware that they may be. It is HAWKER's intent that counts, not whether HUGHES actually believed or even feared that immediate unlawful violence would be used against him. Answers B and C are therefore incorrect.

It is not possible to prove that the victim feared immediate unlawful violence, where it was the intention of the accused to take the victim by surprise so that they did not know they would be assaulted until the act had occurred. The court considered that the accused should have been charged with assault (*Hughes* v *DPP* [2012] EWHC 606 (Admin)). This case shows that if HAWKER simply intended to use immediate and unlawful violence against HUGHES without the required threats, the offence is not made out and therefore answer D is incorrect.

General Police Duties, para. 4.12.6

Answer 12.10

Answer **D** — An offence under s. 4(2) of the Public Order Act 1986 may be committed in a public or private place. However, no offence will be committed where the words or behaviour are used, or the writing, sign or other visible representation is distributed or displayed, by a person inside a dwelling and the other person is also inside that or another dwelling.

Section 8 of the Public Order Act 1986 provides the definition of a dwelling, which is:

> any structure or part of a structure occupied as a person's home or as other living accommodation (whether the occupation is separate or shared with others) but does not include any part not so occupied, and for this purpose 'structure' includes a tent, caravan, vehicle, vessel or other temporary or movable structure.

Therefore, it is not correct to say that where premises are shared by more than one person, no part of the structure can be classed as a dwelling. Living accommodation (such as a person's bedroom) will fall within the definition in s. 8, whether the occupation is separate or shared with others. Answer A is therefore incorrect.

On the other hand, it is also not correct to state that any part of a structure that is shared by more than one person will be classed as a dwelling as defined in s. 8. Even where accommodation is shared, any part of the premises not used as 'living accommodation' will not be classed as a dwelling. Answer B is therefore incorrect.

In *Le Vine* v *DPP* [2010] EWHC 1128 (Admin), a laundry room, commonly used by tenants in sheltered housing, did not form part of a dwelling. Similarly, communal landings which form access routes to separate dwellings have been held not to constitute part of a dwelling even though they could only be entered by way of an entry-phone system (*Rukwira* v *DPP* [1993] Crim LR 882). Answer C is therefore incorrect.

Note that a police cell has been held not to be living accommodation for the purposes of s. 8 (*R* v *Francis* [2006] EWCA Crim 3323).

General Police Duties, para. 4.12.6.1

Answer 12.11

Answer **C** — This question loosely follows the circumstances of *R* v *White (Anthony Delroy)* [2001] 1 WLR 1352, where the Court of Appeal upheld White's conviction for this offence. The court held that the words used are to be construed as they are generally used in England and Wales; and on that basis the word 'African' described a racial group defined by reference to race and therefore answer A is incorrect. This offence can be committed towards people from the same racial group as the accused and answer B is therefore incorrect. This is a crime of 'specific intent' and as such does require the intent to be proven, and therefore answer D is incorrect.

General Police Duties, para. 4.12.7

Answer 12.12

Answer **C** — The Public Order Act 1986, s. 5 states:

> A person is guilty of an offence if he—
> (a) uses threatening or abusive words or behaviour, or disorderly behaviour, or
> (b) displays any writing, sign or other visible representation which is threatening or abusive, within the hearing or sight of a person likely to be caused harassment, alarm or distress thereby.

There needs to be a person within whose sight or hearing the conduct takes place. This requirement was confirmed in *Taylor* v *DPP* [2006] EWHC 1202 (Admin), where it was held that there must be at least evidence that there was someone who could see, or could hear, at the material time, what the individual was doing. It would not be sufficient to show that an 'innocent bystander' may have been caused harassment, alarm or distress; there was no such person present and answer D is therefore incorrect.

The second element that has to be proved is that any of the people present were *likely* to have been caused harassment, alarm or distress by the defendant's conduct. In *Harvey* v *DPP* [2011] EWHC Crim B1 (Admin), the defendant had used bad language when detained by the police (saying, e.g. 'I told you you wouldn't find fuck all') and although this might have been considered abusive, there was no evidence that anyone involved, or any bystanders, had suffered or were likely to have been caused any harassment, alarm or distress. All those involved would have heard such language on many occasions and in consequence the Appeal Court quashed the conviction. Of course, each case will be different, but using the *Harvey* case as an example, it is likely that even if NEWTON had overheard the swearing, he would not have been caused harassment, alarm or distress by the words used by MAHER. The same would be the case in respect of Constable KELLEY and for that reason answers A and B are incorrect.

General Police Duties, para. 4.12.8

Answer 12.13

Answer **A** — Section 6 of the Public Order Act 1986 states that a person is guilty of an offence under s. 5 only if:

> he intends his words or behaviour, or the writing, sign or other visible representation, to be threatening or abusive, or is aware that it may be threatening or abusive, or (as the case may be) he intends his behaviour to be or is aware that it may be disorderly.

This is not an offence which relies only on the intent of the person exhibiting the behaviour; it can also be committed if a person is simply aware that their behaviour is threatening or abusive. Answer B is therefore incorrect. This is also a case of either/or: INCE would either have to intend his behaviour to be threatening or abusive, or he would have to be aware that it was; therefore, answer C is incorrect.

The fact that a person ought to have known that his/her behaviour was threatening or abusive is immaterial, making answer D incorrect. The person's state of mind is often ignored when it comes to charging people with offences under s. 5 (and s. 4). Occasionally, defence solicitors make a point of insisting that their client be interviewed before charge. While it may be impractical to interview all offenders for these offences, it may be worth considering when the facts are unclear.

General Police Duties, para. 4.12.8.1

Answer 12.14

Answer **C** — Section 119(1) of the Criminal Justice and Immigration Act 2008 creates an offence of causing a nuisance or disturbance to an NHS staff member who is working on NHS premises and then failing to leave when required to do so by a constable or an NHS staff member. This section will only apply to people who are not on the NHS premises for the purpose of obtaining medical advice, treatment or care for themselves.

Section 120 of the 2008 Act provides a power for a constable or authorised person to remove a person who has committed an offence under s. 119. Although a non-authorised NHS staff member may ask a person to leave, this does not extend to a power of removal of a person who refuses. Answer B is therefore incorrect.

An authorised officer cannot remove the person if it is reasonably believed they are in need of medical advice etc. or that such removal would endanger their mental or physical health (s. 120(4)). However, a person ceases to be on NHS premises for the purpose of obtaining medical advice, treatment or care for himself or herself in the following two circumstances:

- once the person has received the medical advice (s. 119(3)(a));
- if the person has received the medical advice etc. during the last eight hours (s. 119(3)(b)).

Having received treatment less than eight hours previously, IRWIN is not a patient and may be ejected from the premises. Answers A and D are therefore incorrect.

General Police Duties, para. 4.12.9

Answer 12.15

Answer **A** — Under s. 14(1) of the Public Order Act 1986, if the senior police officer, having regard to the time or place at which and the circumstances in which any public assembly is being held or is intended to be held, reasonably believes that:

(a) it may result in serious public disorder, serious damage to property or serious disruption to the life of the community, or

(b) the purpose of the persons organising it is the intimidation of others with a view to compelling them not to do an act they have a right to do, or to do an act they have a right not to do,

he or she may give directions imposing on the persons organising or taking part in the assembly such conditions as to the place at which the assembly may be (or continue to be) held, its maximum duration, or the maximum number of persons who may constitute it, as appear to him/her necessary to prevent such disorder, damage, disruption or intimidation.

Section 14(1) allows for the police to react to the prevailing circumstances during the assembly; therefore, even though no conditions were set in advance as to the length of the demonstration, provided it appeared necessary to prevent disorder, damage, disruption or intimidation, it was lawful to impose further conditions while the demonstration was being held. Answer C is therefore incorrect.

A direction under s. 14(1) was lawful where a senior police officer imposed a condition that a Climate Camp protest against the G20 Summit in London must stop. The demonstration had lasted the best part of 12 hours and the court held this was quite long enough for the protestors to take advantage of their human rights under Art. 10 (Freedom of Expression) and Art. 11 (Freedom of Assembly and Association) and those wishing to remain were intent on continuing to block the highway, the main thoroughfare into and out of the City. There was no justification to prolong the demonstration and its continuation would cause serious disturbances and disruption to traffic and pedestrians wishing to use the highway. The police had a duty to clear the highway and that could not be done without removing the protestors by force if necessary (*R (On the Application of Moos)* v *Commissioner of Police of the Metropolis* [2011] EWHC 957 (Admin)). Serious disruption is included in this section and answer D is incorrect.

Finally, under s. 14(2), 'the senior police officer' means:

(a) in relation to an assembly being held, the most senior in rank of the police officers present at the scene, and
(b) in relation to an assembly intended to be held, the chief officer of police.

This means that in advance of the assembly, the chief constable was the appropriate officer to impose conditions; however, once it had commenced, any further conditions must be imposed by the senior police officer present at the scene (see *R* v *Lucas* (2014) 17 April 2014 (not reported), where the notice under s. 14 was signed by a chief officer who was not present at the scene, making it invalid). Answer B is therefore incorrect.

General Police Duties, para. 4.12.10.4

Answer 12.16

Answer **D** — Under s. 14A of the Public Order Act 1986, the chief officer of police has the power, if he/she reasonably believes that it is intended to hold a trespassory assembly which may result in serious disruption to the life of the community or significant damage to land or a building or monument which is of historical, archaeological or scientific importance, to apply to the district council for an order prohibiting for a specified period the holding of all trespassory assemblies in the district or part of it. The order must not last for more than four days and must not apply to an area greater than that represented by a circle of five miles radius from a specified centre, and therefore answer C is incorrect. A constable, who must be in uniform, has power to stop someone he/she reasonably believes to be on his/her way to an assembly prohibited by an order under s. 14A and to direct him/her not to proceed in the direction of the assembly, and therefore answer B is incorrect. This power, however, does not apply to vehicles and is restricted to 'stop that person', and answer A is therefore incorrect. Other powers exist to stop the vehicle, however.

General Police Duties, paras 4.12.10.5, 4.12.10.6

Answer 12.17

Answer **C** — Section 1 of the Public Meeting Act 1908 states:

(1) Any person who at a lawful public meeting acts in a disorderly manner for the purpose of preventing the transaction of the business for which the meeting was called together shall be guilty of an offence and shall on summary conviction be liable to imprisonment for a term not exceeding six months or to a fine not exceeding £1,000 or to both...

(2) Any person who incites others to commit an offence under this section shall be guilty of a like offence.

If a constable reasonably suspects any person of committing this offence, he/she *may*, if requested by the person chairing the meeting, require the offender to *declare his/her name and address immediately*. Failing to comply with such a request or giving false details is a summary offence (s. 1(3)). Answers B and D are incorrect.

There is no statutory power of arrest provided by the 1908 Act; therefore, answer A is incorrect. Of course, if the person fails to give their name and address, the arrest may be necessary under s. 24 of the Police and Criminal Evidence Act 1984.

General Police Duties, para. 4.12.10.7

13 Sporting Events

STUDY PREPARATION

The maintenance of public order at sporting events is an important area of responsibility for the police and the service has a far more sophisticated range of measures to help deal with football hooliganism than it did in the 1970s and 1980s. Large sporting events can tie up significant numbers of officers and the emphasis today is on more preventative measures to control spectators.

The Sporting Events (Control of Alcohol etc.) Act 1985 and the Football (Offences) Act 1991 create offences relating to drunkenness and rowdy behaviour at designated sporting events, while the Football Spectators Act 1989 provides the courts with significant powers to issue banning orders against those who are involved with football-related disorder, in connection with regulated football matches both inside and outside the United Kingdom.

The police rely heavily on football clubs to regulate the sale of tickets at major sporting events. The final part of the chapter deals with offences created by the Criminal Justice and Public Order Act 1994 to deal with 'ticket touts', whose actions can undermine attempts to separate home and away supporters.

QUESTIONS

Question 13.1

The police were working at a designated football match when, at half time, the Public Order Commander received a complaint that away fans had been engaged in racialist chanting during the first half. Stewards and the police viewed CCTV and played back images of away supporters shouting, 'You're just a town full of Pakis' at the home fans. They managed to identify the area of the ground where the chanting was coming from and extra stewards and officers were posted to take action if needed.

Considering the offence under s. 3(1) of the Football (Offences) Act 1991 ('racialist' chanting), which of the following statements is correct?

A The prosecution would need to show that the chanting might have been racialist in its nature.

B The prosecution would need to show that the chanting *was* racialist in its nature.

C The prosecution would need to show that the chanting may have been perceived as being racialist in its nature by the people it was directed at.

D The prosecution would need to show that the away fans intended the chanting to be racialist in its nature.

Question 13.2

REYNOLDS was arrested and charged with criminal damage and affray, following an incident which took place while he was on his way to a Premier League football match. REYNOLDS had been drinking heavily in a pub before the match and while he was walking to the ground before kick-off, he stopped at an off-licence to buy some cans of lager. The off-licence owner refused to serve him because he was drunk, and out of anger REYNOLDS caused significant damage to stock in the premises, and smashed a large window on his way out. In court, REYNOLDS admitted the offences and the magistrates were considering imposing a banning order. In response, REYNOLDS claimed that his behaviour was not actually connected to the football match he was attending.

Which of the following statements would be correct in relation to the imposition of a banning order, under s. 14A of the Football Spectators Act 1989?

A The court may decide not to consider a banning order, because REYNOLDS's behaviour was unrelated to the football match.

B The court need not consider a banning order, because REYNOLDS has not used violence towards another person.

C The court need not consider a banning order, because the incident did not take place at the ground.

D The court must consider a banning order, because REYNOLDS was on his way to a football match when he committed the offences.

Question 13.3

CLOWES was the subject of a football banning order, having been convicted of a relevant offence. CLOWES has served one year of the order and has approached a solicitor to enquire whether there was anything that could be done about reducing the period or terminating it altogether.

Which of the following statements is correct, as to whether CLOWES could successfully apply to have the period of the banning order reduced or terminated?

A CLOWES could apply to the court which passed the order for its termination, having served at least two-thirds of its period.

B CLOWES would have to apply to the crown court for its termination, at any time during the period.

C CLOWES could apply to any magistrates' court for its termination, having served at least half of its period.

D CLOWES could apply to the court which passed the order for its termination, within six months of the end of its period.

Question 13.4

CORTEZ is appearing in the magistrates' court due to his part in organising a violent confrontation during a European Champions League football match in Italy. As a result of an undercover operation, the police have been able to demonstrate that CORTEZ was the organiser of violence between fans from an English Premier League club and an Italian club. However, the police have been unable to produce evidence that CORTEZ actually took part in the violence in Italy. An application is being made for a banning order against CORTEZ.

Could such an order succeed in these circumstances?

A Yes, and if it makes an order, the court must require CORTEZ to surrender his passport.

B No, a banning order may only be made when the person has been convicted of a relevant offence.

C Yes, and if it makes an order, the court may require CORTEZ to surrender his passport.

D No, because the incidents of violence occurred abroad, the court must be satisfied that CORTEZ actually took part.

Question 13.5

The police have been looking for JENSEN to serve a notice on him prior to applying for a banning order against him, because of his violent behaviour at Premiership football matches. JENSEN has so far evaded the police, however, officers working at a home tie of a UEFA Champions League match have been circulated his photograph.

JENSEN is spotted outside the ground at the end of the game by Constable BARNETT and because the next game for the club is in two weeks' time, which is the return leg abroad, the officer is keen to detain JENSEN before he disappears again.

Would Constable BARNETT be entitled to detain JENSEN in these circumstances, using powers under s. 21A(2) of the Football Spectators Act 1989?

A No, there is no power of detention at this time because this is not within the control period.

B Yes, JENSEN could be detained for up to a maximum of six hours while a decision is being made whether to serve a notice on him.

C No, JENSEN has not yet been served with a notice outlining that a banning order is to be applied for.

D Yes, JENSEN could be detained for up to a maximum of four hours while a decision is being made whether to serve a notice on him.

Question 13.6

HUNTER was driving a public service vehicle containing a number of passengers who support an English Premier League club. HUNTER was driving the supporters home from a match against another Premier League club. The vehicle was stopped on the motorway by the police, who found that many of the passengers were either in possession of alcohol or drunk. HUNTER admitted stopping at a shop, to allow the passengers to buy alcohol, which they brought onto the vehicle.

Which of the following statements is correct, in relation to offences that may have been committed under the Sporting Events (Control of Alcohol etc.) Act 1985?

A No offences were committed under this Act, as the supporters were not on their way to a designated sporting event.

B HUNTER committed the offence, along with anyone who was drinking alcohol in the vehicle.

C HUNTER committed the offence, along with anyone who was drunk in the vehicle.

D HUNTER committed the offence, along with anyone who was in possession of alcohol or who was drunk in the vehicle.

Question 13.7

GITTENS was involved in an accident while driving to a Premier League football match, which was due to commence in three hours. GITTENS had managed to obtain a distress flare, which was in the car at the time of the accident. Constable MOUNCHER attended the scene and whilst dealing with the accident, the officer saw the flare on the front passenger seat of the car. GITTENS admitted to Constable MOUNCHER that he was intending to smuggle it into the ground.

Would Constable MOUNCHER be able to deal with GITTENS in relation to the flare, under s. 2A of the Sporting Events (Control of Alcohol etc.) Act 1985?

A No, it was outside the period of a designated sporting event.

B Yes, GITTENS was in possession of an article whose main purpose is the emission of a flare.

C Yes, GITTENS had with him an article whose main purpose is the emission of a flare.

D No, GITTENS was not at a designated sports ground, or trying to enter one.

Question 13.8

A Premier League football match was due to commence at 3 pm; however, because of a tube strike fans were unable to get to the ground on time and the kick-off was delayed until 3.30 pm. The match subsequently ended at 5.15 pm (instead of 4.45 pm).

Section 9(4) of the Sporting Events (Control of Alcohol etc.) Act 1985 outlines the period of a 'designated sporting event'. Which of the following statements is correct, in relation to this period?

A The end of the period for this designated sporting event is now 6.15 pm.

B The end of the period for this designated sporting event remains at 5.45 pm.

C The end of the period for this designated sporting event remains at 6.45 pm.

D The end of the period for this designated sporting event is now 7.15 pm.

Question 13.9

WINGROVE supports a football team which is a member of the English Football League, which has qualified for the Champions League. WINGROVE has managed to buy 50 tickets for an away game in Germany and has advertised them for sale on a website. WINGROVE intends making a profit by selling the tickets at more than their market value.

Does WINGROVE commit an offence under s. 166 of the Criminal Justice and Public Order Act 1994, in these circumstances?

A No, the offence does not apply to football matches abroad.

B No, the offence will only be committed when WINGROVE actually sells a ticket.

C No, the offence only applies to international football matches abroad.

D Yes, provided WINGROVE is not authorised by the organisers of the match.

ANSWERS

Answer 13.1

Answer **B** — It is an offence under s. 3(1) of the Football (Offences) Act 1991 to engage or take part in chanting of an indecent or racialist nature at a designated football match.

Section 3(2) goes on to describe the meaning of 'chanting' and 'racialist':

(a) 'chanting' means the repeated uttering of any words or sounds (whether alone or in concert with one or more others); and
(b) 'of a racialist' nature means consisting of or including matter which is threatening, abusive or insulting to a person by reason of his colour, race, nationality (including citizenship) or ethnic or national origins.

The wording of s. 3(2)(b) requires that the chanting *is*, rather than *might be*, threatening, abusive or insulting. Answer A is therefore incorrect.

One way to prove this element of the offence would be the evidence of a person who was threatened, abused or insulted, but this is not expressly required in the Act (and answer C is incorrect). The court is able to make a judgment for itself, for example in *DPP* v *Stoke on Trent Magistrates' Court* [2003] EWHC 1593 (Admin) it was held that shouting 'You're just a town full of Pakis' at supporters from Oldham fell squarely within the definition.

There is no requirement for the prosecution to show that the defendants intended the chanting to be racialist in its nature; they would simply need to demonstrate that it was racialist. Answer D is therefore incorrect.

General Police Duties, para. 4.13.3

Answer 13.2

Answer **A** — Under s. 14A of the Football Spectators Act 1989, the court may make a banning order against a person who is convicted of a relevant offence. The relevant offences are set out in sch. 1 and include offences relating to drunkenness, violence or threats of violence, or public order offences committed at or in connection with a football match *or when travelling to or from a football match* (whether or not the match was actually attended by the offender). Answer C is therefore incorrect.

The order may be made if the court is satisfied that there are reasonable grounds to believe that the order would help to prevent violence or disorder at/in connection with a 'regulated football match'. Violence here includes violence towards property and disorder includes stirring up racial hatred (s. 14C of the 1989 Act). Answer B is therefore incorrect.

However, in *R* v *Elliott* [2007] EWCA Crim 1002, banning orders were quashed where it was found that violence involving a group of men in a public house was unrelated to the match. Therefore, even though REYNOLDS was on his way to a football match when he committed the offences, it *could* be argued that the incident was unconnected to the match itself (and the court may decide not to consider a banning order). Answer A is correct for this reason, and answer D is incorrect.

General Police Duties, para. 4.13.4.1

Answer 13.3

Answer **A** — Banning orders made under s. 14A of the Football Spectators Act 1989 (on conviction of a relevant offence) in addition to an immediate sentence of imprisonment will have a minimum of six and a maximum of 10 years' duration (s. 14F(3)). Other banning orders made under s. 14A (i.e. where they do not accompany a sentence of immediate imprisonment) have a minimum of three and a maximum of five years' duration (s. 14F(4)).

Banning orders made under s. 14B (on complaint by a chief officer of police) have a minimum of three and a maximum of five years' duration (s. 14F(5)).

If a banning order has been in effect for *at least two-thirds of its period*, the person subject to it can *apply to the court which passed the order* for its termination.

Answers B, C and D are therefore incorrect.

General Police Duties, paras 4.13.4.1, 4.13.4.2

Answer 13.4

Answer **A** — Banning orders may be made under s. 14A or s. 14B of the Football Spectators Act 1989. Under s. 14A, the court may make a banning order against a person who is convicted of a relevant offence. The relevant offences are set out in sch. 1 and include offences relating to drunkenness, violence or threats of violence, or public order offences. Under s. 14B, the Chief Officer of police or the Director of Public Prosecutions may submit a request to the court, by way of complaint, to make such an order, even when the person has not been convicted of a relevant offence. Answer B is therefore incorrect.

On application to the court under s. 14B, the magistrates may make an order if the person has at any time *caused or contributed to* any violence or disorder in the United

Kingdom or elsewhere. Therefore, since the police are unable to produce evidence that CORTEZ caused or contributed to violence abroad, answer D is incorrect.

Finally, if the court imposes a banning order in connection with regulated football matches outside the United Kingdom, it *must* require the surrender of the person's passport and/or identity card (s. 14E(3)). Answer C is therefore incorrect.

General Police Duties, para. 4.13.4.2

Answer 13.5

Answer **A** — The Football Spectators Act 1989, s. 21A states:

> (1) This section and section 21B below apply during any control period in relation to a regulated football match outside the United Kingdom or an external tournament if a constable in uniform—
> (a) has reasonable grounds for suspecting that the condition in section 14B(2) above is met in the case of a person present before him, and
> (b) has reasonable grounds to believe that making a banning order in his case would help to prevent violence or disorder at or in connection with any regulated football matches ...
>
> (2) the constable may detain the person in his custody (whether there or elsewhere) until he has decided whether or not to issue a notice under section 21B, and shall give the person his reasons for detaining him in writing.

The condition referred to in s. 21A(1)(a) is that the person has at any time caused or contributed to any violence or disorder in the United Kingdom or elsewhere.

Answer C is incorrect as there is no requirement to serve a notice on a person *before* detaining them under s. 21A(2). The actual purpose of the power is to detain a person in order to decide whether or not to serve a notice of a banning order on him/her.

A person may not be detained under subs. (2) for more than four hours or, with the authority of an officer of at least the rank of inspector, six hours (s. 21A(3)). Therefore, the *maximum* period of detention while deciding whether or not to serve the notice is six hours and answer D is incorrect.

Finally, both answers B and D are also incorrect because the power under s. 21A(2) is only applicable during any control period in relation to a regulated football match outside the United Kingdom or an external tournament. 'Control period' means, in relation to a regulated football match outside England and Wales, the period:

- before the day of the match, and
- ending when the match is finished or cancelled.

This means there is no power to detain JENSEN at this time; however, the opportunity to do so will come before the next game for the club, in the five-day period leading up to the second leg.

General Police Duties, para. 4.13.4.5

Answer 13.6

Answer **D** — Section 1 of the Sporting Events (Control of Alcohol etc.) Act 1985 applies to people who are being conveyed in public service vehicles or railway passenger vehicles, which are being used for the principal purpose of carrying passengers to *or from* designated sporting events (s. 1(1)). Answer A is therefore incorrect.

Under s. 1(2), a person who knowingly causes or permits alcohol to be carried on a vehicle to which the section applies is guilty of an offence (which makes HUNTER guilty of the offence). Other offences are committed by any person who has alcohol in his/her possession while on a vehicle to which this section applies (s. 1(3)), or to a person who is drunk on such a vehicle (s. 1(3)). Since the offence applies to both classes of people, answer C is incorrect.

Section 1 does not actually mention people who are *drinking* alcohol whilst in a vehicle to which this section applies (although by implication, such people are likely to be in possession of alcohol). Since the wording is incorrect (and the offence applies both to people who have alcohol in their possession *and* who are drunk), answer B is incorrect.

General Police Duties, para. 4.13.5

Answer 13.7

Answer **D** — Under s. 2A(1) of the Sporting Events (Control of Alcohol etc.) Act 1985, a person is guilty of an offence if he/she has an article or substance to which this section applies in his/her possession:

(a) at any time during the period of a designated sporting event when he is in any area of a designated sports ground from which the event may be directly viewed, or

(b) while entering or trying to enter a designated sports ground at any time during the period of a designated sporting event at the ground.

Articles include distress flares, smoke bombs, fumigators and fireworks.

However, the offence is not committed when the person is on his/her way to the ground (whether it is inside or outside the period of a designated sporting event). Answers A, B and C are therefore incorrect.

Note that the offence can be committed by being in 'possession' of the article, a broader concept than 'having with him'.

General Police Duties, para. 4.13.7.5

Answer 13.8

Answer **A** — Under s. 9 of the Sporting Events (Control of Alcohol etc.) Act 1985, the period of a 'designated sporting event' is:

> The period beginning two hours before the start of the event or (if earlier) two hours before the time at which it is advertised to start and ending one hour after the end of the event.

Therefore, if the event is delayed, the starting time for the period remains at two hours before the match was advertised to commence. However, the finishing time remains at *one hour after the time the event actually ends*.

Answers B, C and D are incorrect for this reason.

General Police Duties, para. 4.13.7.3

Answer 13.9

Answer **D** — It is an offence under s. 166(1) of the Criminal Justice and Public Order Act 1994 for an unauthorised person to sell a ticket for a designated football match, or otherwise to dispose of such a ticket to another person. A person is 'unauthorised' unless he/she is authorised in writing to sell or otherwise dispose of tickets for the match by the organisers of the match (s. 166(2)(a)).

Section 166(2)(aa) outlines the criteria for 'selling' a ticket, which include offering to sell a ticket, exposing a ticket for sale and advertising that a ticket is available for purchase. Answer B is therefore incorrect.

For the purposes of s. 166(2)(c) a 'designated football match' is described in art. 2(2) of the Ticket Touting (Designation of Football Matches) Order 2007 (SI 2007/790) as an association football match in England and Wales; whereas art. 2(3) designates association football matches *outside* England and Wales involving a national team (of England or Wales), or a team representing a club which is a member of the Football League, the Football Association Premier League, the Football Conference or League of Wales, or matches in competitions or tournaments organised by or under the authority of FIFA or UEFA, in which any of such English or Welsh domestic or national team is eligible to participate or has participated. Answers A and C are therefore incorrect.

General Police Duties, para. 4.13.8

14 Weapons

STUDY PREPARATION

While the definition contained in s. 1 of the Prevention of Crime Act 1953 appears quite simple, you need to know the component parts to fully understand the offence. Learn the meaning of 'lawful authority', 'reasonable excuse', 'has with him' and 'public place'; there are many decided cases to assist (or confuse) you. You must also, of course, learn the three categories of offensive weapons.

Commonly, people tend to confuse the offence under the 1953 Act with the offence of carrying a bladed or sharply pointed article, especially in relation to folding pocket-knives and the length of blades. Remember also where the evidential burden lies in relation to proof for both offences, and the special defences under the Criminal Justice Act 1988.

One of the greatest problems in this very relevant area is separating the different statutory requirements. It is essential to be able to distinguish between the requirements relating to offensive weapons (in the Prevention of Crime Act 1953) and those relating to pointed or bladed instruments as regulated by the Criminal Justice Act 1988. Unless you are very clear about these differences, life will get very confusing. Further legislation in this chapter relates to the carrying of weapons on educational premises and the powers given to staff in such places.

Also, you must be able to tell the difference between an 'offensive weapon' and a 'weapon of offence', as contained in the offence of trespassing with a weapon of offence, under the Criminal Law Act 1977. The manufacture and sale of weapons receive attention, with a long list of weapons that may not be manufactured or sold, etc. Further offences may be committed by selling and marketing knives and articles to children under 16. Do not forget to learn about crossbows and the three offences contained in the Crossbows Act 1987. Also, pay attention to the powers given to a constable to search people and vehicles.

Apart from that, it is very straightforward!

QUESTIONS

Question 14.1

VAUGHAN ordered a novelty item over the Internet, which was delivered directly to his house. The item was a flick-knife which could also be operated as a cigarette lighter. VAUGHAN did not take the flick-knife out of the house, but regularly brought it out to show his friends when they came round.

Considering that the article could be an offensive weapon, which of the following statements is correct, according to s. 1(1) of the Prevention of Crime Act 1953?

A The article is an offensive weapon *per se* and VAUGHAN is guilty of the offence in these circumstances.

B The article is not an offensive weapon *per se*, but VAUGHAN could be guilty of the offence if he intended to use it as one.

C The article is an offensive weapon *per se*, but VAUGHAN is not guilty of the offence in these circumstances.

D The article is not an offensive weapon *per se*, but it has been adapted to be one and VAUGHAN could be guilty of the offence in these circumstances.

Question 14.2

AITKEN had recently split up from SPENCER as a result of suffering serious domestic abuse. She had moved into sheltered accommodation and was living anonymously in a different city. She had managed to secure a job in a bar, which meant she finished work late at night. AITKEN had received a phone call from a friend who told her that SPENCER had found out the area she was living in and to be careful. AITKEN believed that SPENCER was resourceful enough to find her and started carrying a knife in her bag for her own protection and would have used it for self-defence, fearing an imminent attack by her ex-partner.

With these circumstances in mind, which of the following statements is correct, in relation to having a reasonable excuse for having an offensive weapon in a public place?

A Carrying a knife for your own protection will not amount to a reasonable excuse; AITKEN would commit this offence in these circumstances.

B Carrying a knife for your protection may amount to a reasonable excuse provided the person believed he/she was at risk of an imminent attack, and the belief was reasonable.

C Having an offensive weapon with you for self-defence may amount to a reasonable excuse, provided you have armed yourself instantaneously, e.g. immediately prior to an attack.

D Carrying a knife as a general precaution that you may be attacked may amount to a reasonable excuse provided the person believed he/she was at risk of an attack at some time in the future.

Question 14.3

FAWCETT was driving home from work when he caused another car, being driven by GRANT, to brake sharply. GRANT followed him, shouting obscenities and sounding his horn. When FAWCETT stopped at traffic lights, GRANT got out of his car and ran towards him. FAWCETT got out of his own car and picked up a steering wheel lock, and threw it at GRANT, intending to injure him.

Is the steering wheel lock an 'offensive weapon' in these circumstances?

A No, FAWCETT formed the intention to use the article after it came into his possession.

B Yes, as soon as FAWCETT formed the intention to use the article.

C Yes, because FAWCETT used the article, intending to injure GRANT.

D Yes, as soon as FAWCETT picked the article up with the intention to use it.

Question 14.4

Constable BAKER was on patrol when she stopped a vehicle owned and being driven by CLEMENT. HARVEY was in the front passenger seat. Constable BAKER made a search of the vehicle and discovered a flick-knife in the glove compartment.

Could HARVEY and CLEMENT be guilty of an offence under the Prevention of Crime Act 1953?

A No, only CLEMENT may commit the offence, being the owner of the car.

B Yes, the offence is complete against both; no further proof is required.

C No, it is not possible for two people to have the same weapon with them.

D Yes, provided they both knew that the other person had it with him at the time.

Question 14.5

PENFOLD was stopped and searched on his way to a football match while he was walking in High Street. The searching officer, Constable MARRIOTT, discovered in PENFOLD's pocket a number of 50 pence pieces that had been sharpened around the edges. Believing that they were offensive weapons, the officer lawfully arrested PENFOLD.

In order to prove that PENFOLD was guilty of possessing an offensive weapon would Constable MARRIOTT need to prove intent by PENFOLD to use the coins to cause injury?

A No, provided it can be shown that the coins have been made to cause injury.
B Yes, because there is no apparent victim in these circumstances.
C Yes, because the coins are not offensive weapons *per se*.
D No, provided it can be shown the coins have been adapted to cause injury.

Question 14.6

BOSWORTH had gone through a relationship break-up with KINGSTON. BOSWORTH was very upset when he discovered that KINGSTON had started seeing BELL. BOSWORTH found out where BELL worked and drove there one day, carrying a Samurai sword in the car. He waited in the car and as BELL came out of the building, got out carrying the sword. BOSWORTH's intention was to cause BELL serious injury with the sword and he began waving it above his head; however, BELL saw him and ran back into the building, fearing immediate physical harm. BOSWORTH realised the police were likely to be called and got back in the car and drove off.

Considering the offence under s. 1A of the Prevention of Crime Act 1953 (threatening with offensive weapon in public), has BOSWORTH committed this offence?

A Yes, because he intends causing BELL serious physical harm with the sword.
B No, he did not use the weapon in such a way that there was an immediate risk of serious physical harm to BELL.
C Yes, he has unlawfully and intentionally threatened BELL with serious physical harm.
D Yes, BELL was put in fear that he would suffer serious physical harm.

Question 14.7

Constable BRADY stopped and searched CLOUGH in a park one evening, after receiving information that he was carrying a knife. Constable BRADY found a folding knife with a blade of approximately 3.5 inches in length, in CLOUGH's pocket. CLOUGH claimed that he was a scout and bought the knife from a camping shop and it was intended for cutting string.

Which of the following statements is correct, in relation to the knife that Constable BRADY found?

A The knife could be an offensive weapon or a bladed article, depending on CLOUGH's intention.

B The knife could be an offensive weapon depending on CLOUGH's intentions, or a bladed article, regardless of his intention.

C The knife would be an offensive weapon or a bladed article, regardless of CLOUGH's intention.

D The knife could be an offensive weapon depending on CLOUGH's intention; however, it may not be a bladed article, if the length of the blade is under 3.5 inches.

Question 14.8

McGREGOR had been to a traditional Scottish wedding and was wearing the traditional McGregor clan outfit; this included carrying a Skean Dhu knife in a sheath in his right sock. Later in the evening, Constable KEEN was on foot patrol in the city centre and saw McGREGOR standing with a group of people in the street outside a pub. The officer saw that McGREGOR was holding the knife and approached to speak to him. McGREGOR stated that he was simply showing the knife to his friends and had no intention of using it to hurt anyone.

Under what circumstances could McGREGOR claim a defence in relation to the knife, under s. 139 of the Criminal Justice Act 1988?

A If he could demonstrate to the court that he had no intention of using the knife to cause injury and it was part of a national costume.

B If he could demonstrate to the court that he had a good reason for having it with him and it was part of a national costume.

C If he could demonstrate to the court that he had it with him as part of a national costume.

D If he could demonstrate to the court that he had no intention of using the knife to cause injury.

Question 14.9

Constable LLOYD stopped GREGSON, who was driving a motor vehicle on a road, and conducted a search under s. 1 of the Police and Criminal Evidence Act 1984. The officer discovered a Stanley knife underneath GREGSON's seat. Constable LLOYD was of the opinion that GREGSON had concealed the knife in this location and consequently arrested him for having an offensive weapon, contrary to s. 1(1) of the

Prevention of Crime Act 1953. GREGSON was later charged with the offence, but pleaded not guilty, stating that he had a 'good reason' for having the weapon: that he undertook casual work at a relative's factory and used the knife for opening boxes. He claimed that he had forgotten that the knife was under the seat, because he had not worked at the factory for a couple of weeks.

Which of the following statements is correct, in relation to GREGSON's claim of 'good reason'?

A Forgetfulness could amount to a 'good reason' for having it; GREGSON must show beyond reasonable doubt that he had a reasonable excuse for having it.

B The prosecution must show beyond reasonable doubt that GREGSON did not have a 'good reason' for having the weapon.

C Forgetfulness would not amount to a 'good reason' for having it; GREGSON has no defence to this charge.

D Forgetfulness could amount to a 'good reason' for having it; GREGSON must show on the balance of probabilities that he had a reasonable excuse for having it.

Question 14.10

Constable O'NEIL attended a local high school in relation to SPEARS, who had been involved in a violent incident. On arrival, the officer discovered that SPEARS, aged 17, had been excluded the year before and had gone to the premises whilst drunk in possession of a screwdriver and had threatened one of the teachers.

Which of the following statements is correct, in relation to an offence under s. 139AA of the Criminal Justice Act 1988?

A This offence is incomplete in these circumstances because SPEARS was not a pupil at the school.

B This offence is complete if it can be shown that SPEARS threatened someone with the screwdriver.

C This offence is complete if it can be shown that SPEARS threatened someone with the screwdriver and there was an immediate risk of serious physical harm to that person.

D This offence is incomplete in these circumstances because a school premises is not a public place.

Question 14.11

PIETERSEN, a head teacher of a high school in England, was contacted by a member of staff stating that CHAVEZ, a pupil at the school, had been seen carrying a knife on school premises. The teacher kept CHAVEZ under observation until PIETERSEN arrived. Utilising powers under s. 550ZA of the Education Act 1996, PIETERSEN searched CHAVEZ but did not find the knife. CHAVEZ was carrying a bag and the member of staff suggested that CHAVEZ may have hidden the knife inside it.

What authority would PIETERSEN have to search CHAVEZ's possessions under this legislation?

A None, possessions may not be searched under this legislation, only a pupil may be searched.

B A pupil's possessions may be searched, but only in the pupil's presence and in the presence of another member of staff.

C A pupil's possessions may be searched, but only in the presence of another member of staff and with the pupil's permission.

D A pupil's possessions may be searched, but only in the presence of another member of staff.

Question 14.12

MEARS was a pupil of a high school in England on a field trip. The teacher in charge, SMITH, was told by another pupil that MEARS had taken a flick-knife on the trip and had hidden it in a coat pocket. SMITH told MEARS to hand over the weapon; however, MEARS denied being in possession of a knife.

What powers, if any, would SMITH have to search for the weapon, under s. 550ZA of the Education Act 1996?

A SMITH may have searched MEARS, using force if necessary.

B None, as they were not on school premises.

C None, only a head teacher may search a pupil under this legislation.

D SMITH may have searched MEARS, but not by the use of force.

Question 14.13

JENKINGS is the male head teacher of a high school in England and was informed that a female pupil, STILLWELL, had been seen in the classroom with a knife by a female teacher, CHAN. It was believed STILLWELL had hidden the knife in the lining of her jacket and she was taken into an empty classroom.

Which of the following statements is correct, in relation to who may have the authority to search STILLWELL for the knife?

A Only CHAN may search STILLWELL, but she may not require her to remove any clothing.

B Only CHAN may search STILLWELL, but JENKINGS may be present; there are no restrictions on teachers of the opposite sex being present.

C Either CHAN or JENKINGS may search STILLWELL, because it is not likely to involve the removal of more than outer clothing.

D Only CHAN may search STILLWELL, but JENKINGS may be present if it is not reasonably practicable for another teacher of the same sex to be present.

Question 14.14

FLETCHER is the head teacher of a primary school in England and has been informed that a pupil, CARTER, aged 10, has been seen in the playground with a knife by another teacher.

Would FLETCHER have the authority to search CARTER for the knife in these circumstances?

A No, this power does not apply to primary schools.

B No, because CARTER is under the age of 14.

C No, because CARTER is under the age of 11.

D Yes, regardless of CARTER's age, the power applies in these circumstances.

Question 14.15

CRUZ was employed as a computer software programmer, but was sacked for selling material to a rival company. CRUZ returned to the company offices one night, entering the gated compound using an electronic pass that had not been confiscated. CRUZ's intention was to sabotage the company software, by loading a virus onto the server. CRUZ was in possession of a knife, intending to use it to threaten the night security guard if necessary. However, CRUZ was unable to get into the main company building as the electronic pass did not work. CRUZ was disturbed by the security guard and ran off.

Has CRUZ committed an offence contrary to s. 8(1) of the Criminal Law Act 1977 (trespassing with a weapon of offence)?

A No, CRUZ has not entered a dwelling with a weapon of offence.

B Yes, CRUZ has entered premises with a weapon of offence.

C No, CRUZ has not entered a building with a weapon of offence.

D No, CRUZ has not entered a dwelling, or land adjacent to a dwelling with a weapon of offence.

Question 14.16

STONE owns a shop which sells second-hand goods and has a reputation for being able to supply unusual weapons. COLLINS entered the shop looking for some weapons for himself and his friends for a football match the following week. STONE indicated that he could get his hands on some knuckle dusters, which he could sell at a good price. COLLINS agreed to return three days later to buy them.

At what point, if any, would STONE commit an offence under the Criminal Justice Act 1988?

A Not until he actually sells the weapons to COLLINS.
B Not until he is in possession of the weapons with intent to sell them.
C When he offered to sell the weapons to COLLINS.
D Not until he has the weapons with him with intent to sell them.

Question 14.17

FAHEY is aged 18 and works in a hardware shop. McKAY, aged 17, came into the shop one day and selected a pocket-knife from the display, intending to buy it. The pocket-knife had a blade with a cutting edge of 3.5 inches.

Considering offences under s. 141A of the Criminal Justice Act 1988, could FAHEY lawfully sell this pocket-knife to McKAY?

A Yes, because FAHEY is over 18.
B Yes, because McKAY is over 16.
C No, because McKAY is under 18.
D Yes, this offence does not apply to folding pocket-knives.

Question 14.18

Constable SHAPIRO received a complaint of persons dangerously firing a crossbow in the back garden of a dwelling. On arrival, neighbours showed the officer some bolts from the crossbow, which had penetrated the hedge separating their gardens. Constable SHAPIRO could see BARRYMORE alone in the garden, but there was no sign of a crossbow. BARRYMORE appeared to be about 14 years of age.

Does Constable SHAPIRO have the power to enter the garden and search BARRYMORE for the crossbow in these circumstances?

A Yes, there is a power to enter any land other than a dwelling house in order to conduct such a search.

B No, there is no power to enter land, which forms part of a dwelling under this legislation.

C Yes, there is a power to search any premises or vehicle under this legislation.

D No, a constable only has the power to search a person or a vehicle.

ANSWERS

Answer 14.1

Answer **C** — Under s. 1(1) of the Prevention of Crime Act 1953, any person who without lawful authority or reasonable excuse, the proof whereof shall lie on him, has with him in any public place any offensive weapon shall be guilty of an offence.

An offence under this section can only be committed in a public place, therefore answers A, B and D are incorrect.

In relation to the article itself, it has been held that a flick-knife that also operates as a lighter remains an offensive weapon *per se* despite its alternative function (*R* v *Vasili* [2011] EWCA Crim 615). Therefore, if it *had* been in possession of the person in a public place, answers B and D would have been incorrect for this reason also.

General Police Duties, paras 4.14.2, 4.14.2.5

Answer 14.2

Answer **B** — To prove an offence contrary to s. 1(1) of the Prevention of Crime Act 1953, the prosecution must first show, beyond reasonable doubt, that the defendant had an offensive weapon with him/her. The burden of proof then shifts to the defendant to show that he/she had a 'reasonable excuse' for having the weapon.

There are several overlapping cases that deal with the issue of carrying an offensive weapon, or a bladed or sharply pointed article in a public place in self-defence or to prevent an attack. The common themes with these cases are

- the defendant's own belief that he/she may be attacked;
- how reasonable that belief was;
- how imminent the attack is likely to be.

The *reasonableness* of the belief was examined in *N* v *DPP* [2011] EWHC 1807 (Admin). The court found that the defence of reasonable excuse was *not* made out where a person picked up a metal bar for protection having been threatened five minutes earlier by a group of young men in a car who were found to have no weapons. Even if the defendant did believe that he was at risk of an imminent attack, the court held that his belief was not a reasonable one in the circumstances.

Also, it is *not* reasonable to have a weapon with you as a general precaution in case you are attacked (*Evans* v *Hughes* [1972] 1 WLR 1452) and the court is more likely to uphold an appeal if the fear is reasonable that an attack is imminent, rather than an imprecise attack some time in the future (*R* v *McAuley* [2009] EWCA Crim 2130). Answer D is therefore incorrect.

On the other hand, it *may* be reasonable to have a weapon if you have good grounds to anticipate an unprovoked or unlawful attack, for example for a person guarding cash transits (*Malnik* v *DPP* [1989] Crim LR 451), or if you could show on the balance of probabilities that you were in fear of an imminent attack (see *McAuley* noted previously). This approach was confirmed by the Court of Appeal in *R* v *Emmanuel* [1998] Crim LR 347, where it was accepted that 'good reason' could include self-defence. Answer A is therefore incorrect.

None of these cases suggests that this defence is *only* applicable if you have armed yourself instantaneously, for example immediately prior to an attack, and therefore answer C is incorrect.

General Police Duties, paras 4.14.2.2, 4.14.4.1

Answer 14.3

Answer **A** — The expression 'has with him' will not in most cases include circumstances where a person has an 'innocent' article, which he/she uses offensively. The purpose of the Prevention of Crime Act 1953 is to prevent people from arming themselves for some future event, and the intention of the Act is to deal with preventative issues.

The case of *Ohlson* v *Hylton* [1975] 1 WLR 724 demonstrates this. The defendant had a bag of tools with him in the course of his trade. He produced a hammer from the bag and used it to hit someone. The court held that, as he had formed the intention to use the hammer *after* it came into his possession, the offence was not made out (answers B and C are therefore incorrect). This decision was followed by several other similar cases (*Bates* v *Bulman* [1979] 1 WLR 1190, *R* v *Dayle* [1974] 1 WLR 181 and *R* v *Humphreys* [1977] Crim LR 225).

This is not to say that 'innocent' articles may never become offensive weapons, such as people carrying screwdrivers to defend themselves: it depends on the immediacy of the conversion from one to another, and therefore answer D is incorrect.

General Police Duties, paras 4.14.2.2, 4.14.2.3

Answer 14.4

Answer **D** — It is possible for more than one person to have the same weapon 'with them' (*R* v *Edmonds* [1963] 2 QB 142), and therefore answers A and C are incorrect.

It would be necessary to prove that they knew of the existence of the weapon in the hands of the other.

In this case it was decided that both parties knew of the existence of the weapon and that they knew the other party had it 'with him' at the time of the offence. Answer B is incorrect as the offence is not complete until this is proved.

General Police Duties, para. 4.14.2.3

Answer 14.5

Answer **D** — The prosecution would have to show that the coins have been adapted to cause injury in order to show that they are offensive weapons. However, once the prosecution have proved this, there is no need to show an intention to use them to cause injury (*Davis* v *Alexander* (1970) 54 Cr App R 398).

Answer A is incorrect because the coins have not been 'made' to cause injury; they are not offensive weapons *per se*. However, the fact that they are not offensive weapons *per se* still does not place a burden upon the prosecution to prove intent to use them (*Davis* v *Alexander*), which is why answer C is incorrect.

Answer B is incorrect because it is the adaptation of the article that is relevant, not the intention of the person carrying it (*Bryan* v *Mott* (1976) 62 Cr App R 71).

If PENFOLD were charged under the third leg of the definition, where the weapon is intended to cause injury, the prosecution would have to prove an intention to cause injury by PENFOLD. This would obviously be a harder case to prove than adaptation in these circumstances.

General Police Duties, para. 4.14.2.5

Answer 14.6

Answer **B** — Under s. 1A(1) of the Prevention of Crime Act 1953, a person is guilty of an offence if that person—

(a) has an offensive weapon with him/her in a public place,
(b) unlawfully and intentionally threatens another person with the weapon, and
(c) does so in such a way that there is an immediate risk of serious physical harm to that other person.

This offence is meant to bridge the gap between someone who is simply carrying an offensive weapon and someone who actually commits an assault with one. The essence of this offence, therefore, is that a person (A) must have an offensive weapon with him/her and intentionally *uses* the weapon to threaten another (B) creating an immediate risk of serious physical harm to B. While there is no doubt that BOSWORTH had with him an offensive weapon and intended to use it, it would be difficult to argue that BELL was in *immediate* risk of serious physical harm—had he not seen BOSWORTH and run away, matters may have been different. Answers A and C are therefore incorrect.

The fear of the 'victim' that he/she may suffer serious physical harm is not essential to proving the offence (although the evidence may be useful in any trial). It is the intention of the defendant that counts and for that reason answer D is incorrect.

General Police Duties, para. 4.14.3

Answer 14.7

Answer **B** — Under s. 1(1) of the Prevention of Crime Act 1953, any person who without lawful authority or reasonable excuse, the proof whereof shall lie on him, has with him in any public place any offensive weapon shall be guilty of an offence.

Under s. 139 of the Criminal Justice Act 1988, a person commits an offence if he/she has a bladed or sharply pointed article in a public place.

Offensive weapons (under s. 1(1)) fall into three categories for the purposes of this offence, namely, articles:

- made for causing injury (offensive weapons *per se*);
- adapted for causing injury; and
- intended by the person who has them, for causing injury.

The knife carried in this scenario would not count as an offensive weapon *per se* (such as a flick knife or gravity knife) as it was not made for causing injury. Neither has it been adapted for causing injury. It is simply a knife that may be used as a tool, therefore, to prosecute the person under this section, you would have to prove that the person who had the knife intended using it for causing injury. Answer C is incorrect, because the person's intention *is* relevant.

Turning to offences under the Criminal Justice Act 1988, a person commits the offence either by carrying a sharply pointed instrument or a bladed instrument. There is no mention of the intent to use the article for any purpose—having it with you is enough. Answer A is therefore incorrect.

There are defences of lawful authority and reasonable excuse (or good reason) for both offences, and folding pocket knives are excluded *unless* the cutting edge of the blade exceeds 3 inches (7.62 cm) and not 3.5. Answer D is therefore incorrect.

General Police Duties, paras 4.14.2.5, 4.14.4

Answer 14.8

Answer **C** — Under s. 139 of the Criminal Justice Act 1988, a person commits an offence if he/she has a bladed or sharply pointed article in a public place.

Section 139 contains two specific defences:

> (4) It shall be a defence for a person charged with an offence under this section to prove that he had good reason or lawful authority for having the article with him in a public place.
>
> (5) Without prejudice to the generality of subsection (4) above, it shall be a defence for a person charged with an offence under this section to prove that he had the article with him—
>
> (a) for use at work;
>
> (b) for religious reasons; or
>
> (c) as part of any national costume.

Therefore, under s. 139, the intention of the person is irrelevant when it comes to these specific defences and answers A and D are incorrect.

The general defence under s. 139(4) is available for people who are carrying weapons that are not covered by the defence contained in subsection (5). McGREGOR would only have to demonstrate to the court that he had it with him as part of a national costume and answer B is incorrect.

General Police Duties, para. 4.14.4.1

Answer 14.9

Answer **D** — To prove an offence contrary to s. 1(1) of the Prevention of Crime Act 1953, the prosecution must first show, beyond reasonable doubt, that the defendant had an offensive weapon with him. The burden of proof then shifts to the defendant to show that he/she had 'good reason' or a reasonable excuse for having the weapon. Answer B is incorrect, as the prosecution bears no further burden once it can be shown that the person has an offensive weapon with him/her.

The burden of proof on the defendant will be judged on the balance of probabilities, and not beyond reasonable doubt; therefore, answer A is incorrect.

Forgetting that you have the article with you is not a general defence (see *DPP* v *Gregson* (1993) 96 Cr App R 240 and *R (On the application of Hilton)* v *Canterbury Crown Court* [2009] EWHC 2867 (Admin)). However, the courts and commentators have debated the issue of forgetfulness in this context and the relevance of 'forgetting' you have a knife or other article with you. The issues were summarised by the Court of Appeal in *R* v *Jolie* [2003] EWCA Crim 1543:

While it is clear that forgetfulness alone cannot be a 'good reason', from a policing perspective the main thing is to gather any evidence that the defendant had the article with him/her in a public place and to record any explanation given. Whether the defendant had a 'good reason' (which might include forgetfulness combined with other circumstances) is then a matter for the court.

The issue was further examined in *R* v *Chahal* [2010] EWHC 439 (Admin), where the court quashed a conviction under this section. The court held that relevant consideration should have been given where the defendant, who undertook casual work at a relative's factory, forgot about a knife he was carrying. Therefore, the court *could* take this defence into account, and for that reason answer C is incorrect.

General Police Duties, para. 4.14.4.1

Answer 14.10

Answer **C** — Under s. 139AA(1) of the Criminal Justice Act 1988, a person is guilty of an offence if that person:

(a) has an article to which this section applies with him or her in a public place or on school premises,
(b) unlawfully and intentionally threatens another person with the article, and
(c) does so in such a way that there is an immediate risk of serious physical harm to that other person.

This offence is similar to that created in s. 1A of the Prevention of Crime Act 1953 and includes threats to those made on school premises or in a public place. Answer D is incorrect.

The fact that the person is not a pupil of the school is irrelevant and answer A is incorrect.

It must be shown that the person threatened someone with an offensive weapon or a sharply pointed article or article having a blade *and* there was an immediate risk of serious physical harm to that person. Answer B is therefore incorrect.

General Police Duties, para. 4.14.5.1

Answer 14.11

Answer **B** — Section 550ZA(1) of the Education Act 1996 states that when a member of staff of a school in England has reasonable grounds for suspecting that a pupil at the school may have a prohibited item with him/her, or in his/her possessions, the member of staff may search that pupil. According to s. 550ZA(3), a prohibited item is:

(a) an article to which section 139 of the Criminal Justice Act 1988 applies (knives and blades etc.), or
(b) an offensive weapon (within the meaning of the Prevention of Crime Act 1953).

A member of staff for these purposes is any teacher who works at the school and any other person who, with the authority of the head teacher, has lawful control or charge of pupils for whom education is being provided at the school (s. 550ZA(5)). Answer A is incorrect because possessions may be searched as well as the pupil themselves.

A pupil's possessions may not be searched under this section except in their presence and in the presence of another member of staff (s. 550ZB(7)). Since the pupil needs to be present, answer D is incorrect. However, the search may take place without the pupil's permission—indeed, as much force as is reasonable may be used in exercising this power (see s. 550ZB(5)). Answer C is therefore incorrect.

The person carrying out a search may only require the removal of outer clothing; they must be of the same sex and carry out the search in the presence of another member of staff also of the same sex as the pupil if it is reasonably practicable (s. 550ZB(6)).

Note that the powers in relation to prohibited items only apply in England. In Wales the power of members of staff to search pupils is restricted to knives, blades, etc. and other offensive weapons (s. 550AA).

General Police Duties, para. 4.14.5.6

Answer 14.12

Answer **A** — Section 550ZA(1) of the Education Act 1996 states that when a member of staff of a school in England has reasonable grounds for suspecting that a pupil at the school may have a prohibited item with him/her, or in his/her possession, the member of staff may search that pupil. According to s. 550ZA(3), a prohibited item is:

(a) an article to which section 139 of the Criminal Justice Act 1988 applies (knives and blades etc.), or
(b) an offensive weapon (within the meaning of the Prevention of Crime Act 1953).

Under s. 550ZB(4), a search may be carried out only where the member of staff and the pupil are on school premises; or they are elsewhere and the member of staff has lawful control or charge of the pupil. Answer B is therefore incorrect.

A person may carry out a search under this section only if he/she is the head teacher of the school; or he/she has been authorised by the head teacher to carry out the search (see s. 550ZB(1)). Answer C is therefore incorrect.

Finally, such a search may take place without the pupil's permission—indeed, as much force as is reasonable may be used in exercising this power (see s. 550ZB(5)). Answer D is therefore incorrect.

Note that the powers in relation to prohibited items only apply in England. In Wales the power of members of staff to search pupils is restricted to knives, blades, etc. and other offensive weapons (s. 550AA).

General Police Duties, para. 4.14.5.6

Answer 14.13

Answer **D** — Section 550AA(1) of the Education Act 1996 states that a member of the staff of a school in England, who has reasonable grounds for suspecting that a pupil at the school may have with him/her or in his/her possession:

(a) an article to which section 139 of the Criminal Justice Act 1988 applies (knives and blades, etc.), or
(b) an offensive weapon (within the meaning of the Prevention of Crime Act 1953), may search that pupil or his/her possessions for such articles and weapons.

A search under this section may only be conducted by a head teacher, or a person authorised by the head teacher in the presence of another member of staff.

Section 550AA(5) of the Act places certain restrictions on the conduct of the search. The person conducting the search may not require the pupil to remove any clothing *other than outer clothing*; therefore, STILLWELL may be required to remove her jacket and answer A is incorrect.

There *are* restrictions on who may be present at the search; it must be carried out in the presence of another member of staff of the same sex, *unless it is not reasonably practicable for such a person to be present.* Answer B is incorrect.

The person carrying out the search must *always* be of the same sex as the pupil, regardless of the extent of the search; therefore, answer C is incorrect.

Note that the powers in relation to prohibited items only apply in England. In Wales the power of members of staff to search pupils is restricted to knives, blades, etc. and other offensive weapons (s. 550AA).

General Police Duties, para. 4.14.5.6

Answer 14.14

Answer **D** — Section 550AA(1) of the Education Act 1996 states that a member of the staff of a school in England, who has reasonable grounds for suspecting that a pupil at the school may have with him/her or in his/her possession:

(a) an article to which section 139 of the Criminal Justice Act 1988 applies (knives and blades, etc.), or
(b) an offensive weapon (within the meaning of the Prevention of Crime Act 1953), may search that pupil or his/her possessions for such articles and weapons.

A search under this section may only conducted by a head teacher, or a person authorised by the head teacher in the presence of another member of staff.

'School', under s. 4(1) of the Education Act 1996, means an educational institution which is outside the further education sector and the higher education sector and is an institution for providing:

(a) primary education,
(b) secondary education, or
(c) both primary and secondary education,
whether or not the institution also provides further education.

Section 550AA does not specify that primary schools are excluded and there is no mention of a minimum age for searching pupils. Answers A, B and C are therefore incorrect.

General Police Duties, para. 4.14.5.6

Answer 14.15

Answer **B** — Under s. 8(1) of the Criminal Law Act 1977, a person who is on any premises as a trespasser, after having entered as such, is guilty of an offence if, without lawful authority or reasonable excuse, he/she has with him/her on the premises any weapon of offence.

Under s. 12 of the 1977 Act, 'premises' for this purpose means:

(1) any building; or
(2) any part of a building under separate occupation;
(3) *any land adjacent to and used/intended for use in connection with a building;*
(4) the site comprising any building(s) together with ancillary land;
(5) any fixed structure;
(6) any movable structure, vehicle or vessel designed or adapted for residential purposes.

Any building, or land adjacent to a building (not just a dwelling), is covered by s. 8(1), therefore CRUZ has committed the offence and for that reason answers A, C and D are incorrect.

General Police Duties, para. 4.14.6

Answer 14.16

Answer **C** — Section 141 of the Criminal Justice Act 1988 makes it an offence to manufacture, sell, hire, offer for sale or hire, expose, have in possession for the purpose of sale or hire, or lend or give to another person, any weapon listed in the schedule to the Act (knuckle dusters are included).

The offence may be committed by making an offer—the Act makes no mention of being in possession of the article when the offer is made, which is why answer C is correct (this is similar to a case of offering to supply drugs under the Misuse of Drugs Act 1971).

Although offences would be made out in answers A and B, the offence has already been committed.

Answer D would be an incorrect answer in any circumstances, as unlike the original 1953 Act, which requires a person to have the weapon with him, this offence deals with possession for the purpose of sale or hire.

General Police Duties, para. 4.14.7

Answer 14.17

Answer **C** — Under s. 141A of the Criminal Justice Act 1988, it is an offence for any person to sell to a person under 18 a knife, blade, razor blade, axe, or any article which has a blade or sharp point and is made or adapted for causing injury.

Previously, a person would have committed an offence by selling such an article to a person under the age of 16 (and no offence would have been committed in these circumstances). However, the Violent Crime Reduction Act 2006 increased the age limit, so that a sale to any person under the age of 18 is an offence and therefore answer B is incorrect.

The offence does not apply to a razor blade in a cartridge, where not more than 2 mm of the blade is exposed or to a folding pocket-knife with a blade of less than 3 inches. Since the blade in this question was 3.5 inches, it is covered by s. 141A and therefore answer D is incorrect.

The age of the person making the sale is not relevant (which is why answer A is incorrect).

General Police Duties, para. 4.14.8.1

Answer 14.18

Answer **A** — Under s. 3 of the Crossbows Act 1987, a person under the age of 18 who has with him a crossbow which is capable of discharging a missile, or parts of a crossbow which together (and without any other parts) can be assembled to form a crossbow capable of discharging a missile, is guilty of an offence, unless he is under the supervision of a person who is 21 years of age or older.

Under s. 4(1), if a constable reasonably suspects a person is committing or has committed an offence under s. 3, they may search the suspected person or their vehicle for the crossbow (or part of a crossbow). Under s. 4(4), for the purposes of exercising the powers under s. 4(4), a constable may also enter any land other than a dwelling house in order to conduct the search.

In contrast to searches conducted under s. 1 of PACE (where a person cannot be searched in their own garden), the term 'dwelling house' under the Crossbows Act 1987 appears to mean just that—a house. Therefore, there is no power to search 'any premises' under this section and answer C is incorrect. However, there *is* a power to enter other land which is not a dwelling house (such as a garden) in order to search a person or vehicle. Answer B is therefore incorrect.

Lastly, the powers of search under this legislation are not restricted to a search of a person or their vehicle in a public place. Answer D is therefore incorrect.

General Police Duties, para. 4.14.9

15 Domestic Violence and Trade Disputes

STUDY PREPARATION

Domestic violence and abuse are a significant feature of police patrol work and the subject has received a great deal of political and legislative attention over the years. This chapter covers the powers created by the Crime and Security Act 2010 to secure the immediate protection of victims of domestic violence and abuse through Domestic Violence Protection Notices (DVPNs), Domestic Violence Protection Orders (DVPOs) and the Domestic Violence Disclosure Scheme. Additional protection is given to victims through a civil route, under the Family Law Act 1996, which is also dealt with here.

Finally, the chapter deals with criminal offences that may be committed during industrial and trade disputes.

QUESTIONS

Question 15.1

Section 76 of the Serious Crime Act 2015 provides for an offence of 'controlling or coercive behaviour in an intimate or family relationship'.

Which of the following statements best describes how 'controlling or coercive behaviour' can be committed?

A Behaviour that generates serious alarm or distress that has a substantial effect on the victim's day-to-day activities.

B Behaviour that is severe and persistent and capable of causing serious mental health problems for the victims.

C Behaviour that causes the victim to fear that violence will be used against them on at least two occasions.

D Behaviour that causes the victim to fear that violence will be used against them on at least two occasions, or that generates serious alarm or distress that has a substantial effect on the victim's day-to-day activities.

Question 15.2

MILLS and STANTON are in a long-term relationship; they live together and are sexual partners. MILLS has a strong personality and persuaded STANTON to become a sex worker. STANTON commits acts of prostitution regularly and gives MILLS all the money she earns. MILLS does not use violence or threats to force STANTON to live this life, but does make regular threats that her friends and family will be told if she does not continue her prostitution.

Is this behaviour by MILLS covered by the Home Office definition of domestic abuse?

A No, MILLS's behaviour towards STANTON is not violent or sexual.

B No, the definition is limited to violent or physical behaviour against another.

C Yes, this behaviour amounts to domestic abuse according to the definition.

D Yes, if STANTON perceives the behaviour to be controlling.

Question 15.3

HARRIS and WILLIS are both aged 30 and have lived together for three years. WILLIS has made numerous complaints to the police after being assaulted by HARRIS; however, each allegation was withdrawn before the courts were able to hear the case. HARRIS is now in police detention for committing another serious assault on WILLIS. The officer in the case is considering whether it would be appropriate for a Domestic Violence Protection Notice (DVPN) to be issued against HARRIS, in order to protect WILLIS from further violence.

Section 24 of the Crime and Security Act 2010 outlines the procedures for issuing such a notice. In relation to this power, which of the following statements is correct?

A The application for a DVPN must be made to a magistrate, provided HARRIS is charged with the assault on WILLIS.

B The application for a DVPN must be made to a magistrate, but this is not dependent on HARRIS being charged with the assault on WILLIS.

C The DVPN may be issued by a senior police officer, but this is not dependent on HARRIS being charged with the assault on WILLIS.

D The DVPN may be issued by a senior police officer, following consultation at a Multi-Agency Risk Assessment Conference (MARAC), but this is not dependent on HARRIS being charged with the assault on WILLIS.

Question 15.4

An emergency Multi-Agency Risk Assessment Conference (MARAC) is meeting to discuss NEWMAN, the victim of serious domestic abuse. In the last 24 hours, NEWMAN has supported a prosecution against WILSON for assault, and the defendant is currently in police custody waiting to go to court, having been charged with assault. However, NEWMAN has indicated an intention to withdraw the allegation at WILSON's court appearance tomorrow. The various agencies at the MARAC have discussed whether or not a Domestic Violence Protection Notice (DVPN) should be issued against WILSON; however, the meeting has been informed that NEWMAN would be hostile to such a notice being issued.

Which of the following statements is correct in respect of whether a DVPN may be issued against NEWMAN's wishes, under s. 24 of the Crime and Security Act 2010?

A Section 24(3)(b) provides that the opinion of the victim be sought before a DVPN is issued; it may not, therefore, be issued without NEWMAN's consent.

B A DVPN may be issued without NEWMAN's consent, provided either the victim or some other member of the household is under 18.

C A DVPN may not be issued without NEWMAN's consent; only a Domestic Violence Protection Order (DVPO) may be issued in these circumstances.

D The authorising authority may issue a DVPN in these circumstances, even if NEWMAN does not consent to it.

Question 15.5

Constable PENGELLI works in the Public Protection Department and has just read an intelligence log concerning ARMAND, whom the officer knows is a previous victim of domestic abuse. ARMAND's ex-partner, KIFF, was convicted 12 months ago for an assault relating to the abuse and is currently in prison; however, the intelligence log Constable PENGELLI has read indicates that ARMAND has moved in with a new partner, whose convictions for domestic abuse are worse than KIFF's.

Considering the Domestic Violence Disclosure Scheme (DVDS), what action should Constable PENGELLI take?

A None, this scheme relates to requests for information from members of the public, who are concerned about people they are in a relationship with.

B Constable PENGELLI should make appropriate police checks and consult with statutory partners, and a decision should be made by the appropriate police officer as to whether disclosure should be made to ARMAND.

C None, intelligence logs are not accurate enough documents to commence an investigation to decide whether to make a disclosure about a person's criminal convictions.

D Constable PENGELLI should make appropriate police checks and pass the matter to statutory partners, who should make a decision as to whether disclosure should be made to ARMAND.

Question 15.6

VIVIERS recently ended a five-year relationship with SIMMS because of SIMMS's alcoholism. SIMMS has a 14-year-old daughter, CLAIRE, from a previous relationship; CLAIRE has no contact with her father. VIVIERS assumed parenting responsibility for CLAIRE while he lived with her, although he did not formally adopt her. CLAIRE is still in regular contact with VIVIERS and has recently disclosed that SIMMS is regularly violent towards her, but she does not wish to contact the police. VIVIERS has contacted a solicitor in relation to taking out a non-molestation order against SIMMS, on CLAIRE's behalf.

Under the Family Law Act 1996, can VIVIERS apply for a non-molestation order in these circumstances?

A No, because he is not CLAIRE's natural or adopted parent.

B No, because he does not have current parental responsibility for CLAIRE.

C Yes, because he had previous parental responsibility for CLAIRE.

D Yes, but only if the court agrees that VIVIERS should have parental responsibility for the child and he is applying for such.

Question 15.7

DANIELS and EVERSHAM used to share a house as friends, but not as cohabitants. Over a period of time, DANIELS became fixated with EVERSHAM. The behaviour caused EVERSHAM considerable distress and she eventually moved out. DANIELS then began following EVERSHAM home from work and she genuinely feared for her safety. EVERSHAM visited a solicitor with a view to obtaining a non-molestation order against DANIELS.

Would EVERSHAM be likely to succeed in obtaining such an order, under s. 42 of the Family Law Act 1996?

A No, DANIELS has not been made subject to a court order under this Act.

B Yes, an application may be made in these circumstances.

C No, DANIELS and EVERSHAM were not cohabitants, or spouses or related to each other.

D No, such an order may only be made to prevent the molestation of a child.

Question 15.8

HANSEN has been made subject to a non-molestation order under the Family Law Act 1996. The family court made the order *ex parte*, in HANSEN's absence, following evidence from the petitioner, BAIG. The terms of the order state that HANSEN must not contact BAIG in any way. HANSEN has breached the order by telephoning BAIG.

What action could be taken, in respect of HANSEN's breach of the non-molestation order?

A HANSEN could be arrested for a criminal offence, but a lack of knowledge of the order may provide a defence.

B HANSEN can be arrested for a criminal offence; lack of knowledge is no defence—this is an absolute offence.

C No action can be taken, as HANSEN was not in court when the order was made.

D BAIG must return to the family court and request that a power of arrest is attached to the order before HANSEN can be arrested.

Question 15.9

ASHTON has been sacked from his job at an aeronautical factory. He complains to his union, which takes four weeks to decide his case. The union eventually decides to authorise industrial action and to picket the aeronautical factory. In the intervening period, however, the firm has moved premises and no longer occupies the premises where ASHTON worked. A considerable amount of land at the new factory is private.

In relation to picketing, which of the following is true?

A The pickets cannot enter the private land to picket.

B The pickets could picket the new premises as they are still technically ASHTON's place of work.

C There would be a maximum of six pickets allowed at any one time.

D The right to picket outside the factory is an absolute right and cannot be overridden.

Question 15.10

CALLOWAY works in a factory for a large firm, which recently announced a 1% pay settlement for staff, with the unions. Many people working at the factory disagree with the offer and have decided to call a strike. CALLOWAY is not a union member and has made it clear that she will go to work on the proposed day of industrial action. DAWSON lives next door to CALLOWAY and works in the same factory. A week before the proposed action, he began to abuse her, calling her a 'scab', every time he saw her going in and out of her house. This behaviour carried on until the day of the strike.

Could DAWSON be guilty of an offence under s. 241(1) of the Trade Union and Labour Relations (Consolidation) Act 1992, in these circumstances?

A Yes, provided his actions were intended to compel CALLOWAY to abstain from doing an act which she had a legal right to do (i.e. to go to work on the day of the strike).

B No, DAWSON acted alone in this matter; his behaviour was more likely to amount to a public order or harassment offence.

C Yes, but there is no requirement to prove intent on DAWSON's behalf; his behaviour amounted to an offence under this Act regardless of his aim.

D Yes, provided his behaviour caused CALLOWAY to abstain from doing an act which she had a legal right to do (i.e. to go to work on the day of the strike).

ANSWERS

Answer 15.1

Answer **D** — Section 76 of the Serious Crime Act 2015 provides for an offence of 'controlling or coercive behaviour in an intimate or family relationship'.

Controlling or coercive behaviour is defined under this section as causing someone to fear that violence will be used against them on at least two occasions, or generating serious alarm *or* distress that has a substantial effect on their usual day-to-day activities.

Answers A, B and C are therefore incorrect.

General Police Duties, para. 4.15.2

Answer 15.2

Answer **C** — The shared ACPO, CPS and government definition of domestic violence and abuse, as contained in Home Office Circular 003/2013, is:

> Any incident or pattern of incidents of controlling, coercive or threatening behaviour, violence or abuse between those aged 16 or over who are or have been intimate partners or family members regardless of gender or sexuality.

The behaviour can encompass, but is not limited to, psychological, physical, sexual, financial or emotional abuse. Answers A and B are incorrect.

Controlling behaviour is: a range of acts designed to make a person subordinate and/or dependent by isolating them from sources of support, exploiting their resources and capacities for personal gain, depriving them of the means needed for independence, resistance and escape and regulating their everyday behaviour.

Coercive behaviour is: an act or a pattern of acts of assault, threats, humiliation and intimidation or other abuse that is used to harm, punish or frighten their victim.

The behaviour in the question could fall under the definition of 'controlling' or 'coercive' behaviour. However, in either case, the perception of the victim is irrelevant; indeed, many victims of domestic abuse do not see themselves as such because of the unfortunate situations they often find themselves in. Answer D is therefore incorrect.

General Police Duties, para. 4.15.2

Answer 15.3

Answer **C** — Section 24 of the Crime and Security Act 2010 creates a power for a Domestic Violence Protection Notice (DVPN) to secure the immediate protection of a victim of domestic violence from future violence or a threat of violence from a suspected perpetrator. The DVPN is intended to prohibit the perpetrator from molesting the victim of domestic abuse and, where they cohabit, may require the perpetrator to leave those premises.

The DVPN provides an interim solution to protect a vulnerable victim of domestic abuse, pending an application to the magistrates' court for a Domestic Violence Protection Order (DVPO). A DVPN must be issued by a police officer, of at least the rank of superintendent (s. 24(1)). Answers A and B are therefore incorrect.

By its nature, the DVPN is meant to provide a short-term respite, outside the criminal justice system, for the victim, while seeking a longer-term solution through the courts. It is not dependent on the perpetrator being charged with an offence; answer A is also incorrect for this reason.

Under s. 24(3), before issuing a DVPN, the authorising officer must, in particular, consider the opinion of the victim and, if necessary, any person who lives with the victim. However, he or she is not required to consult with a Multi-Agency Risk Assessment Conference (MARAC) beforehand. That said, Home Office guidance suggests that the success of the process will be reliant on the partnership work with other agencies and organisations including those that contribute to MARACs and service providers for Independent Domestic Violence Advocates (IDVAs). If there is time, partners may be consulted, but this is not compulsory and answer D is therefore incorrect.

General Police Duties, para. 4.15.2.1

Answer 15.4

Answer **D** — Section 24 of the Crime and Security Act 2010 creates a power for a Domestic Violence Protection Notice (DVPN) to be issued to secure the immediate protection of a victim of domestic violence from future violence or a threat of violence from a suspected perpetrator. The DVPN is intended to prohibit the perpetrator from molesting the victim of domestic abuse and, when they cohabit, may require the perpetrator to leave those premises. The purpose of a DVPN is to provide an interim solution to protect a vulnerable victim of domestic abuse, pending an application to the magistrates' court for a Domestic Violence Protection Order (DVPO).

Section 24(3)(b) *does* provide that the opinion of the victim should be sought, before a DVPN is issued. The authorising officer should also seek to establish whether the *suspect* wishes to make any representations (s. 24(3)(c)), or any other associated person who lives at the premises who may be affected by the DVPN (s. 24(3)(d)). However, s. 24(5) states that the *authorising officer may issue a DVPN in circumstances where the person for whose protection it is issued does not consent to the issuing of the DVPN*. Answers A and C are therefore incorrect.

Finally, before issuing a DVPN, the authorising officer must, in particular, consider the welfare of any person under the age of 18 whose interests the officer considers relevant to the issuing of the DVPN (whether or not that person is an associated person) (s. 24(3)(a)). However, this does not mean that a DVPN may *only* be issued without consent when the victim or some other member of the household is under 18. Answer B is therefore incorrect.

General Police Duties, para. 4.15.2.1

Answer 15.5

Answer **B** — The principal aim of the Domestic Violence Disclosure Scheme is to introduce recognised and consistent procedures for disclosing information which will enable a partner (A) of a previously violent individual (B) to make informed choices about whether and how A takes forward that relationship with B.

There are two distinct entry routes that may lead to a disclosure being made. The first entry route—'right to ask'—is modelled closely on the existing Child Sex Offender Disclosure Scheme, and is triggered when a person makes a direct application to the police for information about B.

The second entry route—'right to know'—is triggered when the police receive indirect information or intelligence about the safety of A and where, after appropriate checks are made, the police judge that a disclosure should be made to safeguard A (answer A is therefore incorrect). An intelligence log *could* trigger an investigation under the scheme (although more checks would be required) and therefore answer C is incorrect.

The decision-makers are definitely the police (although it is expected that statutory partners should be consulted unless the matter is urgent). Answer D is incorrect for that reason.

General Police Duties, para. 4.15.2.2

Answer 15.6

Answer **C** — Section 42 of the Family Law Act 1996 provides for 'non-molestation' orders. Under s. 42(1), a 'non-molestation order' means an order containing either or both of the following provisions:

(a) provision prohibiting a person ('the respondent') from molesting another person who is associated with the respondent;
(b) provision prohibiting the respondent from molesting a relevant child.

Section 62(3) of the Act describes 'associated' persons who may either be the petitioner or respondent for a non-molestation order. A non-molestation order may be applied for by anyone who is 'associated' with the respondent, including former cohabitants.

Under s. 62(4), a person will be 'associated' with a child if:

(a) he is a parent of the child; or
(b) he has or has had parental responsibility for the child.

Therefore, the fact that VIVIERS does not currently have parental responsibility for CLAIRE, or is not her natural or adopted parent, is irrelevant and he may apply for an order. Answers A and B are therefore incorrect.

There is no mention in s. 42 or s. 62 of the petitioner having to apply for a formal parental role in relation to children before an order can be made—this is about preventing an individual from molesting another and therefore answer D is incorrect.

General Police Duties, para. 4.15.2.4

Answer 15.7

Answer **B** — Under s. 42(1) of the Family Law Act 1996, a 'non-molestation order' means an order containing a provision prohibiting a person ('the respondent') from molesting another person who is associated with the respondent or from molesting a relevant child. Since the provisions do not only apply to children, answer D is incorrect.

Under s. 42(2)(a), the court may make a non-molestation order when an application has been made by a person who is associated with the respondent whether or not any other family proceedings have been instituted. Answer A is therefore incorrect.

Section 62 contains a long list of people who are 'associated' with the respondent, including relatives, children, spouses, cohabitants and civil partners (and people who formerly enjoyed such a status). Under s. 62(3)(c), they also include people who live, or have lived, in the same household, otherwise than merely by reason of one of them being the other's employee, tenant, lodger or boarder. Answer C is therefore incorrect.

General Police Duties, para. 4.15.2.4

Answer 15.8

Answer **A** — Section 42A of the Family Law Act 1996 states:

(1) A person who without reasonable excuse does anything that he is prohibited from doing by a non-molestation order is guilty of an offence.
(2) In the case of a non-molestation order made by virtue of s. 45(1), a person can be guilty of an offence under this section only in respect of conduct engaged in at a time when he was aware of the existence of the order.

Consequently, this provides a power of arrest for the breach of a non-molestation order under the provisions of s. 24(1) of the Police and Criminal Evidence Act 1984. Answer D is incorrect as there is no longer a requirement to attach a power of arrest to an order before a person can be arrested.

In relation to subs. (2), non-molestation orders made by virtue of s. 45(1) are *ex parte* orders where the respondent has not been present at the proceedings when the order was made. This section makes it clear that if the defendant was not in court *and* he/she was not aware of its existence, he/she cannot be found guilty of the offence—but this does not mean that the person cannot be arrested until the facts have been established. Answers B and C are therefore incorrect.

General Police Duties, para. 4.15.2.5

Answer 15.9

Answer **A** — Although picketing is lawful under s. 220 of the Trade Union and Labour Relations (Consolidation) Act 1992, there are some restrictions. It is lawful to picket your former place of work if the action is as a result of the termination of your employment. However, a person's place of work does not include new premises of an employer who has moved since dismissing the people picketing (*News Group Newspapers Ltd* v *SOGAT '82* (*No. 2*) [1987] ICR 181), and therefore answer B is incorrect. The 1992 Act does not place restrictions on the number of pickets; the number six is from the agreed Code of Practice on picketing, which has no legal force, and therefore answer C is incorrect.

Note, however, that if numbers are large enough, there might be a presumption that the pickets intend to intimidate others, which would make the action unlawful (*Broome* v *DPP* [1974] AC 587). If there is a real danger of any offence (e.g. public disorder) being committed, the pickets have no right to attend at the factory to picket under s. 220 (*Piddlington* v *Bates* [1960] 1 WLR 162), and therefore answer D is incorrect.

Section 220 does not authorise pickets to enter onto private land (*British Airports Authority* v *Ashton* [1983] 1 WLR 1079).

General Police Duties, para. 4.15.3.1

Answer 15.10

Answer **A** — Under s. 241(1) of the Trade Union and Labour Relations (Consolidation) Act 1992:

> A person commits an offence who, with a view to compelling another person to abstain from doing or to do any act which that person has a legal right to do or abstain from doing, wrongfully and without legal authority—
> (a) uses violence to or intimidates that person or his spouse or civil partner or children, or injures his property,
> (b) persistently follows that person about from place to place,
> (c) hides any tools, clothes or other property owned or used by that person, or deprives him of or hinders him in the use thereof,
> (d) watches or besets the house or other place where that person resides, works, carries on business or happens to be, or the approach to any such house or place, or
> (e) follows that person with two or more other persons in a disorderly manner in or through any street or road.

There are five different ways to commit this offence, by the defendant behaving in one of the ways just described. In these circumstances, DAWSON used intimidation with a view to compelling another person (CALLOWAY) to abstain from doing any act which she had a legal right to do (i.e. to go to work on the day of the strike). It is only when a person is accused of committing the offence under s. 241(1)(e) that there needs to be more than one person involved and answer B is incorrect.

'With a view to compelling' means with *intent* to compel and since this is an offence of specific intent, it must be shown that the defendant acted with a view to bringing about the consequences previously described. Answer C is therefore incorrect.

On the other hand, because this is a crime of specific intent, it is irrelevant whether or not the defendant's behaviour actually brought about the desired consequences and answer D is incorrect.

General Police Duties, para. 4.15.3.3

16 Protection of People Suffering from Mental Disorders

STUDY PREPARATION

The Mental Health Act 1983 provides for the care and treatment of people suffering from mental disorders and supplies powers for enforcing some of its provisions.

If those powers are executed in good faith, the 1983 Act also provides some protection against criminal and civil liability for the police officers and care workers who use them (s. 139).

The 1983 Act is supported by a Code of Practice that sets out guidance for the police and other agencies when dealing with people suffering from mental disorders.

QUESTIONS

Question 16.1

Constable MERALES was called to an incident in the High Street; on arrival, the officer came across ALLINGTON, who was sat in a public fountain. The officer made enquiries with people in a crowd that had gathered and was considering dealing with ALLINGTON under s. 136 of the Mental Health Act 1983.

Considering powers under s. 136 of the Act, which of the following statements is correct?

A Constable MERALES may arrest ALLINGTON under s. 136, for her own safety.

B Constable MERALES may remove ALLINGTON under s. 136, for her own interests or for the protection of other persons.

C Constable MERALES may remove ALLINGTON under s. 136, if she represents a danger to herself.

D Constable MERALES may remove ALLINGTON under s. 136, if she represents a danger to herself or other members of the public.

Question 16.2

HENDERSON was taken to a dedicated police station by Constable ANACHO. The officer had removed him using powers under s. 136 of the Mental Health Act 1983, from a busy shopping centre, because of concerns over his mental wellbeing. The officer had taken HENDERSON there to have him assessed under the Act.

Considering s. 136 of the Mental Health Act 1983, how long could HENDERSON be detained at a place of safety?

A A period not exceeding 24 hours.

B A period not exceeding 36 hours.

C A period not exceeding 48 hours.

D A period not exceeding 72 hours.

Question 16.3

Magistrates have issued a warrant under s. 135(1) of the Mental Health Act 1983 in relation to SHORT, whose family has been concerned that his mental health has deteriorated significantly recently. The warrant authorises SHORT to be removed to a place of safety.

Which of the following statements is correct, in relation to the execution of the warrant issued by the court?

A The warrant must be executed by a constable, who must be accompanied either by a mental health professional or a registered medical practitioner.

B The warrant must be executed either by a mental health professional or a registered medical practitioner, who may ask for a constable to be present if there is reason to believe SHORT may become violent.

C The warrant may be executed either by a constable or a mental health professional, who must be accompanied by a registered medical practitioner.

D The warrant must be executed by a constable, who must be accompanied by a mental health professional and a registered medical practitioner.

Question 16.4

Constable TOWNSEND has attended single-crewed to assist LIANG, a mental health professional, and BAIG, a registered medical practitioner. The officer has been asked to assist in executing a warrant under s. 135(1) of the Mental Health Act 1983 in relation to PHELPS, whose mental health has caused some concern recently. They were granted access to PHELPS's home by a family member and Constable TOWNSEND assisted in taking him outside to a waiting vehicle; however, without any warning, PHELPS escaped before being placed securely inside. Constable TOWNSEND gave chase but lost sight of PHELPS in a busy shopping centre. Some four hours later, PHELPS was seen on CCTV walking along the High Street and officers are making their way to the scene.

Which of the following statements is correct, in relation to re-taking PHELPS under s. 138 of the Mental Health Act 1983?

A Because the warrant has been executed, the police will only have the power to remove PHELPS to a place of safety under the power of a new warrant.

B The police will have the power to remove PHELPS to a place of safety in these circumstances without a warrant.

C The police will have the power to remove PHELPS to a place of safety in these circumstances under the power of the existing warrant, which has not yet been executed.

D Because PHELPS was detained under a warrant, officers will have to apply the principles of s. 136(1) if they are to remove PHELPS to a place of safety.

Question 16.5

PCSO DALTON was on patrol when she was approached by HOUGHTON who came out of a nearby house. HOUGHTON asked her for assistance—she had been visiting her brother who lived in the house and stated that he suffered from severe alcohol problems. Her brother had fallen over in the house and cut his head; he was conscious but bleeding heavily. HOUGHTON had called 999, but had been told that there would be a delay in an ambulance attending; she wanted to take him to hospital herself but he was refusing. PCSO DALTON walked to the front door with HOUGHTON and could see her brother in the hallway. When he saw her, HOUGHTON's brother started shouting, 'Get her away from my house, I'm not going anywhere.' He was covered in blood and the head wound appeared to be serious. PCSO DALTON wanted to enter the house and help HOUGHTON take her brother to the hospital, because she believed it was in his best interests.

Considering powers under the Mental Capacity Act 2005, which of the following statements is correct?

A PCSO DALTON could enter the house in order to help remove HOUGHTON's brother to the hospital.

B PCSO DALTON could not enter the house in order to remove HOUGHTON's brother unless she was accompanied by a police officer.

C PCSO DALTON does not have the authority to enter the house for the purposes of this Act; only a police officer would be able to do so in these circumstances.

D Neither PCSO DALTON nor any police officer could deal with HOUGHTON's brother under this Act because he is not in a public place; the officer attending must use powers under s. 17(1) of PACE (entry to save life or limb).

ANSWERS

Answer 16.1

Answer **B** — Section 136 of the Mental Health Act 1983 creates a power for police officers to remove such a person under certain conditions; if a constable finds in a place to which the public have access a person who appears to him/her to be suffering from mental disorder and to be in immediate need of care or control, the constable may, if he/she thinks it necessary to do so in the *interests of that person or for the protection of other persons*, remove that person to a place of safety.

Section 136 does not mention danger—this power is more to do with caring for individuals and removing them to a place where they can receive appropriate treatment. Answers C and D are therefore incorrect.

Further, there is no power of arrest under s. 136—the person is not being dealt with for an offence, rather, they are being removed to the most appropriate location to deal with their illness. Answer A is therefore incorrect.

General Police Duties, para. 4.16.2

Answer 16.2

Answer **D** — Where a person has been removed to a place of safety by a constable, under s. 136 of the Mental Health Act 1983, he or she may be detained there for a period not exceeding *72 hours* for the purpose of enabling him/her to be examined by a registered medical practitioner and to be interviewed by an approved mental health professional and of making any necessary arrangements for his/her treatment or care.

Answers A, B and C are therefore incorrect.

General Police Duties, para. 4.16.2

Answer 16.3

Answer **D** — Under s. 135(1) of the Mental Health Act 1983, where there is reasonable cause to suspect that a person believed to be suffering from a mental disorder:

(a) has been, or is being ill-treated or neglected, or
(b) is unable to care for himself/herself and is living alone,

a warrant may be issued by a magistrate authorising a *constable* to enter any premises specified and to remove the person to a place of safety.

Answers B and C are therefore incorrect.

In doing so, the officer *must* be accompanied by an approved mental health professional and a registered medical practitioner. Answer A is therefore incorrect.

General Police Duties, para. 4.16.3

Answer 16.4

Answer **B** — Section 138 of the Mental Health Act 1983 provides a power to re-take people who have been in legal custody under the 1983 Act, who subsequently escape while being taken to or detained in a place of safety. This power applies whether or not the person was removed to a place of safety under s. 136 or whether they were removed under a warrant (under s. 135). Also, this will be a simple matter of detaining the person because he/she has escaped—there is no requirement to consider whether the principles of s. 136(1) apply in the circumstances. Answer D is therefore incorrect.

There is no requirement for the police to utilise powers under the existing warrant, or apply for a new warrant, and therefore answers A and C are incorrect.

Note, there is also a power for a court to issue a warrant for the arrest of a convicted mental patient who is unlawfully at large (Criminal Justice Act 1967, s. 72(3)), but this is not applicable in these circumstances.

General Police Duties, para. 4.16.4

Answer 16.5

Answer **A** — Section 5 of the Mental Capacity Act 2005 states:

(1) If a person (D) does an act in connection with the care or treatment of another person (P), the act is one to which this section applies if—
  (a) before doing the act, D takes reasonable steps to establish whether P lacks capacity in relation to the matter in question, and
  (b) when doing the act, D reasonably believes—
    (i) that P lacks clarity in relation to the matter and
    (ii) that it will be in P's best interests for the act to be done.

(2) D does not incur any liability in relation to the act that he would not have incurred if P—
  (a) had had capacity to consent in relation to the matter, and
  (b) had consented to D's doing the act.

The Act was brought into force to provide a statutory framework to empower and protect vulnerable people who are not able to make their own decisions. Importantly, it can provide police officers with a power to act in a person's best interests, effectively as if they had the person's consent. However, the power is not just given to police officers but to *anyone* acting in the person's best interests. This would include PCSO DALTON or any other person (although you would anticipate the PSCO calling a police officer to the scene to assist). Answers B, C and D are incorrect for this reason.

There is no mention in s. 5 as to *where* the power may be exercised; therefore, it has to be assumed that it may be utilised anywhere. Similarly, the section does not mention whether or not the person assisting has a power to enter premises—therefore, provided the person is doing an act *in connection with the care or treatment of another person*, their actions will be lawful under s. 5. Answers B, C and D are also incorrect for this reason.

General Police Duties, para. 4.16.6.4

17 Offences Relating to Land and Premises

STUDY PREPARATION

The Criminal Justice and Public Order Act 1994 created several offences which have the effect of allowing the criminal courts to deal with offences of trespass. This chapter deals with offences such as trespassing with intent to disrupt lawful activities, trespassing with intent to reside on land, raves and residing in vehicles on land, all of which are very topical. Each offence has several elements to it, but there are common themes throughout, such as authorising officers, offences of failing to leave land when directed to do so and returning within three months of a direction being given.

The Criminal Law Act 1977 makes up the bulk of the second part of the chapter. Offences under s. 6 and s. 7 of the Act are rarely used, but remain useful pieces of legislation, especially that of using violence for securing entry to premises.

Lastly, do not ignore the offences of being found on enclosed premises and causing a nuisance on educational premises; both are useful offences to remember.

QUESTIONS

Question 17.1

A new football stadium is being built on the outskirts of a town. Vehicles belonging to the building company have been parked in an enclosed warehouse situated adjacent to the building site, which is due to be demolished after the stadium is completed. Environmental protestors have been attempting to stop the building work.

The builders arrived for work one morning and as they opened the doors to the warehouse, a number of protestors stormed in and chained themselves to the vehicles. Building work was disrupted for several hours as the police were called to remove them. It was a peaceful protest; no property was damaged and no one was threatened.

Have the protesters committed an offence under s. 68 of the Criminal Justice and Public Order Act 1994 (aggravated trespass), in these circumstances?

A No, as the protestors were not on land in the open air.

B Yes, the offence is complete in these circumstances.

C No, as the protestors were not on land where the building work was due to take place.

D No, as the protestors did not threaten or intimidate the builders, or cause damage.

Question 17.2

OSMAND and NERO entered a building site as trespassers; they were protesting against the construction of a new shopping centre. They had with them a large concrete tube, which they placed on the ground in the middle of the site. OSMAND and NERO then connected their arms through the tube with a padlocked chain. Inspector CORP was the senior officer to arrive and concluded that they had committed an offence contrary to s. 68 of the Criminal Justice and Public Order Act 1994 (aggravated trespass) and directed them to leave. OSMAND and NERO stated that they were unable to leave because they had no key to the padlock. Eventually a locksmith was called to the scene and when they were released, OSMAND and NERO were arrested for failing to leave when directed, under s. 69 of the Act. They were charged with the offence under s. 69 and later in court, claimed they had a reasonable excuse for failing to leave as soon as practicable—that they were unable to do so until they were released.

Could OSMAND and NERO's defence succeed in these circumstances?

A No, they did not leave the site as soon as practicable.

B Yes, they left the site as soon as practicable after they were released.

C No, their intention was to frustrate the police utilising their powers under this Act and they succeeded.

D No, their intention when they chained themselves to the tube is irrelevant; they succeeded in disrupting lawful activities on the site.

Question 17.3

PARSONS, a farmer, agreed to allow a family of travellers to stay on his land for a week. Between them, the travellers had two caravans and two cars. After two weeks, they were still on the land and PARSONS asked them to leave. When they refused, he contacted the police.

Would the officers have the power, under s. 61 of the Criminal Justice and Public Order Act 1994, to direct the family to leave the land?

A No, because the family did not have more than 12 vehicles between them.

B Yes, they could direct the family to leave the land, with their vehicles.

C No, because the family were originally given permission to stay by the landowner.

D No, because the family have not caused damage or used threatening/insulting behaviour.

Question 17.4

Following numerous complaints from residents, Sergeant BISLAND attended a gathering of people in the early hours of the morning with several constables. On their arrival, the officers saw that approximately 100 people were dancing to loud music. The people had entered land which belonged to the local authority that was adjacent to a beach. Sergeant BISLAND believed the people were trespassing on the land and that the gathering amounted to a rave. The sergeant has contacted Inspector MORGAN for advice as to how to remove the people from the area, and how this decision should be communicated to those present.

Which of the following statements is correct, in relation to the decisions that may be made, under s. 63 of the Criminal Justice and Public Order Act 1994?

A Inspector MORGAN may declare that the gathering is a rave, but any of the officers may communicate this decision to those present.

B Only a superintendent may declare that the gathering is a rave and any of the officers may communicate this decision to those present.

C As the senior officer at the scene, Sergeant BISLAND may declare the gathering is a rave; any of the officers may communicate this decision to those present.

D Only a superintendent may declare the gathering is a rave and only Sergeant BISLAND may communicate this decision to those present, as the senior officer at the scene.

Question 17.5

On a Saturday morning, the police received complaints from residents about a group of people gathered on a beach. The group had arrived the previous evening and were partying all night. The police attended and saw 20 people listening to loud, amplified music. The group stated they intended staying until the Monday as it was a bank holiday weekend and that the music would carry on that night and on the Sunday.

Would a senior officer have sufficient evidence at this stage to reasonably believe that a 'gathering' is taking place, as defined in s. 63(1) of the Criminal Justice and Public Order Act 1994?

A Yes, there were at least ten people gathering at the site of a rave.

B No, the people gathering were not trespassing on land.

C Yes, there is sufficient evidence at this time to define this as a 'gathering'.

D No, s. 63(1) does not apply in the daylight hours, the senior officer would have to wait until night-time to make this decision.

Question 17.6

Constable BERNARD was working a Friday late shift. The officer knew that the previous weekend, on the Sunday, officers had disrupted a rave involving a group of people who had been trespassing in a field. A direction had been given for people to leave the land, under s. 63 of the Criminal Justice and Public Order Act 1994. Constable BERNARD had been given instructions to patrol the area and had details of the people and vehicles involved the previous weekend. Whilst on patrol, the officer visited the field and saw a van being unloaded by two people who appeared to be setting up sound equipment. One of the people, SWAINE, was the owner of the van and was on the officer's list.

Given that SWAINE was aware of the direction to leave the land the previous weekend, has an offence been committed under s. 63, in these circumstances?

A Yes, it is within seven days of the direction being given.

B No, 24 hours have elapsed since the direction was given.

C No, seven days have not elapsed since the direction was given.

D Yes, it is within three months of the direction being given.

Question 17.7

MASON was a private landlord and was renting a flat out to BIEL, who had failed to pay rent for the past three months. MASON had been unable to contact BIEL, but knew that the tenant was still using the flat as a resident. One day, MASON arranged for a friend, DAVIDSON, to attend the flat and change the locks, to prevent BIEL from entering.

Which of the following statements is correct, in relation to MASON's liability for an offence under s. 1 of the Protection from Eviction Act 1977?

A MASON would be guilty of unlawfully depriving BIEL from residency of the property in these circumstances.

B MASON would not be guilty of depriving BIEL from residency of the property; this offence is committed by persistent withdrawal of services to force a person to leave.

C MASON would not be guilty of depriving BIEL from residency of the property; this is a civil matter between the two parties.

D MASON could be guilty of unlawfully depriving BIEL from residency of the property, but may have a defence because of BIEL's failure to pay the rent.

Question 17.8

SCOTT and his partner jointly owned their house, but they had been through difficult times recently. As a result, SCOTT was spending a lot of time drinking in the local pub. One evening, he returned home after several hours drinking, and found that his partner had changed the locks to the front door and left several bin liners outside the house containing his belongings. The police were called to the address by neighbours because SCOTT was causing a disturbance. When the police arrived, SCOTT was in the garden, shouting, 'If you don't let me in, I'm going to kick the fucking door in'.

Considering the offence under s. 6 of the Criminal Law Act 1977 (violence for securing entry), which of the following statements is correct?

A The offence is not complete because SCOTT has not actually used violence to gain entry to the premises.

B The offence is complete because SCOTT has threatened to use violence to gain entry to the premises.

C Because SCOTT has a proprietary interest in the property, he cannot commit this offence.

D SCOTT is not a displaced residential occupier, therefore, this offence is not designed for such behaviour and he cannot commit this offence.

Question 17.9

SCOTT lived next door to a house which had been vacant for three years, while the elderly occupant was in a residential home. SCOTT and his wife had gone through a break-up during this time and she asked him to leave. He left his home and broke into the house next door, taking up residence so that he could be near his children. SCOTT had been living in the house for six months when a distant relative of the elderly owner, STEED, turned up stating that her relative had died and she had been left the property in the will. STEED asked SCOTT to leave the premises because she intended taking up residence. SCOTT told her he would leave if she could prove this; otherwise he would not be going anywhere. STEED reported the matter to the police stating that SCOTT was trespassing on the premises and refusing to leave.

What defence would be available to SCOTT, for an offence under s. 7 of the Criminal Law Act 1977 (person failing to leave premises)?

A That he had asked STEED to produce written evidence of her right to tenancy of occupancy of the premises and she had failed to do so.

B That he had asked STEED to produce written evidence of her right to tenancy of occupancy of the premises and she had refused to do so.

C SCOTT would have no defence because STEED owned the house and had stated her desire to live there.

D That STEED was required to produce written evidence of her right to tenancy of occupancy of the premises when she had asked him to leave and she did not do so.

Question 17.10

LEHMAN is living in rental property and has been in a long-standing dispute with the owner, CAHIL, over a failure to conduct adequate repairs to the property. LEHMAN's Tenancy Agreement has ended; however, she is refusing to leave because CAHIL has refused to return a bond of £250. CAHIL, on the other hand, is refusing to hand over the bond until LEHMAN allows access to the property for inspection. CAHIL has discovered that LEHMAN's friend MENCE has also moved into the property—MENCE has never been on the Tenancy Agreement. CAHIL has persuaded a court to issue an Eviction Notice in respect of LEHMAN and MENCE and the Notice outlines that if they fail to leave, they will be regarded as trespassers.

Who, if either, of LEHMAN and MENCE would be guilty of an offence under s. 144 of the Legal Aid, Sentencing and Punishment of Offenders Act 2012 (squatting in a residential building), in these circumstances?

A Neither, as long as MENCE is there with LEHMAN's permission.

B Only MENCE; LEHMAN does not commit this offence, provided she does not leave the premises and re-enter.

C Both persons commit the offence as they are now trespassing.

D Only MENCE; LEHMAN does not commit this offence, whether or not she leaves the property and re-enters.

Question 17.11

The police attended an alarm at an office building in a city centre. They made a search of the premises and found PECK, who was hiding in one of the offices. The officers recognised PECK as a homeless person with whom police regularly had dealings. Following questioning, the officers decided that there was insufficient evidence to arrest PECK for burglary. PECK was then arrested for being found on enclosed premises.

Would the premises that PECK was found on amount to an 'enclosed premises', for the purposes of offences under s. 4 of the Vagrancy Act 1824?

A No, 'enclosed premises' will only include outhouses and land ancillary to buildings.

B No, if the person is found in a building, that building must be a dwelling for the purposes of this offence.

C Yes, provided the person is found in a building, or outhouse or land ancillary to a building; it doesn't matter what type of building.

D No, a room within an office building will not amount to an enclosed area for the purposes of this offence.

Question 17.12

Constable PEARCE has been liaising with BENT, a Local Authority Housing Officer, about anti-social behaviour at a house maintained by them, which is being rented out to ALLSOPP. Complaints are received regularly from nearby residents about people committing anti-social behaviour while visiting ALLSOPP's house. Numerous supportive interventions have been attempted to persuade ALLSOPP to take responsibility, including a Community Protection Notice, but these have all failed. The partners are now considering a repossession order under the Housing Act 1985.

Which of the following statements is correct in relation to the granting of such an order, in these circumstances?

A An order may only be granted if it can be shown that ALLSOPP was involved in the anti-social behaviour committed by the other people.

B An order may only be granted if it can be shown that ALLSOPP had been convicted of committing a criminal offence on the premises.

C An order may be granted if it can be shown that the people visiting ALLSOPP were guilty of causing nuisance or annoyance to people living in the locality.

D An order may only be granted if it can be proved that ALLSOPP had failed to control the nuisance or annoyance being caused to people living in the locality.

Question 17.13

Constable PARRY was called to a high school at 4 pm on a Saturday by the caretaker, POINTER. It would appear that teenagers, who attended the school, were entering the playing fields on weekends and using them as a meeting area. POINTER stated that the teenagers were generally well-behaved, but their presence meant that he had to work extra hours on weekends, to make sure they did not cause a disturbance.

Considering s. 547(1) of the Education Act 1996, have the children committed an offence in this situation?

A No, there is no evidence that the children are causing a disturbance.

B No, the children are gathering when the school is closed, therefore they are not causing a nuisance to anyone.

C Yes, they could be causing a nuisance or disturbance to the annoyance of POINTER, who lawfully uses the premises.

D No, even though they may be causing a nuisance or disturbance to the annoyance of POINTER, they are not interrupting lessons at the school.

ANSWERS

Answer 17.1

Answer **B** — Under s. 68(1) of the Criminal Justice and Public Order Act 1994, a person commits the offence of aggravated trespass if he/she trespasses on land and, in relation to any lawful activity which persons are engaging in or are about to engage in on that or adjoining land, does there anything which is intended by him/her to have the effect:

(a) of intimidating those persons or any of them so as to deter them or any of them from engaging in that activity,
(b) of obstructing that activity, or
(c) of disrupting that activity.

Therefore, even though the protestors did not threaten or intimidate the builders, or cause damage, their actions were sufficient to obstruct and disrupt the activity. Answer D is therefore incorrect.

The offence is committed when a person trespasses on land where the activity is due to take place or on *adjoining* land (which makes answer C incorrect).

Section 68 originally included the phrase 'in the open air' but it was removed by the Anti-social Behaviour Act 2003. In *DPP* v *Chivers* [2010] EWHC 1814 (Admin), it was held that the purpose and effect of this amendment was quite plainly to include buildings. This situation remains the same and answer A is incorrect.

Note that in order to establish the offence of aggravated trespass under s. 68, you must prove that the defendant had committed the act(s) complained of in the physical presence of a person engaged or about to engage in the lawful activity with which the defendant wished to interfere (*DPP* v *Tilly* [2001] EWHC 821 (Admin)).

General Police Duties, para. 4.17.2

Answer 17.2

Answer **B** — Section 68(1) of the Criminal Justice and Public Order Act 1994 states that a person commits the offence of aggravated trespass if he trespasses on land and, in relation to any lawful activity which persons are engaging in or are about to engage in on that or adjoining land, does there anything which is intended by him/her to have the effect:

(a) of intimidating those persons or any of them so as to deter them or any of them from engaging in that activity,
(b) of obstructing that activity, or
(c) of disrupting that activity.

The intent of the defendant *is* relevant—if they have not committed the offence of aggravated trespass, then the order under s. 69 directing them to leave is invalid; answer D is therefore incorrect.

It is a defence for the accused to show that they were not trespassing on the land, or had a reasonable excuse for failing to leave the land as soon as practicable or for again entering the land as a trespasser (s. 69(4)).

In circumstances similar to this question, the court quashed the appellants' convictions for failing to leave a shop premises as soon as practicable when so directed by the police, because they were physically unable to move until they had been unchained, and had left as soon as this was done. Answer A is therefore incorrect.

The court also held that what they did was designed to disrupt the shop's trade, not to frustrate the operation of s. 69; the fact that they had voluntarily (and deliberately) placed themselves in a situation in which they could not leave when directed was held to be irrelevant (see *Nero* v *DPP* [2012] EWHC 1238 (Admin) and *Richardson* v *Director of Public Prosecutions* [2014] UKSC 8). Answer C is therefore incorrect.

General Police Duties, paras 4.17.2, 4.17.2.1, 4.17.2.2

Answer 17.3

Answer **C** — To prove the offence under s. 61 of the Criminal Justice and Public Order Act 1994, you need to show that at least two people are trespassing on land with a common purpose of residing there and reasonable steps have been taken to ask them to leave.

If these conditions are apparent, you must then show that:

- they have damaged land; *or*
- they have used threatening etc. behaviour; *or*
- they have between them *six* or more vehicles.

As none of these applies, answers B and D are incorrect. Under s. 61(2), if the people had been given permission to stay on the land but had subsequently become trespassers, the officers would have to satisfy themselves that one of the conditions in s. 61(1) had occurred after they had become trespassers.

The original 1994 Act specified 12 vehicles, but this has been amended to six and therefore answer A is incorrect.

(It should be noted that the Home Office has issued guidance to the police on the use of the powers under s. 61. It advises that the police must be able to demonstrate that all eviction and enforcement decisions are 'proportionate' in weighing individual harm against the wider public interest.)

General Police Duties, para. 4.17.3

Answer 17.4

Answer **B** — The elements of a 'gathering' for a rave are found in s. 63(1) of the Criminal Justice and Public Order Act 1994. The senior officer (a superintendent) would have to be satisfied that these elements are present before giving a direction for people to leave under this section. Those elements are that:

- the gathering is on land in the open air;
- the gathering is likely to be attended by 20 or more persons (whether or not they are trespassers);
- amplified music is played during the night (with or without intermissions), which by reason of its loudness and duration and the time at which it is played, is likely to cause serious distress to the inhabitants of the locality.

Under s. 63(2) of the Act, when these elements are present, a direction may be given for the people gathered there to leave the land and take any vehicles or property with them. Such a direction may only be made by an officer of at least the rank of *superintendent*. Answers A and C are therefore incorrect.

Section 63(3) states that if the direction under s. 63(2) is not communicated to the people at the scene by the officer making the direction, it may be communicated to them by *any constable at the scene*. Answer D is therefore incorrect.

General Police Duties, paras 4.17.5, 4.17.5.1

Answer 17.5

Answer **C** — The elements of a 'gathering' for a rave are found in s. 63(1) of the Criminal Justice and Public Order Act 1994. The senior officer (a superintendent) would have to be satisfied that these elements are present before giving a direction for people to leave under this section. Those elements are that:

- the gathering is on land in the open air;
- the gathering is likely to be attended by 20 or more persons (whether or not they are trespassers);

- amplified music is played during the night (with or without intermissions), which by reason of its loudness and duration and the time at which it is played, is likely to cause serious distress to the inhabitants of the locality.

Taking matters in order, the superintendent must first believe that a gathering of 20 people is likely to take place—not ten. This is the figure described in s. 63(2)(b), which is the preventative element of this section, where officers can tell people to leave to prevent the rave from taking place. Answer A is therefore incorrect.

It is irrelevant whether the gathering is trespassing and answer B is incorrect. (Note that s. 63(1A) of the Act deals specifically with gatherings where people are trespassing.)

Generally, the amplified music must be played during the night; however, there will be occasions where raves take place over several days. This is provided for in s. 63(1)(a), which states that this section applies when:

> such a gathering continues during intermissions in the music and, where the gathering extends over several days, throughout the period during which amplified music is played at night (with or without intermissions).

Therefore, as the officers attending the scene (and their superintendent) had reason to believe that a rave would take place the same evening, they would not have to wait until the evening before taking action. Answer D is therefore incorrect.

General Police Duties, para. 4.17.5.1

Answer 17.6

Answer **A** — A superintendent may give a direction under s. 63(2) of the Criminal Justice and Public Order Act 1994 for people to leave land when he/she reasonably believes that they are making preparations or gathering for a rave. Under s. 63(6) of the Act, if a person knowing that a direction under s. 63(2) has been given which applies to him/her:

> (a) fails to leave the land as soon as reasonably practicable, or
> (b) having left again enters the land within the period of 7 days beginning with the day on which the direction was given,
>
> he/she commits an offence...

Therefore, the offence is committed when a person re-enters the land *within* seven days (not three months) as opposed to after seven days have elapsed. Answers C and D are incorrect.

A further offence is committed under s. 63(7A), when a person knows that a direction under s. 63(2) has been given which applies to him/her, and he/she makes preparations for or attends a gathering to which this section applies within the period of 24 hours. This section was created to prevent people from closing down a rave when a direction has been given and moving immediately to a different location to set up another one. Whilst it is obviously connected to the offence in s. 63(6), it is meant for an entirely different purpose and answer B is incorrect.

General Police Duties, para. 4.17.5.2

Answer 17.7

Answer **A** — Under s. 1(3) of the Protection from Eviction Act 1977:

> If any person with intent to cause the residential occupier of any premises—
> (a) to give up the occupation of the premises or any part thereof; or
> (b) to refrain from exercising any right or pursuing any remedy in respect of the premises or part thereof;
>
> does acts likely to interfere with the peace or comfort of the residential occupier or members of his household, or persistently withdraws or withholds services reasonably required for the occupation of the premises as a residence, he shall be guilty of an offence.

Since the offence may be committed either by 'interference with the peace or comfort' of the resident, *or* by withholding services, answer B is incorrect.

Landlords changing the locks of an entrance door while the residential occupier is out *would* amount to an offence under s. 1(3) (*Costelloe* v *Camden London Borough Council* [1986] Crim LR 249)—it is not a civil matter between parties and therefore answer C is incorrect.

To have a defence under this section, a person would either have to show that they had reasonable cause to believe that the residential occupier had ceased to reside in the premises (which is not the case here) or that he/she had reasonable grounds for doing the acts or withdrawing or withholding the services in question. This offence is designed to prevent acts such as this and ensure landlords act responsibly by using legal remedies to resolve disputes—the actions are not reasonable and they amount to an offence; therefore, answer D is incorrect.

General Police Duties, para. 4.17.7.1

Answer 17.8

Answer **B** — Under s. 6(1) of the Criminal Law Act 1977, any person who, without lawful authority, uses or threatens violence for the purpose of securing entry into any premises for himself or for any other person is guilty of an offence, provided that:

(a) there is someone present on those premises at the time who is opposed to the entry which the violence is intended to secure; and
(b) the person using or threatening the violence knows that that is the case.

The offence may be committed by a person who *threatens* violence to secure entry to premises and it is not necessary to show that violence was actually used. Answer A is therefore incorrect.

This offence is not restricted to occasions involving 'residential occupiers' and the fact that a person has any right or interest in premises will not constitute 'lawful authority' to use violence to secure entry into those premises (s. 6(2)). Additionally, it is immaterial whether the violence used/threatened is against a person or property, or whether the purpose of the entry is to gain *possession* of the premises or any other purpose (s. 6(4)).

Simply using or threatening to use violence to gain entry would amount to an offence under s. 6 and answers C and D are incorrect.

General Police Duties, para. 4.17.7.2

Answer 17.9

Answer **A** — Section 7(1) of the Criminal Law Act 1977 states that subject to the following provisions of this section and to s. 12A(9) (which provide defences to this offence), any person who is on any premises as a trespasser after having entered as such is guilty of an offence if he/she fails to leave those premises on being required to do so by or on behalf of:

(a) a displaced residential occupier of the premises; or
(b) an individual who is a protected intending occupier of the premises.

There is no doubt that in these circumstances SCOTT was trespassing on the premises and should not have been living there. It is possible that STEED was, in fact, a protected intending occupier and, if she was, SCOTT would commit the offence under s. 7(1) because he failed to leave when requested by such a person.

However, if the defendant can show that he/she asked the protected intending occupier to produce written evidence of his/her right to tenancy of occupancy of the premises and that person *failed* to do so, he/she may have a defence (s. 12A(9)). Answer B is incorrect because a simple failure (not a refusal) could provide a defence.

The onus is not on the protected intending occupier to produce the relevant document to back up his/her request for the person to leave; the defence is triggered when the defendant asks for such proof and the other party fails to produce it. Answer D is incorrect.

Finally, a defence may be claimed by a person if they can prove that either he/she believed that the person requiring him/her to leave the premises was not a protected intending occupier, or that he/she had asked the person to produce the relevant documentation and that person had failed to do so. Since there is a defence available to SCOTT, answer C is incorrect.

General Police Duties, para. 4.17.7.4

Answer 17.10

Answer **D** — Section 144(1) of the Legal Aid, Sentencing and Punishment of Offenders Act 2012 states:

(1) A person commits an offence if—
  (a) the person is in a residential building as a trespasser having entered it as a trespasser,
  (b) the person knows or ought to know that he/she is a trespasser, and
  (c) the person is living in the building or intends to live there for any period.

However, the offence is not committed by a person holding over after the end of a lease or licence *even if the person leaves and re-enters the building* (s. 144(2)) and therefore answers B and C are incorrect.

For the purposes of this section the fact that a person derives title from a trespasser, or has the permission of a trespasser, does not prevent the person from being a trespasser (s. 144(4)). In other words, even though MENCE is on the premises with LEHMAN's permission, she is a trespasser and could commit this offence. Answer A is therefore incorrect.

General Police Duties, para. 4.17.7.5

Answer 17.11

Answer **D** — It is a summary offence under s. 4(1) of the Vagrancy Act 1824 for any person to be found in or upon any dwelling house, warehouse, coach house, stable or outhouse or in any enclosed yard, garden or area for *any unlawful purpose*. This ancient offence was created to prevent vagrancy and the original definition gives a clue as to the type of premises that might be considered enclosed:

(i) every person wandering abroad and lodging in any barn or outhouse, or in any deserted or unoccupied building, or in the open air, or under a tent, or in any cart or waggon, and not giving a good account of himself or herself;
(ii) every person being found in or upon any dwelling house, warehouse, coach-house, stable, or outhouse, or in any enclosed yard, garden, or area, for any unlawful purpose;

commits an offence.

Answers A and B are incorrect as the Act covers many buildings that are not merely dwellings or outhouses and land ancillary to buildings.

However, a room within an office building has been held *not* to amount to an enclosed area for the purposes of this offence (*Talbot* v *Oxford City Justices* [2000] 1 WLR 1102). Answer C is therefore incorrect.

General Police Duties, para. 4.17.7.6

Answer 17.12

Answer **C** — Under housing legislation, landlords may apply to the county court to evict tenants who are behaving anti-socially using the relevant 'ground for possession'. These are ground 2 of sch. 2 to the Housing Act 1985 for secure tenants (mostly tenants of local authorities) and ground 14 of sch. 2 to the Housing Act 1988 for assured tenants (tenants of housing associations and landlords in the private rented sector), respectively. These grounds are discretionary; that is, the court must be satisfied that anti-social behaviour has occurred and that it would be reasonable to grant possession.

Section 94 of the Anti-social Behaviour, Crime and Policing Act 2014 inserted a s. 84A and sch. 2A into the 1985 Act providing landlords with an 'absolute ground for possession for anti-social behaviour'. The relevant grounds on which a court may order repossession under these provisions are that the tenant or a person residing in or visiting the dwelling-house:

(a) has been guilty of conduct causing or likely to cause a nuisance or annoyance to a person residing, visiting or otherwise engaging in a lawful activity in the locality; or
(b) has been convicted either of using the dwelling-house or allowing it to be used for immoral or illegal purposes, or of an indictable offence committed in, or in the locality of, the dwelling-house.

Therefore, there is no requirement to demonstrate that the tenant was engaged in the anti-social behaviour (it is sufficient that people visiting the dwelling are). Neither is there a requirement to prove that the tenant had failed to control people visiting him/her (although the failure of the supportive interventions would be good evidence in attempting to secure the order). In these circumstances, it would be sufficient to show the court that the tenant or a person residing in or visiting the dwelling-house had been guilty of 'conduct causing or likely to cause a nuisance or annoyance to a person residing, visiting or otherwise engaging in a lawful activity in the locality'. Answers A and D are therefore incorrect.

Answer B is incorrect because although criminal behaviour at the premises *may* give rise to an order being made, this is not the only route the partners can take and the court may grant the order equally if the premises are associated with anti-social behaviour.

General Police Duties, para. 4.17.7.7

Answer 17.13

Answer **C** — Under s. 547(1) of the Education Act 1996:

> Any person who without lawful authority is present on premises to which this section applies and causes or permits nuisance or disturbance to the annoyance of persons who lawfully use those premises (whether or not any such persons are present at the time) [shall be guilty of an offence].

Obviously, this offence is designed to deal with nuisance such as disturbing lessons or other school-related activities, however, the offence may still be committed when the people who usually use the school (pupils and teachers) are not present. Answers B and D are therefore incorrect.

The offence may be committed by causing a nuisance *or* a disturbance to the annoyance of persons who lawfully use those premises. A caretaker would qualify as such a person and while the children may not have been causing a disturbance, they were most certainly causing a nuisance. Answer A is therefore incorrect.

General Police Duties, para. 4.17.7.8

18 Licensing and Offences Relating to Alcohol

STUDY PREPARATION

The Licensing Act 2003 brought licensing and licensed premises into line with the Government's effort to place crime and disorder matters at the top of the policing agenda. Licensing matters are dealt with by licensing authorities (made up of local authority members).

Operating schedules place the emphasis firmly on the holders of personal licences to run orderly premises, taking into account such matters as crime and disorder, public safety and protection of children. Knowledge of the different types of licences and the new system of objecting to them is critical. You should also learn the powers to enter premises and, once inside, how to deal with offences and/or drunkenness.

Ages are important, and most of the original offences of under-age drinking under the 1964 Act have remained.

The Anti-social Behaviour, Crime and Policing Act 2014 introduced the Public Spaces Protection Order, which provides for an order to be made prohibiting the consumption of alcohol in designated public places, as well as dealing with any other particular nuisance or problem in a particular area.

Further powers of enforcement are provided, allowing the courts to make an order requiring licensed premises to be closed.

The Gambling Act 2005 reformed the laws relating to gambling and introduced a licensing system to regulate operating licences, personal licences, premises licences and temporary use of premises notices. The responsibility for granting licences is shared between the Gambling Commission and local licensing authorities.

QUESTIONS

Question 18.1

CALE is the chair of a residents' association on a housing estate. The public house on the estate, the Anchor, has caused considerable concern recently due to the number of public order incidents that have occurred in the vicinity of the premises on weekends. CALE and other residents have raised the issue several times in PACT meetings; however, their perception is that the police and the local authority are reluctant to take action against the licensee.

In which circumstances could CALE and the residents' association apply to the licensing authority for a review of the premises licence, under s. 51 of the Licensing Act 2003?

A The residents' association may apply for a review of the premises licence if there have been incidents of serious crime or serious disorder or both.

B There is no facility for the residents' association to request a review of the premises licence; they would have to rely on the police or the local authority licensing department to act on their behalf.

C The residents' association may apply for a review of the premises licence, or the application may be made by the police or the local authority licensing department if necessary.

D The residents' association may apply for a review of the premises licence, if they are asked to do so following an investigation by the police or the local authority licensing department.

Question 18.2

A request has been made by the local police for an accelerated review of the conditions of the licence of the Horse and Jockey public house, because of the number of serious disorder incidents that have occurred there recently.

Within what period of time must such an application be considered?

A Within 24 hours.

B Within 36 hours.

C Within 48 hours.

D Within seven days.

Question 18.3

In the last four weeks, the police have been called to numerous violent incidents at the Railway public house, which reopened two months ago after refurbishment, with a new personal licence holder and extended opening times. During this period, two people have been stabbed and this weekend another person received serious facial injuries after being hit with a beer glass. The police are considering making a request for an accelerated review of the conditions of the licence because of the serious disorder.

How must an application be pursued under the terms of s. 53A of the Licensing Act 2003?

A A senior police officer or a senior representative of the local authority must present the application to the licensing authority.

B A senior police officer must present the application to the licensing authority.

C A senior police officer must present the application to the magistrates' court.

D A senior representative from any responsible authority must present the application to the licensing authority.

Question 18.4

Section 97 of the Licensing Act 2003 provides a power of entry for a constable to enter and search any premises which hold a club premises certificate.

What restrictions are placed on this power of entry and search?

A Entry is allowed to detect licensing offences or to prevent a breach of the peace only.

B Entry is allowed to prevent a breach of the peace only.

C Entry is allowed to detect licensing offences, to search for offences relating to the supply of drugs, or to prevent a breach of the peace.

D Entry is allowed to search for offences relating to the supply of drugs, or to prevent a breach of the peace only.

Question 18.5

The West End Social Club has been closed for some time because, due to financial hardships experienced by members, the club was not making enough money to survive. A group of local residents is seeking to reopen the premises as a qualifying club, with a view to forming a committee and applying for a club premises certificate. Their intention is to seek a licence to serve alcohol on the weekends only, with the proceeds being invested back into the club. The committee is concerned about the number of members it will attract.

Which of the following statements is correct, in relation to the committee's concerns?

A There must be at least 20 members for the club to qualify as a qualifying club.
B There must be at least 25 members for the club to qualify as a qualifying club.
C There must be at least 50 members for the club to qualify as a qualifying club.
D There must be at least 100 members for the club to qualify as a qualifying club.

Question 18.6

COURTNEY is the holder of a personal licence and is the manager of the Railway public house, a premises situated in a small village. Residents of the village wish to start a commercial venture by renting out their village hall to wedding parties. The hall is situated in a picturesque location, next to the church and a river. The intention is to rent the hall out during the summer months on Saturdays only and the committee has approached COURTNEY to manage a bar for the weddings.

Which of the following statements is correct, in relation to COURTNEY being able to apply for a temporary event notice (TEN), to be able to assist?

A As a personal licence holder, COURTNEY could apply for five TENs in a calendar year.
B As a personal licence holder, COURTNEY could apply for 12 TENs in a calendar year.
C As a personal licence holder, COURTNEY could apply for 20 TENs in a calendar year.
D As a personal licence holder, COURTNEY could apply for 50 TENs in a calendar year.

Question 18.7

Constable KHAN was on duty as part of a plain-clothes team of police officers, working with LEWIS, a licensing officer from the local authority and a person authorised under the Licensing Act 2003. The team was tasked with visiting public houses in the locality to identify licensing offences. They arrived at the Royal Oak public house at 10.50 pm and identified themselves to GEORGE, the door supervisor, and asked to enter the premises. GEORGE refused, stating the premises were about to close. The operating schedule stated that the premises should close at 11 pm.

Does either Constable KHAN or LEWIS have the power to enter the premises using reasonable force under the Licensing Act 2003?

A No, the power to enter by reasonable force is restricted to uniformed officers only.
B Constable KHAN only; LEWIS does not have a power to enter by force in these circumstances.
C Yes, both have the power to enter using reasonable force in these circumstances.
D Yes, but only if they have reason to believe that offences are being committed.

Question 18.8

HORAN is a committee member of the East Side Social Club, premises which have had problems recently with the licensing authority. The premises are covered by a club premises certificate, however, the licensing authority recently withdrew its authorisation to provide entertainment in the form of live acts due to numerous complaints from residents. HORAN has been under pressure from members to reintroduce the live acts, many of whom have stated they will drink elsewhere if the entertainment is not resumed. HORAN has agreed to do so and has arranged for ZANE to provide entertainment this evening.

If ZANE were to perform at the club tonight, would any offences be committed under s. 136 of the Licensing Act 2003?

A Yes, by HORAN, for allowing a licensable activity to take place.
B Yes, by HORAN, for allowing a licensable activity to take place and by ZANE for actually carrying on a licensable activity.
C No, this offence does not cover activities on premises with a club premises certificate.
D No, this is not a licensable activity, as it does not involve the sale of alcohol.

Question 18.9

RICHARDS entered the Horse and Groom public house in an intoxicated condition and was served a pint of beer by HOPKINS. RICHARDS walked away from the bar and began abusing other customers. RICHARDS was ejected from the premises before drinking any of the beer. HOPKINS is a bar worker and is neither the holder of a premises licence nor the designated premises supervisor.

Has HOPKINS committed an offence by selling alcohol to a person who is drunk, under s. 141 of the Licensing Act 2003?

A Yes, HOPKINS would commit the offence in these circumstances.
B No, the offence will only be committed by the holder of a premises licence and the designated premises supervisor.

C No, as RICHARDS did not consume the drink.

D No, the offence will only be committed by the holder of a premises licence.

Question 18.10

HOULIE was in the Glendale public house one evening and was asked to leave by GREEN, the holder of the premises licence. HOULIE was drunk and abusive towards the bar staff. HOULIE left the premises voluntarily. However, once outside, he began banging on the door trying to get back into the pub. GREEN ignored HOULIE and contacted the police and when they arrived, HOULIE was walking away from the premises.

Has HOULIE committed an offence under s. 143 of the Licensing Act 2003 in these circumstances?

A No, because HOULIE has not actually re-entered the premises after being asked to leave.

B No, as no one has requested that he not re-enter the pub.

C Yes, as he was trying to regain entry to the pub in which he was drunk and disorderly.

D Yes, as it is an offence to be or have been drunk and disorderly on licensed premises.

Question 18.11

Constable TERRY was called to the garden of a house in the early hours of the morning. On arrival, Constable TERRY found COYLE drunk and asleep in a flowerbed. COYLE woke up as a result of being prodded by the officer. COYLE stood up, but was clearly unsteady and out of concern for his safety, Constable TERRY took hold of COYLE by the arm and led him out of the garden. Once they reached the street, COYLE became violent and disorderly towards Constable TERRY. The officer then decided to arrest COYLE for being drunk and disorderly.

Would COYLE's behaviour amount to an offence of drunk and disorderly, under s. 91(1) of the Criminal Justice Act 1967?

A No, the original incident took place in a private place, where the offence cannot be committed.

B Yes, COYLE's disorderly behaviour occurred before being arrested by Constable TERRY.

C No, COYLE's disorderly behaviour occurred after being taken hold of by the officer, which amounts to an arrest.

D Yes, it is irrelevant where Constable TERRY took hold of COYLE, this offence may be committed in a private place, as well as a public place.

Question 18.12

BRUNT was in the garden of a pub on a hot sunny day, accompanied by her two children, PAUL and CARRIE, aged 8 and 6 years respectively. BRUNT had consumed so much alcohol that she could barely stand up and other customers were so concerned for the welfare of the children that they called the police.

Given BRUNT's condition, could she be dealt with by the police for being drunk in charge of a child, under s. 2 of the Licensing Act 1902, in these circumstances?

A No, both children are over 5 years of age.

B Yes, but only in respect of CARRIE.

C Yes, in respect of both children.

D No, this offence cannot be committed on licensed premises; there are other offences under the Licensing Act 2003 to deal with this offence.

Question 18.13

BATES is 15 years of age and was in the Railway public house. She was waiting for her parents to arrive as they were due to have a family meal. While she was waiting, she went to the bar and bought a glass of coke from PEARSON, the designated premises supervisor. When her parents arrived, BATES consumed a meal, but only drank the coke she had bought earlier.

Which of the following is correct, in relation to any offences that may have been committed under the Licensing Act 2003?

A BATES committed an offence by being on the premises whilst unaccompanied by an adult; PEARSON committed an offence by allowing her to be there.

B No offences were committed because BATES was over the age of 14.

C Only PEARSON committed an offence by allowing BATES to be on the premises whilst unaccompanied by an adult.

D No offences were committed because BATES did not purchase or consume alcohol on the premises.

Question 18.14

JABLONOWSKI is working in the Masons Arms public house. She serves TINNEY who is aged 16 and, generally speaking, looks his age. JABLONOWSKI believes TINNEY is 18 years of age, but asks for identification to impress her boss and TINNEY produces a student ID card stating he is 18; the card, however, is a very poor fake and should have been easily perceived as such. JABLONOWSKI, however, serves TINNEY alcohol.

Which of the following is true in relation to selling alcohol to someone under 18?

A JABLONOWSKI has a defence in that she honestly believed that TINNEY was over 18.

B JABLONOWSKI has a defence in that she asked for evidence of his age and it was produced.

C JABLONOWSKI has a defence in that she believed TINNEY was over 18 *and* she asked for evidence of his age.

D JABLONOWSKI has no defence as TINNEY produced fake evidence and it should have been obvious to her it was fake.

Question 18.15

During the summer months, DENNIS organised a series of Twenty 20 cricket matches. DENNIS was granted temporary event notices to sell alcohol at each of the matches. After the first week, the police received information that alcohol was being sold to young people. They conducted test purchase operations over the next two weeks and, on two occasions, alcohol was sold to different young people under the age of 18. DENNIS was responsible for both sales.

Would DENNIS be guilty of an offence under s. 147A of the Licensing Act 2003 (persistently selling alcohol to children) in these circumstances?

A No, the alcohol was sold to different individuals.

B Yes, regardless of the fact that alcohol was sold to different individuals.

C No, there is only evidence that alcohol was sold to individuals on two occasions.

D No, this section does not apply to premises authorised to be used for permitted temporary activities.

Question 18.16

GREEN owns an off-licence which is being monitored by the local Neighbourhood Policing Team, because of complaints that alcohol is being sold to young people on a regular basis. During an operation in March, the police caught GREEN selling alcohol to ZENDEN, aged 16. In April, the police again detected GREEN selling alcohol to ZENDEN on one other occasion.

Would GREEN's behaviour amount to an offence under s. 147A of the Licensing Act 2003 (persistently selling alcohol to children under the age of 18)?

A Yes, GREEN has sold alcohol to a person under 18, on two or more occasions, in two consecutive months.

B No, GREEN has not sold alcohol to a person under 18, on three or more occasions, in three consecutive months.

C No, GREEN has not sold alcohol to a person under 18, on two or more occasions, in three consecutive months.

D No, GREEN has not sold alcohol to a person under 18, on four or more occasions, in three consecutive months.

Question 18.17

KELLY is 17 years of age and was in the Swan public house with his parents; they were at the premises having a family meal. Halfway through the meal, KELLY's father gave him £20 to go to the bar to buy drinks for the people at the table. KELLY bought two glasses of wine for his parents and a pint of lager for himself. KELLY returned to the table and consumed the lager.

Which of the following is correct, in relation to any offences KELLY may have committed under the Licensing Act 2003?

A KELLY committed two offences; first, when he bought the lager and later when he consumed it.

B KELLY committed an offence by buying the lager for himself; however, as his parents are over 18, he committed no offence by buying the wine for them.

C KELLY committed no offences, because he was accompanied by an adult and consuming the lager with a table meal.

D KELLY committed an offence by buying the lager for himself; however, he did not commit an offence when he consumed it at the table.

Question 18.18

FABIEN, aged 21, was entering an off-licence one evening when a group of young people were standing outside. One of the group asked FABIEN to buy four cans of lager for them. FABIEN suspected that the young people were under age, but agreed to buy the cans. However, the conversation was overheard by the owner of the off-licence, who refused to sell the lager to FABIEN.

Does FABIEN commit an offence under s. 149 of the Licensing Act 2003, in these circumstances?

A No, because the shop owner refused to sell the alcohol to FABIEN.

B No, the alcohol was not intended for consumption on relevant premises.

C No, both because the shop owner refused to sell the alcohol to FABIEN *and* it was not intended for consumption on relevant premises.

D Yes, regardless of whether the shop owner refused to sell the alcohol to FABIEN, or where it was to be consumed.

Question 18.19

QUINCY is the premises licence holder for Travellers Rest. The premises has a restaurant which is set aside for table meals and contains a small bar where people can buy alcohol for consumption with their meals. STAINES is 17 years of age and was working at the bar in the restaurant area. QUINCY was busy in the main bar and asked the restaurant manager, SANCHEZ, to authorise STAINES's sales of alcohol. However, SANCHEZ was also busy and forgot to do this. Consequently, STAINES sold alcohol to several customers to have with their meals, without this authorisation.

Has either QUINCY or SANCHEZ committed an offence under s. 153 of the Licensing Act 2003, in these circumstances?

A Yes, both persons have committed the offence.

B Only QUINCY has committed the offence, because this responsibility cannot be simply passed on to another member of staff.

C Only SANCHEZ has committed the offence, because QUINCY has not knowingly allowed the unauthorised sale of alcohol.

D Neither person has committed the offence in these circumstances.

Question 18.20

Constable PERRY was walking through the Anchor public house one evening. The officer saw FLETCHER sitting at a table with a group of people, drinking a pint of beer. On two occasions in the past six months, Constable PERRY had confiscated alcohol from FLETCHER in a public place, and was aware that the person was under 18 years of age.

Has FLETCHER committed an offence under s. 30(1) of the Policing and Crime Act 2009 (persistently possessing alcohol in a relevant place) in these circumstances?

A No, a public house is not a relevant place for the purposes of this section.

B Yes, FLETCHER has been in possession of alcohol in a relevant place on two or more occasions in six consecutive months.

C Yes, FLETCHER has been in possession of alcohol in a relevant place on three or more occasions in 12 consecutive months.

D Yes, FLETCHER has been in possession of alcohol in a relevant place on three or more occasions in six consecutive months.

Question 18.21

Whilst on patrol in a park in the evening, Constable MANNING saw a group of four young people, all drinking from bottles of beer. The officer discovered that three of the group were 17 years of age and the youngest, GRANT, was under 15. Constable MANNING confiscated the alcohol from the group and disposed of it.

What does s. 1 of the Confiscation of Alcohol (Young Persons) Act 1997 state about the actions Constable MANNING should now take?

A Constable MANNING may take names and addresses from all of the group and may remove GRANT to his place of residence or a place of safety.

B Constable MANNING must take names and addresses from all of the group and must remove GRANT to his place of residence or a place of safety.

C Constable MANNING must take names and addresses from all of the group and may remove GRANT to his place of residence or a place of safety.

D Constable MANNING must take names and addresses from all of the group and may remove everyone in the group to their place of residence or a place of safety.

Question 18.22

Constable SINGH was walking through a park when he came across two young people, who were intoxicated. He discovered they were 15 years old and that they had been given drink by HAWKINS. Constable SINGH intercepted HAWKINS, who was walking away from the park, and saw that he was in possession of a can of lager from which he was drinking. HAWKINS is over 18 years old.

What are Constable SINGH's powers to deal with HAWKINS in these circumstances?

A He has the power to confiscate the alcohol from HAWKINS and demand his name and address.

B He has no powers, as HAWKINS did not intend to supply the alcohol to a person under 18.

C He has no powers, as HAWKINS is not under 18.

D He has no powers, as HAWKINS is not in the company of a person under 18 to whom he intends to supply the alcohol.

Question 18.23

The police have conducted a series of test purchase operations over a period of a month at the Railway public house, due to suspected under-age drinking. The officers conducting the exercise have reported that GREEN, the premises licence holder, served alcohol to five under-age drinkers during this period. The duty inspector considers that an offence has been committed under s. 147A of the Licensing Act 2003, and a closure notice should be served on GREEN, to prevent further sales to young people.

Which of the following statements is correct, in relation to such a notice, under s. 169A of the Act?

A The inspector may authorise a closure notice, provided GREEN accepts responsibility for the offence under s. 147A.

B The inspector may authorise a closure notice in these circumstances alone.

C A superintendent may authorise a closure, provided GREEN accepts responsibility for the offence under s. 147A.

D A superintendent may authorise a closure, provided there is a realistic prospect of prosecuting GREEN for an offence under s. 147A.

Question 18.24

A Public Spaces Protection Order has been made, under s. 59 of the Anti-social Behaviour, Crime and Policing Act 2014, in relation to an area adjacent to a leisure centre. Residents living nearby had been suffering anti-social behaviour over a significant period of time because of an alcohol-related problem and had asked the police for a long-term solution to the problem.

Which of the following statements is correct in relation to the duration of the order once it is in place?

A The order may last for up to 12 months.

B The order may last for up to two years.

C The order may last for up to three years.

D There is no maximum time limit for such an order, provided it is reviewed every 12 months.

Question 18.25

Staff from a Neighbourhood Policing Team have been meeting with partners from the local authority to discuss problems relating to ongoing serious anti-social behaviour on a housing estate. Consideration is being given to making a Public Spaces Protection Order to assist the partners in dealing with the problem.

Which of the following statements is correct, in relation to making such an order, under s. 59 of the Anti-social Behaviour, Crime and Policing Act 2014?

A The order may be made either by a superintendent or an equivalent person in the local authority, provided it can be demonstrated that they have consulted with each other.

B The order must be made and publicised by the local authority, in consultation with the chief officer of police, the Police and Crime Commissioner and any representatives of the local community they consider appropriate.

C The order may be made either by a superintendent or an equivalent person in the local authority, provided it can be demonstrated that they have consulted with each other and publicised the details of the order locally.

D The order may be made either by an inspector or an equivalent person in the local authority, in consultation with any representatives of the local community they consider appropriate.

Question 18.26

The Swan public house is situated on a housing estate and there have been complaints by residents that at weekends customers are allowed to drink in the car park at the premises long after the pub closes and that their rowdy behaviour causes a disturbance until the early hours of the morning. The licence holder, MARTIN, has been visited by licensing officers and has been instructed to put an action plan in place to address the issue. However, residents say that the problem is still ongoing and a licensing review is due to take place. One suggestion being put forward is to make a Public Spaces Protection Order prohibiting the consumption of alcohol at the location.

Which of the following statements is correct, in relation to the suggestion to make such an order, under s. 59 of the Anti-social Behaviour, Crime and Policing Act 2014?

A This power only applies to public places, and premises in respect of which a premises licence is in place may not be designated.

B This power generally only applies to public places; however, the car park of premises in respect of which a premises licence is in place may be designated, but not the premises itself.

C This power generally only applies to public places; however, since MARTIN is failing to comply with the conditions of the licence, an order may be made in respect of the car park.

D This power generally only applies to public places; however, since the alcohol is being consumed when the premises is closed, an order may be made in respect of the car park.

Question 18.27

Constable PARIS was on patrol in a public park, where a Public Spaces Protection Order is in place, under s. 59 of the Anti-social Behaviour, Crime and Policing Act 2014. The notice identifies the park as a designated area where alcohol may not be consumed. Constable PARIS saw BELL sitting on a park bench with four unopened cans of lager. BELL was intoxicated, but did not consume alcohol from the cans in the officer's presence.

What power was available to Constable PARIS to deal with BELL under these circumstances?

A Constable PARIS had a power to direct BELL not to drink from the cans.

B None, Constable PARIS did not see BELL drinking from the cans.

C None, as the cans were unopened.

D Constable PARIS had a power to confiscate the cans, but not to dispose of them.

Question 18.28

A licensing authority is considering imposing a Late Night Levy on all licensed premises in a city centre in its area, to raise revenue in relation to the costs of policing and the reduction and prevention of crime and disorder during the night.

Which of the following statements is correct, in relation to the time parameters for such a levy, under s. 125 of the Police Reform and Social Responsibility Act 2011?

A It may be applied for any period of time between midnight and 6 am, but the time parameters must be the same every day.

B It may be applied for any period of time between midnight and 6 am and the time parameters may vary, depending on the specific requirements of the area.

C It may be applied for any period of time between 2 am and 6 am, but the time parameters must be the same every day.

D It may be applied for any period of time between 10 pm and 6 am and the time parameters may vary, depending on the specific requirements of the area.

Question 18.29

The licensing authority in a local area is considering a proposal by licensing officers to issue an Early Morning Alcohol Restriction Order in a city centre. Evidence has been produced that there has been a significant increase in alcohol-related violence in the early hours of the morning, in a small geographical area that contains eight licensed premises. The licensing officers have asked for an order to be temporarily implemented in relation to these premises while they work with the licence holders on solving the problem.

Which of the following statements is correct in relation to the licensing authority's powers in these circumstances?

A An order may allow the authority to restrict the sale of alcohol between midnight and 6 am while they seek to promote the licensing objectives.

B An order may allow the authority to restrict the sale of alcohol between 2 am and 6 am while they seek to promote the licensing objectives.

C An order may allow the authority to restrict the sale of alcohol between 3 am and 6 am while they seek to promote the licensing objectives.

D An order provides limitless powers to the authority and they may restrict the sale of alcohol at any time while they seek to promote the licensing objectives.

Question 18.30

Local licensing officers working in partnership have met urgently on a Saturday morning to discuss the Carpenters Arms public house, which has been the location of serious disorder over the last three weekends. A closure notice had been issued to the licence holder the previous evening following a fight between two rival gangs at the premises. The officers were preparing a file to take to court to apply for a closure order to prevent the premises opening again that night, because intelligence had shown that further violence was likely to occur.

Which of the following statements is correct, in relation to an application for a closure order, under s. 160 of the Licensing Act 2003?

A The application may be made by an inspector or an equivalent person from the local authority.
B The application may be made by a superintendent or an equivalent person from the local authority.
C The application may only be made by a superintendent.
D The application may only be made by a member of the licensing authority for the area.

Question 18.31

A closure order has been made in respect of the Heathcock public house, which has been the location of serious disorder over the weekend. The request was made for the order to allow the local licensing authority to meet urgently to discuss the problems at the premises and any potential solutions.

If the order was granted, how long would it last, according to s. 160 of the Licensing Act 2003?

A The premises could be closed for a period not exceeding 24 hours.
B The premises could be closed for a period not exceeding 48 hours.
C The premises could be closed for a period not exceeding seven days.
D The premises could be closed for a period not exceeding 14 days.

Question 18.32

The Duke of Wellington public house has been the subject of a closure order, which has been served on the licence holder, MARLEY, prohibiting him from opening the pub today. The police are monitoring the premises because intelligence has been received that they will be opened, contrary to the order. Officers observe a number of customers going inside and then enter the premises themselves. Inside, they find the designated premises supervisor, JAMES, and two members of staff serving customers; however, MARLEY is not present.

Who would be liable, in these circumstances, for an offence under s. 160(4) of the Licensing Act 2003?

A JAMES only, as the person who opened the premises contrary to the order.
B MARLEY and JAMES; this is an absolute offence for the premises supervisor and the licence holder.
C JAMES and the staff serving customers; MARLEY would only be guilty if he knew the premises were open and allowed them to be so.

D JAMES and MARLEY only; MARLEY would only be guilty if he knew the premises were open and allowed them to be so.

Question 18.33

Constable WARREN works as a Licensing Officer based in a co-located office with the local authority Licensing Department. Constable WARREN has attended premises in High Street with CANTEBURRY, a local authority Licensing Officer. They have received intelligence that NEWMAN is using the premises for the unlicensed sale of alcohol. Their intention is to gather evidence and, if necessary, close the premises down.

Section 19 of the Criminal Justice and Police Act 2001 allows for a closure notice to be served in respect of unlicensed premises. In respect of this power, which of the following statements is correct?

A A closure notice may be served by Constable WARREN only, provided this is done in consultation with the local authority (which would include consulting with CANTEBURRY).

B Either Constable WARREN or CANTEBURRY could serve a closure notice in these circumstances.

C A closure notice may only be served by an inspector; neither Constable WARREN nor CANTEBURRY has the authority to do so in these circumstances.

D A closure notice may only be authorised by a magistrate; either Constable WARREN or CANTEBURRY would have to apply to the court for such a notice.

ANSWERS

Answer 18.1

Answer **C** — Section 51 of the Licensing Act 2003 allows for an application for a review of a premises licence by a responsible authority *or any other person*. Answer B is therefore incorrect.

It is not necessary to wait for an investigation to take place by the police or the local authority licensing department—the whole point of the 2003 Act is that processes must be transparent and communities are encouraged to contribute to matters that affect them and their families and neighbours. Similarly, there is no need for a member of the public to wait for an incident of serious crime or serious disorder to occur before challenging the activities of a licensed premises. The *licensee* is required to demonstrate through the licensing objectives how he/she is going to contribute to the prevention of crime and disorder—the onus is on him/her to resolve this issue, not the community. Answers A and D are therefore incorrect.

General Police Duties, para. 4.18.4.2

Answer 18.2

Answer **C** — Section 53A of the Licensing Act 2003 provides for an accelerated review of licensed premises by a licensing authority, and the attaching of temporary conditions to a premises licence pending a full review of the licence.

The procedure provides for a senior police officer (of or above the rank of superintendent) to certify to a licensing authority, that he/she considers licensed premises to be associated with serious crime and/or serious disorder.

On receiving the application the licensing authority will be obliged to consider *within 48 hours* whether it is necessary to take interim steps pending a full review of the licence, which must take place within 28 days. Answers A, B and D are therefore incorrect.

General Police Duties, para. 4.18.4.2

Answer 18.3

Answer **B** — There is a general provision under s. 51 of the Licensing Act 2003 for an interested party or responsible authority to apply to a relevant licensing authority for a review of the premises licence. For example, a local resident may consider that the measures taken by the licensee to prevent public nuisance are insufficient and request that they be reviewed. Similarly, the police may consider that the measures put in place to prevent crime and disorder are not being effective and need to be reviewed.

However, s. 53A of the Act provides for an accelerated review of licensed premises by *a licensing authority*, and the attaching of temporary conditions to a premises licence pending a full review of the licence. Answer C is therefore incorrect.

The procedure involves a senior police officer—of or above the rank of superintendent—certifying to a licensing authority that he/she considers licensed premises to be associated with serious crime and/or serious disorder. Answers A and D are therefore incorrect.

General Police Duties, para. 4.18.4.2

Answer 18.4

Answer **D** — Under s. 97 of the Licensing Act 2003, where a club premises certificate has effect in respect of any premises, a constable may enter and search the premises if he/she has reasonable cause to believe:

(a) that an offence under section 4(3)(a), (b) or (c) of the Misuse of Drugs Act 1971 (supplying or offering to supply, or being concerned in supplying or making an offer to supply, a controlled drug) has been, is being, or is about to be, committed there, or
(b) that there is likely to be a breach of the peace there.

This section does not allow a constable to enter the premises to detect licensing offences; therefore, answers A and C are incorrect. Entry is allowed (using reasonable force if necessary) in order to detect offences under the Misuse of Drugs Act 1971, or if a breach of the peace is likely to occur in the premises. Answers A and B are incorrect for this reason.

General Police Duties, para. 4.18.4.4

Answer 18.5

Answer **B** — Under s. 60 of the Licensing Act 2003, a club premises certificate may be granted by a licensing authority certifying that the premises may be used by the club for one or more qualifying club activities specified in the certificate, and that the club is a qualifying club in relation to each of those activities (s. 60). One of the general conditions that applies for a club to qualify as a qualifying club under s. 62 is that *the club has at least 25 members*.

Answers A, C and D are therefore incorrect.

General Police Duties, para. 4.18.4.4

Answer 18.6

Answer **D** — A Temporary Event Notice (TEN), issued by the licensing authority, is required where a person (the premises user) intends to carry out a licensable activity on unlicensed premises or wishes to operate outside the terms of their existing premises licence or club premises licence (s. 100 of the 2003 Act).

A 'licensable activity' is the sale or supply of alcohol, regulated entertainment (e.g. music, singing or dancing), or provisions of late night refreshment (hot food or drink between the hours of 2300 and 0500). Such activities might include a publican engaged to run a temporary bar for a wedding at a venue not licensed for the sale of alcohol, or a person not being the holder of a personal licence who may wish to run a bar and provide a band at a party to celebrate a significant anniversary.

A personal licence holder is permitted *50* TENs per calendar year and an individual who is not the holder of a personal licence is permitted five TENs a year. Answers A, B and C are incorrect for this reason.

Note, while a personal licence holder is permitted 50 TENs, all *premises* are limited to *15* TENs in a calendar year.

General Police Duties, para. 4.18.4.5

Answer 18.7

Answer **C** — Under s. 179 of the Licensing Act 2003, where a constable or an authorised person has reason to believe that any premises are being, or are about to be, used for a licensable activity, they may enter the premises with a view to seeing whether the activity is being, or is to be, carried on under and in accordance with an authorisation (s. 179(1)). A person exercising the power conferred by this section may, if necessary, use reasonable force (s. 179(3)). Since the power under this section is not restricted to police officers, answer B is incorrect. Also, there is no requirement for a police officer to be in uniform, therefore answer A is incorrect.

There is a separate power, under s. 180 of the Act, for a constable to enter premises in order to investigate offences. A constable may enter by reasonable force under this section. However, s. 179 shows that a constable or authorised person may enter premises using reasonable force simply to make sure that licensing activities are being carried out within the law. Answer D is therefore incorrect.

(Note that an authorised person exercising the powers conferred on them must, if so requested, produce evidence of their authority to exercise the power.)

General Police Duties, para. 4.18.5

Answer 18.8

Answer **A** — Section 136(1) of the Licensing Act 2003 states that a person commits an offence if—

(a) he carries on or attempts to carry on a licensable activity on or from any premises otherwise than under and in accordance with an authorisation, or
(b) he knowingly allows a licensable activity to be so carried on.

This offence requires that the person carried on (or attempted to carry on) the licensable activity *either* in a manner not authorised by or in accordance with an appropriate authorisation, or *knowingly* allowed the activity to be carried on in that way. Therefore, the offence could be committed by both persons.

However, where the licensable activity in question is the provision of regulated entertainment, a person will generally *not* commit an offence under this section if his/her only involvement in the provision of the entertainment is that he/she played the music, performed the dance, etc. (see s. 136(2)). Answer B is therefore incorrect.

'Licensing activity' includes any activity mentioned on the licence which is covered by the licence; it could include serving alcohol, but could equally include providing live entertainment. Answer D is therefore incorrect.

'Authorisation' here means activities at premises with a premises licence, a club premises certificate or a temporary event notice in respect of which the relevant conditions have been met. While some offences apply only to 'relevant premises', s. 136(1) is wider than that and applies to any premises. Answer C is therefore incorrect.

General Police Duties, para. 4.18.7.1

Answer 18.9

Answer **B** — The Licensing Act 2003, s. 141 states:

(1) A person to whom subsection (2) applies commits an offence if, on relevant premises, he knowingly—

(a) sells or attempts to sell alcohol to a person who is drunk, or
(b) allows alcohol to be sold to such a person.

This subsection applies:

(2) (a) to any person who works at the premises in a capacity, whether paid or unpaid, which gives him authority to sell the alcohol concerned,
(b) in the case of licensed premises, to—
(i) the holder of a premises licence in respect of the premises, and
(ii) the designated premises supervisor (if any) under such a licence.

Under s. 141(2)(a), the offence may be committed by any person who works on the premises, whatever their capacity. However, on licensed premises (which is the case in this question) the offence is covered by s. 141(2)(b), which restricts liability to the holder of a premises licence and/or the designated premises supervisor. Answers A and D are therefore incorrect. It is irrelevant that RICHARDS did not consume the drink—the offence is complete when the alcohol is sold to a person who is intoxicated. Answer C is therefore incorrect.

General Police Duties, para. 4.18.7.5

Answer 18.10

Answer **B** — Under s. 143(1)(a) of the Licensing Act 2003, a person who is drunk or disorderly commits an offence if, without reasonable excuse, he/she fails to leave relevant premises when requested to do so by a constable or by a person to whom subs. (2) applies (the holder of a premises licence in respect of the premises, and/or the designated premises supervisor). Since HOULIE left when requested by GREEN, no offence was committed under this subsection; answer D is therefore incorrect.

Under s. 143(1)(b) of the Act, a further offence is committed if a person enters or attempts (answer A is therefore incorrect) to enter relevant premises after a constable or a person to whom subs. (2) applies has requested him/her not to enter. HOULIE was not so requested and therefore would also not commit this offence; answer C is therefore incorrect.

General Police Duties, para. 4.18.7.7

Answer 18.11

Answer **B** — Under s. 91(1) of the Criminal Justice Act 1967, a person commits an offence if, in a public place, he/she is guilty, while drunk, of disorderly conduct. Since the offence may only be committed in a public place, answer D is incorrect.

The offence will not be committed when a person does not commit a disorderly act until after their arrest (*H* v *DPP* (2006) 170 JP 4). However, in *McMillan* v *Crown Prosecution Service* [2008] EWHC 1457 (Admin), it was held that where a police officer took hold of a drunken person by the arm to steady them for their own safety it was not an arrest. The circumstances in this case entailed the officer leading the drunken person from a private garden to a public place. It was then legitimate for the officer to arrest for this offence where the accused then displayed disorderly behaviour. The circumstances in *McMillan* mirror those in this question—it is irrelevant where the original incident commenced, the disorderly behaviour occurred in a public place, *before* the officer decided to make an arrest. Answers A and C are therefore incorrect.

General Police Duties, para. 4.18.7.8

Answer 18.12

Answer **B** — Under s. 2 of the Licensing Act 1902:

(1) If any person is found drunk in any highway or other public place, whether a building or not, or on any licensed premises, while having the charge of a child apparently under the age of seven years, he may be apprehended ...
(2) If the child appears to the court to be under the age of seven, the child shall, for the purposes of this section, be deemed to be under that age unless the contrary is proved.

Although this is a rather dated piece of legislation, this section is still being used for its specific purpose, that is, the safety of young children (see *R (On the application of A)* v *Lowestoft Magistrates' Court* [2013] EWHC 659 (Admin)).

The offence is complete in relation to the 6-year-old child only; therefore, answers A and C are incorrect.

Although there may be other Licensing Act 2003 offences that can be considered, the offence under s. 2 may be committed on licensed premises and answer D is incorrect.

General Police Duties, para. 4.18.7.10

Answer 18.13

Answer **C** — Under s. 145(1) of the Licensing Act 2003, an offence is committed by the relevant person who allows an unaccompanied child to be on the premises at a time when they are open for the purposes of being used for the supply of alcohol for consumption there.

A child is unaccompanied if he/she is under 16 and is not in the company of an individual aged 18 or over (s. 145(2)(a) to (b)). Answer B is therefore incorrect.

The offence may be committed by any person who works at a licensed premises in a capacity, whether paid or unpaid, which authorises him/her to request the unaccompanied child to leave the premises. The offence is not committed by the child himself/herself. Answer A is therefore incorrect.

It is irrelevant whether or not the child purchased or consumed alcohol on the premises; the offence is complete by the child simply being on the premises unaccompanied and answer D is incorrect.

General Police Duties, para. 4.18.8.1

Answer 18.14

Answer **D** — It is an absolute offence to sell alcohol to someone who is under 18, but there are some defences available.

To begin with, the person selling the alcohol must believe the person is aged 18 or over; lack of this belief loses the defence immediately. However, this belief must then be supported by either of the following circumstances:

- nobody could reasonably have suspected from the individual's appearance that he/she was aged under 18; *or*
- all reasonable steps to establish the individual's age had been taken.

JABLONOWSKI's belief is not enough on its own; answer A is therefore incorrect.

In the scenario TINNEY did not look over 18, so JABLONOWSKI would have to follow the reasonable steps route to establish identity.

The Licensing Act 2003 further defines what 'reasonable steps' are in relation to establishing identification. They are:

- the individual was asked for evidence of his/her age; *and*
- the evidence produced would have convinced a reasonable person.

Producing identification does not negate the offence if such identification is obviously fake (as it was in the scenario). Answers B and C are therefore incorrect.

In summary then, for the defence to succeed, the person selling must believe the individual buying to be 18 or over. If it is not obvious to everyone else that this individual, by appearance, is over 18 then proof of age is required; such proof has to be convincing.

General Police Duties, paras 4.18.8.3, 4.18.8.4

Answer 18.15

Answer **B** — Under s. 147A(1) of the Licensing Act 2003, a person is guilty of an offence if:

(a) on 2 or more different occasions within a period of 3 consecutive months alcohol is unlawfully sold on the same premises to an individual aged under 18;
(b) at the time of each sale the premises were either licensed premises or premises authorised to be used for a permitted temporary activity; and
(c) that person was a responsible person in relation to the premises at each such time.

Under s. 147A(5), the individual aged under 18, to whom the sale is made, can be the same person or different people and therefore answer A is incorrect.

The Policing and Crime Act 2009, s. 28, amended s. 147A(1)(a) so that the offence is committed if alcohol is sold on 'two or more different occasions', whereas it was previously 'three or more different occasions'. Answer C is therefore incorrect.

This section *does* apply to premises authorised to be used for permitted temporary activities and for that reason answer D is incorrect.

General Police Duties, para. 4.18.8.6

Answer 18.16

Answer **A** — Under s. 147A(1) of the Licensing Act 2003, a person is guilty of an offence if:

(a) on 2 or more different occasions within a period of 3 consecutive months alcohol is unlawfully sold on the same premises to an individual aged under 18.

The Policing and Crime Act 2009, s. 28, amended s. 147A(1)(a) so that the offence is committed if alcohol is sold on 'two or more different occasions', whereas it was previously 'three or more different occasions'.

Answers B, C and D are therefore incorrect.

General Police Duties, para. 4.18.8.6

Answer 18.17

Answer **D** — Under s. 149(1) of the Licensing Act 2003, an individual aged under 18 commits an offence if he buys or attempts to buy alcohol. It is irrelevant that the person is buying alcohol on behalf of an adult; the offence is committed when the alcohol is purchased and answer B is incorrect.

It is a defence under s. 149(5) to buy alcohol on behalf of a person under 18 when:

- the relevant person (the person purchasing the alcohol) is aged 18 or over,
- the individual is aged 16 or 17,
- the alcohol is beer, wine or cider,
- its purchase or supply is for consumption at a table meal on relevant premises, and
- the individual is accompanied at the meal by an individual aged 18 or over.

This section would provide a defence for KELLY when *consuming* the lager at the table; however, it did not allow him to *purchase* the alcohol. Answers A and C are therefore incorrect.

General Police Duties, para. 4.18.8.7

Answer 18.18

Answer **D** — Under s. 149(3)(a) of the Licensing Act 2003, a person commits an offence if he/she buys or attempts to buy alcohol on behalf of an individual aged under 18. The offence is complete when the person attempts to purchase the alcohol; therefore, answers A and C are incorrect.

There is a separate offence under s. 149(4) of the Act, of a person buying or attempting to buy alcohol on behalf of an individual aged under 18, for consumption on relevant premises—however, since the offence may be committed in either of the circumstances described, answers B and C are incorrect.

General Police Duties, para. 4.18.8.7

Answer 18.19

Answer **D** — Under s. 153(1)(a) of the Licensing Act 2003, a person commits an offence if on any relevant premises he/she knowingly allows an individual aged under 18 to make on the premises any sale of alcohol unless the sale has been specifically approved by that or another responsible person.

A 'responsible person' means, in relation to licensed premises:

- the holder of a premises licence in respect of the premises;
- the designated premises supervisor (if any) under such a licence; or
- any individual aged 18 or over who is authorised for the purposes of this section by such a holder or supervisor.

Generally, either person *could* commit an offence under s. 153, because QUINCY can authorise SANCHEZ to supervise STAINES and claim not to have 'known' they were unauthorised in these circumstances. This procedure is well established in large supermarkets, where a person supervising the till area is unlikely to be the licence holder, or even a designated premises supervisor—such a person would fall under the third category listed earlier.

However, none of this is particularly relevant in these circumstances, because of the exception contained in s. 153(2), which states that subs. (1) does *not* apply where:

- the alcohol is sold or supplied for consumption with a table meal;
- it is sold or supplied in premises which are being used for the service of table meals (or in a part of any premises which is being so used); and
- the premises are (or the part is) not used for the sale or supply of alcohol otherwise than to persons having table meals there and for consumption by such persons as an ancillary to their meal.

Since STAINES was working in the restaurant area at the time, the offence is not committed, which is why answer D is correct and answers A, B and C are incorrect.

General Police Duties, para. 4.18.8.11

Answer 18.20

Answer **A** — Under s. 30(1) of the Policing and Crime Act 2009, a person under the age of 18 is guilty of an offence if, without reasonable excuse, the person is in possession of alcohol in any relevant place on three or more occasions within a period of 12 consecutive months.

Section 30(2) defines a 'relevant place' as:

(a) any public place, other than excluded premises, or
(b) any place, other than a public place, to which the person has unlawfully gained access.

In relation to subs. (2)(a), 'excluded premises' means premises with a premises licence or permitted temporary activity used for the supply of alcohol, and premises with a club premises certificate used for the supply of alcohol to members or guests.

Therefore, while FLETCHER has previously been in possession of alcohol in a relevant place on two occasions in 12 consecutive months, a public house is an 'excluded premises' and the provisions of this section do not apply there. Answers B, C and D are incorrect for this reason.

Answers B and D would also have been incorrect, had FLETCHER been in possession of alcohol in a relevant place, as the time period which triggers this offence is three or more occasions in 12 consecutive months.

General Police Duties, para. 4.18.8.12

Answer 18.21

Answer **C** — Under s. 1 of the Confiscation of Alcohol (Young Persons) Act 1997, apart from the power to confiscate any alcohol from young people under the age of 18 under subss (1) and (2) in certain conditions (which applied in this case), a constable has further duties and powers, as follows:

(1AA) A constable who imposes a requirement on a person under sub-section (1) shall also require the person to state the person's name and address.

(1AB) A constable who imposes a requirement on a person under sub-section (1) may, if the constable reasonably suspects that the person is under the age of 16, remove the person to the person's place of residence or a place of safety.

The duty to ask for the person's name and address under s. 1(1AA) is not just a power, it is a requirement and answer A is incorrect.

On the other hand, the constable is not *required* to remove a person under 16 to their place of residence or a place of safety and this power is not available to the rest of the people in the group, who were over 16. Answers B and D are therefore incorrect.

General Police Duties, para. 4.18.8.13

Answer 18.22

Answer **A** — Under s. 1(1) of the Confiscation of Alcohol (Young Persons) Act 1997, a constable who reasonably suspects that a person who is in a relevant place is in possession of alcohol, may confiscate the alcohol if:

(a) the person is under 18; *or*
(b) the person intends that any of the alcohol shall be consumed by a person under 18 in a relevant place; *or*
(c) the person is with *or* has recently been with a person under 18 and that person has recently consumed alcohol in the relevant place.

Under s. 1(6), a 'relevant place' is:

- any public place, other than licensed premises; or
- any place, other than a public place, to which that person has unlawfully gained access;

and for this purpose a place is a public place if, at the material time, the public or any section of the public has access to it—on payment or otherwise—as of right or by virtue of express or implied permission.

Under para. (c), as HAWKINS has recently been with a person under 18 who has consumed alcohol, regardless of whether he intends to supply more alcohol to the children, the officer will have the power to confiscate the alcohol he is in possession of. Answers B and D are therefore incorrect.

Also, alcohol may be confiscated from a person who is over 18 if he/she has committed an act mentioned under paras (b) and (c)—the power is designed to prevent alcohol either being consumed by, or supplied to, people under 18. Answer C is therefore incorrect.

Note that under subs. (1AA) of the Act (inserted by s. 29 of the Policing and Crime Act 2009), a constable exercising the power under s. 1 *shall* require the person to state their name and address. The previous subsection (now omitted) stated that a constable *may* require the person to give their name and address.

General Police Duties, para. 4.18.8.13

Answer 18.23

Answer **D** — Section 169A of the Licensing Act 2003 provides that a senior police officer (of the rank of superintendent or higher), or an inspector of weights and measures, may give a closure notice where there is evidence that a person has committed the offence of persistently selling alcohol to children at the premises in question. Answers A and B are therefore incorrect.

A further condition exists under s. 169A—the superintendent must consider that the evidence is such that there would be a realistic prospect of conviction if the offender was prosecuted for it. Answer C is therefore incorrect.

General Police Duties, para. 4.18.8.15

Answer 18.24

Answer **C** — Under s. 59 of the Anti-social Behaviour, Crime and Policing Act 2014, a local authority may make a Public Spaces Protection Order if satisfied on reasonable grounds that activities carried on in a public place within the authority's area have had, or are likely to have, a detrimental effect on the quality of life of those in the locality. The authority must also be satisfied on reasonable grounds that the activities are unreasonable and the effect, or likely effect, of the activities is, or is likely to be, of a persistent or continuing nature.

The public space must be identified in the order, as well as the types of activities the order is seeking to restrict (in this case, the anti-social behaviour).

Orders will last for up to three years before requiring a review and there is no limit on the number of times an order can be reviewed and renewed (s. 60).

Answers A, B and D are therefore incorrect.

General Police Duties, para. 4.18.9.1

Answer 18.25

Answer **B** — Under s. 59 of the Anti-social Behaviour, Crime and Policing Act 2014, a local authority may make a Public Spaces Protection Order if satisfied on reasonable grounds that activities carried on in a public place within the authority's area have had, or are likely to have, a detrimental effect on the quality of life of those in the locality. The authority must also be satisfied on reasonable grounds that the activities are unreasonable and the effect, or likely effect, of the activities is, or is likely to be, of a persistent or continuing nature.

The public space must be identified in the order, as well as the types of activities the order is seeking to restrict (in this case, the anti-social behaviour).

The power to make the order lies with the local authority and they must publicise the details of the proposed order and consult the chief officer of police, the Police and Crime Commissioner (or the equivalent in London) and any representatives of the local community they consider appropriate—for example, a local residents' group or a community group that regularly uses the public place.

Answers A, C and D are therefore incorrect.

General Police Duties, para. 4.18.9.1

Answer 18.26

Answer **A** — Under s. 59 of the Anti-social Behaviour, Crime and Policing Act 2014, a local authority may make a Public Spaces Protection Order if satisfied on reasonable grounds that activities carried on in a public place within the authority's area have had, or are likely to have, a detrimental effect on the quality of life of those in the locality. The authority must also be satisfied on reasonable grounds that the activities are unreasonable and the effect, or likely effect, of the activities is, or is likely to be, of a persistent or continuing nature.

The public space must be identified in the order, as well as the types of activities the order is seeking to restrict (in this case, the consumption of alcohol).

However, an order prohibiting the consumption of alcohol cannot be used against licensed premises (s. 62)—regardless of whether they are closed. There are sufficient powers under the Licensing Act 2003 to ensure compliance from the licence holder, which is a more appropriate way of dealing with this problem.

Answers B, C and D are therefore incorrect.

General Police Duties, para. 4.18.9.1

Answer 18.27

Answer **A** — Under s. 59 of the Anti-social Behaviour, Crime and Policing Act 2014, a local authority may make a Public Spaces Protection Order if satisfied on reasonable grounds that activities carried on in a public place within the authority's area have had, or are likely to have, a detrimental effect on the quality of life of those in the locality. The authority must also be satisfied on reasonable grounds that the activities are unreasonable and the effect, or likely effect, of the activities is, or is likely to be, of a persistent or continuing nature.

The public space must be identified in the order, as well as the types of activities the order is seeking to restrict (in this case, the consumption of alcohol).

Section 63(3) of the Act provides a constable or an authorised person (which could be a PCSO or a local authority licensing officer) with powers to deal with people who contravene orders, if he/she reasonably believes that a person is or has been consuming, or intends to consume, alcohol in that place. Answer B is therefore incorrect.

Three distinct powers are given:

- to require the person not to consume alcohol (including a requirement to cease drinking);
- to require the person to surrender the alcohol;
- to dispose of anything surrendered in a manner he/she considers appropriate.

Answer D is incorrect, because the officer may exercise any of these powers and dispose of anything surrendered in such a manner as he/she considers appropriate. The fact that the cans were unopened is not relevant and they may be confiscated utilising the powers described previously. Answer C is therefore incorrect.

General Police Duties, para. 4.18.9.2

Answer 18.28

Answer **A** — Section 125 of the Police Reform and Social Responsibility Act 2011 introduced provisions for a Late Night Levy on licensed premises. The levy may be applied by a licensing authority in its area if it considers it desirable to raise revenue in relation to the costs of policing and other arrangements for the reduction or prevention of crime and disorder, in connection with the supply of alcohol between midnight and 6 am. Answers B and C are therefore incorrect.

The period can be for any length of time within these parameters, *but must be the same every day*. Answers C and D are incorrect for this reason.

The levy is payable by the holders of premises licences or club premises certificates which authorise the supply of alcohol during those hours. The licensing authority is expected to consider the need for a levy with the chief officer of police and Police and Crime Commissioner.

General Police Duties, para. 4.18.10

Answer 18.29

Answer **A** — Sections 172A to 172E of the Licensing Act 2003 give licensing authorities the powers they need to effectively manage and police the night-time economy and take action against those premises that are causing problems.

The Early Morning Alcohol Restriction Orders can be applied to areas between midnight and 6 am, where the licensing authority considers that restricting the late-night supply of alcohol is appropriate to promote the licensing objectives.

Answers B, C and D are therefore incorrect.

General Police Duties, para. 4.18.11

Answer 18.30

Answer **C** — Under s. 160(1) of the Licensing Act 2003, where there is or is expected to be disorder in any local justice area, a magistrates' court acting in the area may make an order requiring all premises which are situated at or near the place of the disorder or expected disorder, and in respect of which a premises licence or a temporary event notice has effect, to be closed for a period, not exceeding 24 hours, specified in the order.

A magistrates' court may make an order under this section only on the application of a police officer who is of the rank of superintendent or above (s. 160(2)).

Answers A, B and D are therefore incorrect.

General Police Duties, para. 4.18.12

Answer 18.31

Answer **A** — Under s. 160(1) of the Licensing Act 2003, where there is or is expected to be disorder in any local justice area, a magistrates' court acting in the area may make an order requiring all premises which are situated at or near the place of the disorder or expected disorder, and in respect of which a premises licence or a temporary event notice has effect, to be closed for a period, not exceeding 24 hours, specified in the order.

Answers B, C and D are therefore incorrect.

General Police Duties, para. 4.18.12

Answer 18.32

Answer **D** — Under s. 160(4) of the Licensing Act 2003, where an order is made under this section, a person to whom subs. (5) applies commits an offence if he/she knowingly keeps any premises to which the order relates open, or allows any such premises to be kept open, during the period of the order. Because the person would have to allow the premises to open knowingly, MARLEY could have a defence and answer B is incorrect.

Section 160(5) outlines who can actually commit the offence; this subsection applies:

(a) to any manager of the premises,
(b) in the case of licensed premises, to—
  (i) the holder of a premises licence in respect of the premises, and
  (ii) the designated premises supervisor (if any) under such a licence, and
(c) in the case of premises in respect of which a temporary event notice has effect, to the premises user in relation to that notice.

Since the offence can be committed by both the licence holder and the premises supervisor (but not the other staff), answers A and C are incorrect.

General Police Duties, para. 4.18.12

Answer 18.33

Answer **B** — Under s. 19 of the Criminal Justice and Police Act 2001, where a constable is satisfied that any premises (including land or any place whether covered or not):

- are being used or
- have been used within the last 24 hours
- for the unlicensed sale/exposure for sale
- of alcohol
- for consumption on or in the vicinity of the premises

he/she may serve a closure notice.

This power is available to any police officer of any rank, therefore, Constable WARREN does not need to call an inspector or go to court. Answers C and D are therefore incorrect.

In addition, under s. 19, the power to serve a notice is available to any police officer of any rank and *may also be exercised by the relevant local authority*. Answer A is therefore incorrect.

General Police Duties, para. 4.18.13

19 Offences and Powers Relating to Information

STUDY PREPARATION

The management—and mismanagement—of information is an area of increasing importance to the police generally and therefore to its supervisors, managers, trainers and examiners.

The key issues here are the statutory restrictions on who can access what type of information and for what purpose. Much accessing of information involves the use of computers and it is therefore necessary to understand the relevant aspects of the Computer Misuse Act 1990.

Also covered are the control measures, which are required to be in place to protect data held on individuals, under the Data Protection Act 1998, and the powers given to the Information Commissioner to regulate the storage of such data.

A large part of this chapter contains the provisions of the Regulation of Investigatory Powers Act 2000 (RIPA), which covers the covert acquisition of information about people, through the use of covert human intelligence sources (CHIS), surveillance and the interception of communications.

QUESTIONS

Question 19.1

BERGMAN is a Dutch national studying for a Ph.D. in Criminology in a university in England and is a temporary resident in the country. BERGMAN is writing a dissertation on the effectiveness of criminal justice interventions in young people's offending and requires statistical information on arrests, methods of disposal and re-offending amongst young people. BERGMAN has written to the Youth Justice Board (YJB) with specific questions relating to these matters, requesting disclosure under the Freedom of Information Act 2000.

Which of the following statements is correct, in relation to BERGMAN's request under the 2000 Act?

A The Act is designed to cover disclosure to organisations as opposed to individuals and the YJB is not obliged to supply this information to BERGMAN.

B Any person or organisation is entitled to request information; however, public authorities are only obliged to supply information to people or organisations who are UK nationals.

C Any person or organisation is entitled to request information, including those who are not UK nationals.

D Any person or organisation is entitled to request information, excluding those who are not UK nationals; however, as a temporary UK resident, BERGMAN is entitled to this information.

Question 19.2

Chief Inspector KEYES works in the Call and Incident Management Department of Eastshire Police and has received an email from the Data Protection Officer. A freedom of information request has been received relating to 101 call-handling statistics. The applicant has requested information on how many of the 101 calls received in the last calendar year were dealt with by the police, and how many of the 101 calls were passed on to the local authority because they related to non-police incidents. Chief Inspector KEYES has replied that the department receives about 10,000 101 calls every month and the Force's command and control system does not allow a search identifying how such calls were dealt with; to comply with the request, the department would have to set aside significant resources to gather accurate information and the chief inspector has refused to do this.

Which of the following statements is correct, in relation to Chief Inspector KEYES's refusal to comply with the request?

A Eastshire Police must provide this information; it may only refuse to do so if disclosing such information is not in the public interest.

B Eastshire Police may decide not to provide this information, if the costs associated with retrieving the information are disproportionate compared to the request.

C Eastshire Police must provide this information; it may only refuse to do so if disclosing such information is prejudicial to law enforcement, national security or legal professional privilege.

D Eastshire Police may decide not to provide this information, but it may only do so if it considers that the application is repeated or vexatious.

Question 19.3

Section 1 of the Computer Misuse Act 1990 makes provision in relation to unauthorised access to computer material.

Where a person is not authorised and they have the required intent and knowledge, at which point would an offence under this section first be committed?

A When the computer is switched on.

B When the 'log on screen' is filled out.

C When they are successfully logged onto the system.

D When the actual program is accessed.

Question 19.4

BIGNELL worked for a large bank and was dating BRADY who, unknown to her, had ties with an organised crime gang. BRADY persuaded BIGNELL to access information from customers' accounts and pass the details to him. BIGNELL was afraid to ask BRADY why he wanted the information and was unaware that he was selling on the data to credit card forgers.

What would have to be proved, in order to convict BIGNELL of an offence contrary to s. 1 of the Computer Misuse Act 1990?

A That she was not authorised to access the data and that she knew this was the case.

B That she was not authorised to access the data and that she knew this was the case, or was reckless as to whether or not this was the case.

C Only that she was not authorised to access the data.

D That she was not authorised to access the data and that she knew what the information was being used for.

Question 19.5

DAVIDSON is a computer programmer who has been asked by JELLIS to assist in a crime. JELLIS wants him to access the computer records of a Ferrari dealership's new customers' accounts and add JELLIS's details as a bona fide customer. This will, he believes, enable him to test drive a Ferrari. He intends not to return the car but take it for a 'joy-ride', amounting to an offence under s. 12(1) of the Theft Act 1968 (taking a motor vehicle or other conveyance without authority etc.). DAVIDSON 'hacks' into the company's computer and makes the changes. However, in reality, JELLIS will not be able to carry out his plan as the company always sends a representative on the test drive.

Has DAVIDSON committed an offence under s. 2 of the Computer Misuse Act 1990 (unauthorised access with intent to commit or facilitate commission of further offences)?

A Yes, even though the commission of the offence intended was impossible.

B Yes, even though he was merely facilitating the crime.

C No, as the intention to commit the crime lay with JELLIS.

D No, as the offence intended is not covered by s. 2.

Question 19.6

LENNON was a computer software engineer who worked for a company which distributed electronic equipment bought by customers online. LENNON was sacked by the company for allegedly stealing. Seeking revenge, LENNON devised a program which sent three million emails to the company's inbox in one day. LENNON hoped that the volume of emails would cause the company's online computer package to crash. However, another software engineer working for the company realised what was happening and implemented a program which intercepted the emails. In the end, no damage was done to the company.

If LENNON were to be prosecuted for an offence under s. 3 of the Computer Misuse Act 1990, which of the following statements would be correct in respect of the 'intent' required for this offence?

A The prosecution would have to show that LENNON intended causing an economic loss to the company.

B The prosecution must show that LENNON intended to impair the operation of the company's software program.

C The prosecution would have to show that LENNON intended to impair the operation of the company's software program, or was reckless as to whether it would be impaired.

D The prosecution would have to show that LENNON intended causing permanent damage to the company's computer program.

Question 19.7

PREEDY is a security guard in a hospital and suspects a colleague, WALL, of stealing from patients' lockers. PREEDY approached Constable HARPER with his concerns.

There was insufficient evidence to act on at this stage. Constable HARPER asked PREEDY to keep an eye on WALL and to report any unusual activity. PREEDY decided to take matters a step further and undertook some covert questioning of WALL, trying to get information on the thefts. WALL inadvertently let slip where some of the stolen property was hidden and PREEDY contacted Constable HARPER to pass on the information.

In relation to PREEDY, could he be described as having acted as a covert human intelligence source (CHIS), in these circumstances?

A Yes, when Constable HARPER asked PREEDY to keep an eye on WALL, they established a relationship.
B Yes, when PREEDY undertook covert questioning of WALL, he established a relationship.
C Yes, but only when PREEDY passed on the information to Constable HARPER.
D No, Constable HARPER did not task PREEDY or direct his activities.

Question 19.8

Constable PETERS is a member of a Neighbourhood Policing Team on a housing estate which suffers from a significant drug problem. The officer has formed a good relationship with young people in the area and has been approached by GAMLIN who lives on the estate and is aged 14. GAMLIN has disclosed to the officer that her older brother, whom she lives with, but does not get on with, is actively dealing heroin. She told Constable PETERS that she would like to give regular information about her brother's activities. The officer has returned to the station and has sought advice from the Dedicated Source Unit (DSU).

In these circumstances, could the DSU officers seek authority to recruit GAMLIN as a CHIS?

A No, on no occasion should the use or conduct of a CHIS be authorised when he/she is under 16 years of age.
B Yes, subject to the special provisions that apply to all juvenile CHISs.
C No, on no occasion should the use or conduct of a CHIS under 16 years of age be authorised to give information against someone in the same household as the person.
D No, on no occasion should the use or conduct of a CHIS under 16 years of age be authorised to give information against someone in the same family as the person.

Question 19.9

Detective Inspector GREEN has been telephoned by Detective Constable CALDWELL, an officer working in the Drug Squad. The officer has received information that a large quantity of drugs is due to be moved into the area within the next hour, to an address well known to the team. Detective Constable CALDWELL is at court applying for a warrant to search the premises, but wishes to set up a directed surveillance operation urgently to monitor the address.

Is Detective Inspector GREEN able to give an urgent authority for directed surveillance?

A No, inspectors are only able to give urgent authorities for CHIS activity.

B Yes, Detective Inspector GREEN may give an urgent authority if it is not reasonably practicable to have the application considered by a superintendent.

C Yes, inspectors are able to give authorities for directed surveillance in any situation; the restrictions relating to urgent authorities apply to CHIS activity.

D No, only a superintendent is able to give urgent authorities.

Question 19.10

Superintendent MILLER has given an urgent authorisation for CHIS activity by ALVIRES, who has passed on information to the police about a potential bomb-making ‘factory’ in a house in the neighbourhood. ALVIRES has been tasked, within strict parameters, to find out more information while the police organise an armed response.

Given that the CHIS has been authorised orally, which of the following statements is correct as to how long the authorisation should last?

A The authorisation will last for 24 hours unless renewed.

B The authorisation will last for 48 hours unless renewed.

C The authorisation will last for 72 hours unless renewed.

D Because it has been given by a superintendent, is will last for 12 months.

Question 19.11

DAWSON was arrested for a series of frauds against elderly people, involving the theft of £250,000. The police believed that SHELLEY, a solicitor, had been passing information to DAWSON about clients and their bank accounts in a conspiracy to commit fraud. DAWSON asked for SHELLEY to represent him while he was in custody. The officer in charge, DCI PATTERSON, considered making an application to place covert listening devices in the police station interview room, to listen in on their consultation.

Which of the following statements is correct, in relation to the police being allowed to use such surveillance methods?

A This is not permissible, as it amounts to directed surveillance.
B This is permissible, as it only amounts to directed and not intrusive surveillance.
C This is permissible, even though it amounts to intrusive surveillance.
D This is not permissible; all communications between lawyers and their clients are subject to legal privilege.

Question 19.12

PLUNKETT and FERRIS had been arrested by the police for conspiracy to commit murder. They had been interviewed over several days in the police station and neither person made any comment during interview. They were charged with the offence and were being taken to court in the back of a police van. Unknown to the pair, a directed surveillance authority had been obtained to place a covert listening device in the vehicle, which recorded crucial evidence pointing to their guilt.

In relation to the authority obtained, which of the following statements is correct?

A This authority was incorrectly given; this amounted to intrusive surveillance because PLUNKETT and FERRIS were in a vehicle.
B This authority was correctly given; the regulations relating to intrusive surveillance apply only on residential premises.
C This authority was incorrectly given; this amounted to intrusive surveillance because information was obtained using a covert listening device.
D This authority was correctly given; this amounted to directed surveillance because PLUNKETT and FERRIS were not inside a private vehicle.

Question 19.13

The police are investigating an organised crime group suspected of committing a series of armed robberies. Intelligence has been received that key members of the group have arranged to meet in a remote hotel in a week's time. Consideration is being given to applying for an authorisation to conduct surveillance at the hotel with audio and visual devices (microphones and cameras). The investigating officers are planning to place devices in common areas, such as the bar and dining room and in hotel rooms.

The Covert Surveillance and Property Interference Code of Practice provides guidance on what is intrusive surveillance. Which of the following is correct in relation to the type of surveillance authorisation the officers would require?

A A directed surveillance authorisation for the common areas and an intrusive surveillance authorisation for the hotel rooms.

B An intrusive surveillance authorisation for the common areas and hotel rooms; a hotel is a 'residential premises' according to the Code.

C A directed surveillance authorisation for the common areas and hotel rooms; a hotel is not a 'residential premises' according to the Code.

D A directed surveillance authorisation for the common areas and an intrusive surveillance authorisation for the hotel rooms; however, if they only plan to use listening devices in the hotel rooms, this would also amount to directed surveillance.

Question 19.14

Undercover police officers have infiltrated a large gang which is organising armed robberies in banks and building societies throughout the country. It is estimated that the gang is responsible for 30 crimes, which have so far yielded over £500,000. The investigating officers believe that the investigation would be assisted by obtaining a warrant to intercept communications between the various members of the gang.

Would the authorising officer be able to agree to such a warrant under s. 5 of the Regulation of Investigatory Powers Act 2000?

A Yes, provided it is suspected that the information would prove valuable to the investigation.

B No, the case is not one which affects the interests of national security.

C No, the case is not one which affects the interests of national security or which would affect the economic well-being of the United Kingdom.

D Yes, provided it is believed that the information would prove necessary for the purposes of the investigation.

Question 19.15

PRIESTLEY is employed by the police as an analyst in a police staff role, in a force intelligence bureau. He goes home one evening and, as a matter of conversation, he tells his wife, a serving police officer, that he saw an interception warrant issued in relation to a local company, but does not mention which company it is.

In relation to unauthorised disclosures, contrary to s. 19 of the Regulation of Investigatory Powers Act 2000, which of the following is true?

A PRIESTLEY cannot commit the offence as he is a member of the support staff.

B PRIESTLEY does not commit the offence as he does not name the company.

C PRIESTLEY commits the offence simply by mentioning it to his wife.

D PRIESTLEY commits the offence, but has a defence that he did not disclose it outside the police service.

Question 19.16

Constable FULLER was called to an incident involving a person in a public place, who was suffering from a mental disorder. The incident eventually led to Constable FULLER conveying the person to the police station, under s. 136 of the Mental Health Act 2007. Constable FULLER spent a considerable time trying to identify the person without success; the person had no identifying papers in his possession and was unable to communicate with the officer to state who he was. The person had a mobile phone with him, but there were no contact numbers on the phone. The mobile had only contacted one number, on several occasions; however, Constable FULLER tried it with no reply. As a last resort, Constable FULLER wondered whether the police could request a telephone subscriber's check, to try to identify the person.

Would Constable FULLER be able to request a telephone subscriber's check in these circumstances?

A No, such a check could only be requested for the purpose of preventing death or serious injury.

B Yes, such a check could be requested where a person is unable to identify themselves because of a mental condition, to assist in identifying them or obtaining information about their next of kin.

C No, such a check could only be requested for the purpose of preventing or detecting crime, preventing disorder, protecting the interests of national security or the economic well-being of the United Kingdom.

D No, such a check could only be requested where a person has died, to assist in identifying them or their next of kin.

ANSWERS

Answer 19.1

Answer **C** — Under s. 1 of the Freedom of Information Act 2000, a public authority is under a duty to comply with properly made requests from any 'person' who makes a request for information in writing and to inform that person whether the public authority holds specified information and if it does, communicate that information to the applicant unless one of the exemptions applies.

The requirement to disclose such information is not restricted to 'organisations'—individuals may make legitimate requests for information. Answer A is therefore incorrect.

The requirement to make a disclosure includes communicating information to a representative organisation or a person who is *not* a UK national and it is irrelevant that BERGMAN is a temporary UK resident. Answers B and D are therefore incorrect.

General Police Duties, para. 4.19.1.1

Answer 19.2

Answer **B** — Under s. 1 of the Freedom of Information Act 2000, a public authority is under a duty to comply with properly made requests from any 'person' who makes a request for information in writing and to inform that person whether the public authority holds specified information and if it does, communicate that information to the applicant unless one of the exemptions applies.

There are significant exemptions to the duty of disclosure and assistance. One of these exemptions will be the practicalities arising from the cost of obtaining the information sought. There are internal costs associated with assimilating and disclosing large amounts of information and, if those costs exceed the appropriate fee payable by the applicant, the public authority will usually be exempt from complying.

There are a number of other exemptions, such as the public interest in withholding the information outweighs that of disclosing it; information which would be prejudicial to law enforcement, national security or defence; information which attracts legal professional privilege or information related to ongoing investigations being conducted by public authorities. The Act also states that the authority must also provide advice and assistance to the person applying *unless* there is an exemption or the application is repeated or vexatious.

However, these exemptions are not stand-alone or exclusive as suggested in the scenario, which means that answers A, C and D are incorrect.

General Police Duties, para. 4.19.1.1

Answer 19.3

Answer **A** — An offence under s. 1 of the Computer Misuse Act 1990 is committed by causing a computer to perform a function, and all the answers would amount to 'functions'. As you were asked at which point an offence would first be committed, answer A is the correct answer. Although answers B, C and D all may fall under the section, they are incorrect, as switching the computer on is the first function that would amount to the offence.

General Police Duties, para. 4.19.2.1

Answer 19.4

Answer **A** — Under s. 1(1) of the Computer Misuse Act 1990, a person is guilty of an offence if:

(a) he causes a computer to perform any function with intent to secure access to any program or data held in any computer;
(b) the access he intends to secure is unauthorised; and
(c) he knows at the time when he causes the computer to perform the function that that is the case.

In order to prove the offence under s. 1, you must also show that the defendant knew the access was unauthorised and that he/she intended to secure access to the program or data. More proof is required than simply showing the defendant was not authorised to access the data and therefore answer C is incorrect.

This is an offence of 'specific intent', therefore lesser forms of *mens rea* such as recklessness will not be sufficient to convict a person. Answer B is therefore incorrect.

The offence is complete when the person knowingly accesses unauthorised data. There is no requirement to show that he/she knew what the information was being used for (albeit, if BIGNELL *did* know what the data was being used for, she could commit an offence under s. 2 of the Act). Answer D is therefore incorrect.

General Police Duties, para. 4.19.2.1

Answer 19.5

Answer **D** — Section 2 of the Computer Misuse Act 1990 requires intent on the part of the defendant; and this is either the intention to commit an offence to which s. 2 applies, or the intention to facilitate the commission of such an offence. DAVIDSON has this intention, as he knows the purpose of his actions and is aware that it will facilitate the taking and driving away (TADA), and therefore answer C is incorrect. Section 2 applies to the particular classes of offences set out in s. 2(2) of the 1990 Act. Section 12(1) of the Theft Act 1968 (taking a motor vehicle or other conveyance without authority etc.) is such a summary offence and therefore does not fall within offences outlined in s. 2(2), and therefore answer B is incorrect. As to impossibility, s. 2(4) of the 1990 Act makes clear that a person may be guilty of an offence even though the facts are such that the commission of the further offence is impossible; but as the offence intended is not covered by s. 2 of the 1990 Act this is immaterial. Therefore, answer A is incorrect.

General Police Duties, para. 4.19.2.3

Answer 19.6

Answer **C** — Under s. 3(1) of the Computer Misuse Act 1990, a person is guilty of an offence if he/she does any unauthorised act in relation to a computer and at the time he/she does the act he/she knows that it is unauthorised; and either subs. (2) or subs. (3) applies.

Under subs. (2), the person must *intend* by doing the act:

(a) to impair the operation of any computer;
(b) to prevent or hinder access to any program or data held in any computer; or
(c) to impair the operation of any such program or the reliability of any such data.

This section is designed to ensure that adequate provision is made to criminalise all forms of denial of service attacks in which the attacker denies the victim(s) access to a particular resource, typically by preventing legitimate users of a service accessing that service. An example of this is where a former employee, acting on a grudge, impaired the operation of a company's computer by using a program to generate and send 5 million emails to the company (*DPP* v *Lennon* [2006] EWHC 1201 (Admin)).

Section 3(3) of the Act states that this subsection also applies if the person is *reckless* as to whether the act will do any of the things mentioned in paras (a) to (c) of subs. (2) above. Therefore, the offence can be committed by a person who intends or is reckless as to whether the program is impaired and answer B is incorrect.

There is no requirement to prove an intent to cause an economic loss to the company and therefore answer A is incorrect.

An 'unauthorised act' can include a series of acts, and a reference to impairing, preventing or hindering something includes a reference to doing so temporarily (s. 3(5)) and therefore answer D is incorrect.

General Police Duties, para. 4.19.2.4

Answer 19.7

Answer **B** — A covert human intelligence source is someone who establishes or maintains a relationship with another person for the *covert* purpose of:

- obtaining information,
- providing access to information

or who *covertly* discloses information obtained by the use of such a relationship.

The main purpose of the Regulation of Investigatory Powers Act 2000 is to control the use of surveillance and covert human intelligence sources (CHIS) operations by public authorities and to ensure that any infringement of a person's human rights is lawful.

The definition would not usually apply to members of the public generally supplying information to the police. Similarly, people who have come across information in the ordinary course of their jobs who suspect criminal activity (such as bank staff, local authority employees, etc.) do not have a covert relationship with the police simply by passing on information. However, if the person supplying the information is asked by the police to do something further in order to develop or enhance it, any form of direction or tasking by the police in this way could make the person a CHIS and thereby attract all the statutory provisions and safeguards.

In the circumstances in this question, the officer has simply asked PREEDY to keep an eye on things and this would not actually amount to 'tasking' or 'directing' a person's activities and Constable HARPER has certainly not asked him to develop a relationship with WALL. Answer A is incorrect, as PREEDY was not acting as a CHIS as a result of his conversation with the officer.

Nevertheless, PREEDY went on to act as a CHIS, according to the above definition, when he covertly questioned WALL for information (and thus formed a 'relationship' with him) and later when he covertly disclosed the information to the officer. Answer D is therefore incorrect. The first point at which this happened was during the questioning; therefore, answer C is incorrect.

General Police Duties, para. 4.19.4.2

Answer 19.8

Answer **B** — The Covert Human Intelligence Sources Code of Practice, Chapter 5, outlines authorisation procedures for the use or conduct of a CHIS. The Code states that on no occasion should the use or conduct of a CHIS under 16 years of age be authorised to give information against his/her *parents or any person who has parental responsibility for him/her*. There is no specific mention of other family members in this Code and answers A, C and D are therefore incorrect.

In other cases involving juvenile CHISs, authorisations should not be granted unless the special provisions contained within the Regulation of Investigatory Powers (Juveniles) Order 2000 (SI 2000/2793) are satisfied.

General Police Duties, para. 4.19.4.4

Answer 19.9

Answer **B** — The Regulation of Investigatory Powers (Directed Surveillance and Covert Human Intelligence Sources) Order 2003 (SI 2003/3171), as amended, sets out the relevant roles and ranks for those who can authorise directed surveillance. In the case of the police the relevant rank will generally be at superintendent level and above, and the authorisation must be in writing except in urgent cases where oral authorisation may be given (s. 43(1)(a)).

Where it is not reasonably practicable to have the application considered by a superintendent or above, having regard to the urgency of the case, then an *inspector may give the relevant authorisation* which will only last 72 hours unless renewed by a superintendent.

Answers A, C and D are therefore incorrect.

General Police Duties, para. 4.19.4.6

Answer 19.10

Answer **C** — If a CHIS authorisation was given orally by a superintendent in an urgent case, it will only last for 72 hours unless renewed. If it is renewed during that time period, it can then last for up to 12 months.

Answers A, B and D are therefore incorrect.

General Police Duties, para. 4.19.4.4

Answer 19.11

Answer **C** — In relation to 'legal privilege' the House of Lords held that the Regulation of Investigatory Powers Act 2000 permits covert surveillance of communications between lawyers and their clients even though these may be covered by legal professional privilege (*Re McE (Northern Ireland)* [2009] UKHL 15). Answers A and D are therefore incorrect.

The Regulation of Investigatory Powers (Extension of Authorisation Provisions: Legal Consultations) Order 2010 (SI 2010/461) provides that directed surveillance carried out in relation to anything taking place on any premises that are being used for the purpose of legal consultations shall be treated as 'intrusive surveillance'. The consultation may be between a professional legal adviser and their client or person representing their client, or with a medical practitioner, where legal proceedings are contemplated and for the purposes of such proceedings.

'Any premises' includes prisons, police stations, legal advisers' business premises and courts. Since the proposal amounts to intrusive surveillance, answers A and B are incorrect.

General Police Duties, para. 4.19.4.6

Answer 19.12

Answer **D** — The Covert Surveillance and Property Interference Code of Practice, Chapter 2, provides guidance on what is intrusive surveillance. Intrusive surveillance is covert surveillance that is carried out in relation to anything taking place on residential premises or in any private vehicle, and that involves the presence of an individual on the premises or in the vehicle or is carried out by a means of a surveillance device. Intrusive surveillance applies to vehicles as well as premises and answer B is incorrect.

In *R* v *Plunkett* [2013] EWCA Crim 261, in admitting evidence of statements and admissions by the accused in a police van which were covertly recorded, it was held that a police van is not a private vehicle for the purposes of s. 26(3) and that the authorisation given by a superintendent under s. 28 of the Regulation of Investigatory Powers Act 2000 (RIPA) for directed surveillance was appropriate. Answer A is therefore incorrect.

In another case, evidence arising from the use of a bug in police transport, which was obtained in circumstances that meant there was a technical breach of the RIPA authority, was held admissible in that the officers had not acted in bad faith knowing they were exceeding their authority (*Khan* v *R* [2013] EWCA Crim 2230).

The definition of surveillance as intrusive relates to the location of the surveillance, and not any other consideration of the nature of the information that is expected to be obtained (see Code 2.12) or the method of obtaining the information. Answer C is therefore incorrect.

General Police Duties, para. 4.19.4.7

Answer 19.13

Answer **A** — The Covert Surveillance and Property Interference Code of Practice, Chapter 2, provides guidance on what is intrusive surveillance and states:

> 2.11 Intrusive surveillance is covert surveillance that is carried out in relation to anything taking place on residential premises or in any private vehicle, and that involves the presence of an individual on the premises or in the vehicle or is carried out by means of a surveillance device.

'Residential premises' are considered to be so much of any premises as is for the time being occupied or used by any person, however temporarily, for residential purposes or otherwise as living accommodation. This specifically includes hotel or prison accommodation that is so occupied or used (s. 48(1)). Answer C is therefore incorrect.

However, common areas (such as hotel dining areas) to which a person has access in connection with their use or occupation of accommodation are specifically excluded (s. 48(7)). Answer B is incorrect.

It is irrelevant for these purposes what kind of device the police intend to use to gather evidence; it is either intrusive surveillance according to the guidelines or not. Answer D is therefore incorrect.

General Police Duties, para. 4.19.4.7

Answer 19.14

Answer **D** — Section 5 of the Regulation of Investigatory Powers Act 2000 allows the Secretary of State to issue interception warrants under certain, very stringent, conditions. Section 5(3) describes when it will be *necessary* to issue such a warrant:

- in the interests of national security;
- for the purpose of preventing or detecting 'serious crime' (including the provisions of any international mutual assistance agreement)—serious crime means offences for which a person aged 21 or over and who has no previous convictions could

reasonably expect to be sentenced to at least three years' imprisonment, or where the conduct involves the use of violence, results in substantial financial gain or is conducted by a large number of persons in pursuit of a common purpose;

- for the purpose of safeguarding the economic well-being of the United Kingdom.

Therefore, although a warrant may be issued when it is necessary in the interests of national security or for the purpose of safeguarding the economic well-being of the United Kingdom, one may also be issued where the offence is one in which people commit offences resulting in substantial financial gain and which involve the use of violence or a large number of people pursuing a common purpose. Answers B and C are therefore incorrect.

It is not enough that the Secretary of State 'suspects' that these threats or needs exist, nor that he/she considers that an interception warrant might be useful, valuable or effective. The Secretary of State must *believe* that the warrant is *necessary* for one of the purposes set out and the methods of recovering that information are proportionate. Answer A is therefore incorrect.

General Police Duties, para. 4.19.4.11

Answer 19.15

Answer **C** — This offence applies to police officers and police staff alike, and would apply to anyone involved in an investigation (answer A is therefore incorrect). It deals with interception warrants, and requires those to whom it applies to keep secret any knowledge they have in relation to that warrant. The offence would be committed by simply mentioning the warrant's existence, irrespective of whether any individual or company was named (answer B is therefore incorrect). Although there is a defence, it relates to the accused taking steps to prevent the disclosure; in the circumstances of the question this is clearly not the case and PRIESTLEY has no defence (answer D is therefore incorrect).

Note that there are other defences available to s. 19, but they relate to communication with legal advisers and the Interception of Communications Commissioner.

General Police Duties, para. 4.19.4.12

Answer 19.16

Answer **B** — Chapter II of the Regulation of Investigatory Powers Act 2000 deals with the concept of 'communications data'. This is broadly information that relates to the use of the particular communications service but not the *content* of the communication itself. The full definition can be found in s. 21(4). Examples of communications data would include:

- itemised telephone bills;
- telephone subscriber details;
- addresses or other marks on the outside of postal packages and letters.

Section 22 of the Act sets out the circumstances when, and the purposes for which, such communications data may be obtained. In order to obtain communications data the designated person must believe it is necessary to obtain the data:

- for the purpose of preventing or detecting crime or preventing disorder;
- in the interests of national security, public safety or the economic well-being of the United Kingdom;
- for the purposes of protecting health or collecting or assessing any tax, duty, etc.;
- in an emergency, for the purpose of preventing (or mitigating) death, injury or damage to a person's physical or mental health;
- to assist investigations into alleged miscarriages of justice;
- for the purpose of assisting in identifying any person who has died otherwise than as a result of crime, or who is unable to identify him/herself because of a physical or mental condition, other than one resulting from crime, or obtaining information about the next of kin or other connected persons of such a person or about the reason for his/her death or condition;
- for any other purpose specified by an order made by the Secretary of State;

and that to do so is *proportionate* to what is sought to be achieved.

Therefore, while the general reason for accessing a telephone subscriber's check might centre on the prevention and detection of serious crime etc., or preventing death or serious injury, subscriber details *may* be requested where a person is unable to identify themselves because of a mental condition, to assist in identifying them or obtaining information about their next of kin.

Answers A, C and D are therefore incorrect.

General Police Duties, para. 4.19.4.15

20 Equality

STUDY PREPARATION

At last, the final chapter!

Although it would be easy to dismiss this area as merely a bit of political correctness, this chapter contains some of the most relevant and important legislation for supervisors and managers.

This area of legislation has undergone a complete overhaul with the Equality Act 2010 pulling together all strands of diversity and discriminatory behaviour under one umbrella.

It is essential that all employers understand their legal obligations in relation to the equal and/or fair treatment of others. You will need to know what will amount to discrimination, how to distinguish between direct and indirect discrimination, and familiarise yourself with the protected characteristics covered in the Act.

It is also as important to understand the concept of victimisation and to recognise when and where it can arise.

When dealing with this area, it is worth remembering that in some circumstances you have to treat everyone in the same way, while in others treating everyone in the same way is discriminatory—and if you don't understand this point, you need to revise this chapter!

QUESTIONS

Question 20.1

Constable LATTON has approached her sergeant and disclosed that she is considering undergoing gender reassignment surgery. However, she is concerned about discrimination and how the operation would affect her work.

In relation to Constable LATTON's concerns, at what point would she be protected by s. 7(1) of the Equality Act 2010 (protected characteristics of gender reassignment)?

A Constable LATTON would be protected by s. 7 when she has undergone the process and returned to work.

B Constable LATTON would be protected by s. 7 when she has undergone the process, but before she returns to work.

C Constable LATTON would be protected by s. 7 when she is undergoing or has undergone the process.

D Constable LATTON would be protected by s. 7 when she is proposing to undergo, is undergoing or has undergone the process.

Question 20.2

Detective Sergeant PORTER works on an operational CID team. The officer has two children, aged 2 and 4 years, and she has recently split up with her long-term partner. Detective Sergeant PORTER has applied for flexible working arrangements to help look after her family, but has been told that her BCU is unable to accommodate a change in her hours. The officer has discovered that a married female detective sergeant in another part of the force, with two young children, has negotiated a change in working hours, which is almost identical to the application rejected in respect of her. Detective Sergeant PORTER has met with the Police Federation to discuss a claim of discrimination under the Equality Act 2010.

Could Detective Sergeant PORTER have a claim of discrimination, under the Equality Act 2010, in these circumstances?

A Yes, this is a clear case of discrimination and Detective Sergeant PORTER could make a claim under the Equality Act 2010.

B No, because Detective Sergeant PORTER is no longer living with her partner, or married, the Equality Act 2010 does not apply to her case.

C No, because Detective Sergeant PORTER is not married, or in a civil partnership, the Equality Act 2010 does not apply to her case.

D No, Detective Sergeant PORTER would have to be married in order to claim discrimination under the Equality Act 2010 in these circumstances.

Question 20.3

Eastshire Constabulary is the respondent in a case of discrimination brought by Chief Inspector ASHTON, who claims that he has been passed over several times for promotion to superintendent because of his sexual orientation.

Which of the following statements is correct in relation to the burden of proof that the court would have to consider?

A Chief Inspector ASHTON must establish facts that point to a presumption of discrimination; the burden of proof then shifts to Eastshire Constabulary to prove that he was not treated unfairly.

B Eastshire Constabulary must establish the facts in their entirety that Chief Inspector ASHTON was not treated unfairly.

C Chief Inspector ASHTON must establish the facts in their entirety that he was treated unfairly by Eastshire Constabulary.

D Eastshire Constabulary must establish that Chief Inspector ASHTON was not treated unfairly; the burden then rests with him to rebut the facts.

Question 20.4

Constable JOHN is a response officer and is the sole carer of his elderly parent, who is 94 years of age. Constable JOHN has submitted a flexible working request to the senior management team, which would mean working fewer night shifts, but would assist the officer financially due to the cost of carers. The senior management team has rejected the application for operational reasons. Constable JOHN is considering taking action against the force for discrimination, citing that the decision of the senior management team is unreasonable.

Which of the following statements would be correct, in relation to Constable JOHN's potential claim of discrimination?

A Constable JOHN would only have to demonstrate that the senior management team's decision was unreasonable, in order to succeed with the claim.

B Constable JOHN could succeed with the claim, by showing that some other hypothetical person would have been treated more favourably.

C Constable JOHN would have to demonstrate that some other person was treated more favourably, in order to succeed with the claim.

D Constable JOHN would have to demonstrate that there would be a tangible or material loss as a result of the decision.

Question 20.5

GIRAUD is a police staff member working in the force Control Room. GIRAUD has been receiving counselling and treatment for depression for a number of years. His GP has recommended a course of medicine which would improve GIRAUD's condition, but would mean that he would need a full night's sleep every night. As a shift worker, this would prove difficult for GIRAUD and he has submitted a request to adjust his shifts to finish at 2 am on night shifts instead of 6 am. The request for reasonable adjustments has been rejected due to operational capacity and GIRAUD has now spoken to a solicitor to discuss a claim of discrimination under the Equality Act 2010.

Which of the following statements would be correct in relation to the level of disadvantage GIRAUD must have suffered, in order for a claim like this to be successful?

A A tribunal would have to conclude that GIRAUD had been placed at a substantial disadvantage by a failure to make reasonable adjustments.

B A tribunal would conclude that even the slightest disadvantage caused to GIRAUD by a failure to make reasonable adjustments would amount to discrimination.

C The threshold for any disadvantage in such a case is that by a failure to make reasonable adjustments, GIRAUD had been caused some disadvantage.

D A tribunal should not have a specific level of disadvantage in mind when deciding whether or not GIRAUD had suffered discrimination; it should make a decision based on the facts presented.

Question 20.6

FINNEGAN was profoundly deaf and was a suspect in a drug dealing case. Officers executed a warrant at FINNEGAN's house and found controlled drugs, for which he was arrested. The team had taken Constable SPEARING with them—a Neighbourhood officer, who had had numerous previous dealings with FINNEGAN and who was confident of being able to communicate the purpose of the search. FINNEGAN later sued the police for a breach of the Equality Act 2010, on the grounds that they had not provided an interpreter, which put him at a substantial disadvantage during the search.

Which of the following statements is correct, in relation to FINNEGAN's claim against the police?

A The claim is out of context; if officers have breached the terms of the Police and Criminal Evidence Act 1984, this is an evidential matter and not an equality issue.

B The Equality Act 2010 applies to operational matters; however, there is no disadvantage if the officers and FINNEGAN were able to communicate without an interpreter.

C The claim is out of context; the Equality Act 2010 does not apply as this is an operational matter and not an employment issue.

D This is a clear breach of the Equality Act 2010 and FINNEGAN should succeed with his claim against the police.

Question 20.7

Constable GILLIS is on the High Potential Development Scheme (HPDS) and works as a staff officer to the ACPO team in her force. The officer is currently on statutory maternity leave, having given birth to her child ten weeks ago. Constable GILLIS had originally stated that she would return to work after 26 weeks (the ordinary maternity leave period), but has now stated that she wishes to take leave for a further 26 weeks (additional maternity leave period). A decision has been taken to move Constable GILLIS to a different post and replace her, because the ACPO team is unable to manage her abstraction for the additional 26 weeks. Constable GILLIS has sought advice from her Federation Representative, believing that she has been treated unfavourably because of her request for additional maternity leave.

Would Constable GILLIS be protected by s. 18 of the Equality Act 2010, in these circumstances?

A No, s. 18 only applies in the period of 26 weeks after the employee has given birth (ordinary maternity leave period).

B Yes, this is sex discrimination by the employer; Constable GILLIS has been treated less favourably because she is female.

C Yes, Constable GILLIS is in the 'protected period', as defined by s. 18, and has been treated unfavourably.

D No, s. 18 only applies during an employee's pregnancy and two weeks after she has given birth.

Question 20.8

Constable DODD has approached her inspector and disclosed that she believes she is suffering sexual harassment from her sergeant. Constable DODD reported that the sergeant often made remarks about her body in front of other members of the team. In private, he would talk about his sex life and would ask Constable DODD about sexual relationships with her partner. Constable DODD said she had confronted the sergeant about the behaviour and that he had told her that she was imagining the behaviour and that it did not amount to harassment.

What matters should be taken into account in relation to Constable DODD's perception of what had happened during any investigation?

A The investigating officer may take into account Constable DODD's perception of what had happened and compare this to the perception of other members of the team.

B The investigating officer may take into account Constable DODD's perception of what had happened and compare this to the perception of the sergeant.

C The investigating officer must take into account Constable DODD's perception of what had happened, regardless of the perception of other people.

D The investigating officer must take into account Constable DODD's perception of what had happened, depending on the evidence disclosed.

Question 20.9

Constable MELROSE has just started work on a response team in a new area. Officers are aware that before moving to the team, Constable MELROSE had made a complaint of racial discrimination against colleagues on another team and that the complaint had been unsubstantiated. Some officers on Constable MELROSE's new team decided to record problems they encountered with the officer, in fear that they may be the subject of a race discrimination claim at some future date.

Would the officers' behaviour amount to victimisation, because of Constable MELROSE's previous complaint?

A Yes, even though the previous complaint was unsubstantiated, this amounts to victimisation.

B No, if a complaint is unsubstantiated, any future complaint of similar actions cannot amount to victimisation.

C No; however, the officers' behaviour could amount to direct discrimination.

D No, the behaviour of the officers concerned would not amount to victimisation in these circumstances.

Question 20.10

Eastshire Constabulary is being sued by Constable AMIR. The claim relates to a failure by the force to allow Constable AMIR time off to attend a number of religious festivals throughout the year. Constable AMIR's line managers have not been cited, as the officer understands the pressures of delivering operational policing; however, the claim is made against the force for failing to have policies and procedures in place to account for the religious beliefs of its staff.

Which of the following statements is correct, in relation to Eastshire Constabulary's liability under s. 42 of the Equality Act 2010?

A Constable AMIR's line managers and the Chief Constable may be liable; the responsible authority is only liable for discrimination by members of staff towards people outside the force.

B The Chief Constable alone may be liable in these circumstances; the responsible authority has no liability under this Act.

C The Chief Constable and the responsible authority may be liable in these circumstances.

D Constable AMIR's line managers may be liable; the Chief Constable and the responsible authority are only liable for discrimination by members of staff towards people outside the force.

Question 20.11

MARLER has made a claim of discrimination under the Equality Act 2010 against her local police force. MARLER applied for a post as a PCSO and passed what amounted to a national selection process. However, she was told that although she had passed, there were insufficient posts to take her on at this time and that she would be contacted at a later time should any further vacancies arise. However, MARLER has been told by someone working in the Recruitment Department that the force had appointed three people from black and minority ethnic (BME) backgrounds who had also passed the process, but who had scored fewer marks than she had. She had been told this had happened because the force was under-represented in this department by people from BME communities.

Would the behaviour of the force amount to discrimination in employment in these circumstances?

A No, the force can select whom it wants from a pool of people who have passed the process.

B Yes, provided MARLER's performance in the process was better than the people selected ahead of her.

C No, if the force is under-represented by people from BME communities, they can be selected ahead of other candidates provided they passed the process.

D No, provided each candidate was given a fair opportunity to pass the assessment, this is an example of positive action, which the force is entitled to undertake.

Question 20.12

Constable STUBBS is currently suing her employers for discrimination in the workplace. She has cited several instances of inappropriate sexual behaviour towards her by her line managers in work. Constable STUBBS has also included evidence in her statement of inappropriate sexual behaviour towards her by work colleagues while they were at a social Christmas function in a nearby public house.

Would Constable STUBBS be able to rely on *all* of this evidence in her claim of discrimination against her employers?

A Yes, she may be able to rely on this evidence because the function was an extension of the workplace.

B No, but she would have been able to if the behaviour had taken place at an off-duty function at her actual workplace.

C Yes, she may rely on evidence of any inappropriate behaviour, inside or outside the workplace.

D No, her employers cannot be held liable for the behaviour of her colleagues outside the workplace.

ANSWERS

Answer 20.1

Answer **D** — Under s. 7(1) of the Equality Act 2010:

> A person has the protected characteristic of gender reassignment if the person is proposing to undergo, is undergoing or has undergone a process (or part of a process) for the purpose of re-assigning the person's sex by changing physiological or other attributes of sex.

A reference to a transsexual person is a reference to a person who has the protected characteristic of gender reassignment (s. 7(2)).

Since the officer is protected by the Act from the time she is proposing to undergo the operation (effectively now), answers A, B and C are incorrect.

General Police Duties, para. 4.20.2.3

Answer 20.2

Answer **C** — Before looking at the legislative aspects of this case, we should examine some practical matters. First, as a caring employer, should Detective Sergeant PORTER's BCU consider her application for flexible working because of the personal circumstances she finds herself in? Yes, of course. Are they obliged to grant her application because of some legislation or regulation outside the Equality Act 2010? Not necessarily.

The Employment Act 2002 first gave the parents of children of a specified age (5 years old at the time) the right to request a flexible working pattern from April 2003. Subsequent changes to the legislation now mean that parents with children aged 16 or under and those with disabled children under 18 now have the right to apply for a flexible working pattern. However, police officers are not 'employees' for most purposes as they are not employed under contracts, which means they are not generally covered by the 2002 Act; they are public office holders (or 'workers' in some cases) (see *Fisher* v *Oldham Corporation* [1930] 2 KB 364 and *Sheikh* v *Chief Constable of Greater Manchester Police* [1990] 1 QB 637).

However, police forces do follow the flexible working requirements covered in the 2002 Act (mirroring the EU Working Time Directive) when it comes to applications to change shift patterns, etc.

Returning to equality legislation now, where does Detective Sergeant PORTER's claim sit within the Equality Act 2010? Section 13(1) of the Equality Act 2010 states:

> A person (A) discriminates against another (B) if, because of a protected characteristic, A treats B less favourably than A treats or would treat others.

Under s. 8(1) of the Act, a person has the protected characteristic of marriage and civil partnership if he/she is married or is a civil partner.

However, people who are not married or civil partners do not have this characteristic, meaning, effectively, people who are single parents, widows, widowers or even common law partners do not enjoy protection under the 2010 Act. The Marriage (Same Sex Couples) Act 2013 extended marriage to same-sex couples, which means that marriage has the same effect in law in relation to such a couple as it does in relation to an opposite-sex couple, but, despite opposition, it gave no extra rights to heterosexual couples, same-sex couples, single parents or anyone else who simply does not want to, or is unable to, marry or enter into a civil partnership.

The effect of this is that, in relation to this question, because Detective Sergeant PORTER is not married, or in a civil partnership, she has no rights whatsoever to make a claim under the Equality Act 2010. Answers A, B and D are therefore incorrect.

General Police Duties, para. 4.20.2.4

Answer 20.3

Answer **A** — Sexual orientation is one of the protected characteristics covered by the Equality Act 2010 and it is unlawful to discriminate against a person due to their sexual orientation.

In proceedings relating to contraventions of the Act the burden of proof initially rests with the complainant. Answers B and D are therefore incorrect.

Once the complainant establishes facts from which it might be presumed that there had been discrimination the burden of proof shifts to the respondent to prove no breach of the principle of equal treatment (s. 136). Answer C is therefore incorrect.

General Police Duties, para. 4.20.3

Answer 20.4

Answer **B** — Section 13(1) of the Equality Act 2010 states:

> A person (A) discriminates against another (B) if, because of a protected characteristic, A treats B less favourably than A treats or would treat others.

Less favourable treatment of a person because that person is associated with a protected characteristic, for example because the person has a friend or partner with a particular protected characteristic, or carries out work related to a protected characteristic, is within the scope of this section. This might include carers of disabled people and elderly relatives, who can claim they were treated unfairly because of duties that they had to carry out at home relating to their care work. For example, the non-disabled mother of a disabled child can be discriminated against because of the child's disability (*Coleman* v *Attridge Law* (Case C-303/06) [2008] IRLR 722). This is known as 'associative discrimination'.

To constitute direct discrimination the treatment experienced by B must be different from that of another person. This difference is often referred to as a 'comparator'. The treatment of B must be less favourable than the treatment afforded a comparator. The comparator can be hypothetical where B can establish direct discrimination by showing that if there was another person in similar circumstances, but without B's protected characteristic, that person would be treated more favourably (for an explanation of hypothetical comparators see *Shamoon* v *Chief Constable of the Royal Ulster Constabulary* [2003] UKHL 11). This is why answer B is correct, and answer C is incorrect.

Less favourable treatment is a broad concept and any disadvantage to which B has been subject will constitute such treatment. B need not have suffered a tangible or material loss (*Chief Constable of West Yorkshire Police* v *Khan* [2001] UKHL 48) and therefore answer D is incorrect.

However, it is not enough merely to show unreasonable treatment (*Bahl* v *The Law Society* [2004] IRLR 799). Answer A is therefore incorrect.

General Police Duties, para. 4.20.3.1

Answer 20.5

Answer **A** — Under s. 20 of the Equality Act 2010, where this Act imposes a duty to make reasonable adjustments, the requirement is that where a provision, criterion or practice puts a disabled person at a *substantial disadvantage* in relation to a relevant matter in comparison with persons who are not disabled, such steps should be taken as it is reasonable to have to take to avoid the disadvantage.

The section contains only one threshold for the reasonable adjustment duty, that of 'substantial disadvantage'; s. 212(1) defines 'substantial' as more than minor or trivial.

Answers B, C and D are therefore incorrect.

General Police Duties, para. 4.20.3.3

Answer 20.6

Answer **B** — Section 13(1) of the Equality Act 2010 states:

> A person (A) discriminates against another (B) if, because of a protected characteristic, A treats B less favourably than A treats or would treat others.

Disability is one of the protected characteristics covered by the 2010 Act and the police service has a general 'public sector duty' as a public authority to eliminate discrimination and promote equality (see s. 149).

Section 20 of the Act outlines what is meant by the duty to make reasonable adjustments for the purposes of the Act and, under s. 20(5), the requirement is:

> where a disabled person would, but for the provision of an auxiliary aid, be put at a substantial disadvantage in relation to a relevant matter in comparison with persons who are not disabled, to take such steps as it is reasonable to have to take to provide the auxiliary aid.

Section 21 provides that a failure to comply with any one of the reasonable adjustment requirements amounts to discrimination against a disabled person to whom the duty is owed.

The requirement to comply with the 2010 Act applies as much in an operational context as it does in employment legislation; the fact that the officers may have breached PACE is irrelevant in some ways; a discrimination case, if brought about, would be treated as a separate matter and could bring punishment on the force regardless of whether FINNEGAN is found guilty of supplying drugs. Answers A and C are therefore incorrect.

However, it was held that police officers lawfully searching the home of a man whom they knew to be profoundly deaf did *not* have any effect on the ability of the man and the officers to communicate with each other effectively without a British Sign Language interpreter being present. Officers who had had previous dealings with the man were satisfied on the basis of these dealings that they could achieve a basic level of communication with him without the benefit of an interpreter (*Finnegan* v *Chief Constable of Northumbria* [2013] EWCA Civ 1191). This case demonstrates that the circumstances in the question were not a *clear* breach of the Equality Act 2010 and answer D is therefore incorrect.

General Police Duties, para. 4.20.3.3

Answer 20.7

Answer **C** — An employee generally has the right to 26 weeks of ordinary maternity leave and 26 weeks of additional maternity leave making one year in total. The combined 52 weeks is known as Statutory Maternity Leave.

Section 18 of the Equality Act 2010 states:

(1) This section has effect for the purposes of the application of Part 5 (work) to the protected characteristic of pregnancy and maternity.
(2) A person (A) discriminates against a woman if, in the protected period in relation to a pregnancy of hers, A treats her unfavourably—
    (a) because of the pregnancy, or
    (b) because of illness suffered by her as a result of it.
(3) A person (A) discriminates against a woman if A treats her unfavourably because she is on compulsory maternity leave.
(4) A person (A) discriminates against a woman if A treats her unfavourably because she is exercising or seeking to exercise, or has exercised or sought to exercise, the right to ordinary or *additional* maternity leave.

The duration of the protected period depends on the statutory maternity leave entitlements as set out in the Employment Rights Act 1996, which defines the right to compulsory, ordinary and additional maternity leave. The protected period starts when a woman becomes pregnant and ends either:

- if she has the right to ordinary and additional maternity leave, at the end of the additional maternity leave period or (if earlier) when she returns to work after the pregnancy; or
- if she does not have that right, at the end of the period of two weeks beginning with the end of the pregnancy.

Answer A is incorrect, because compulsory maternity leave is only one of the areas covered by s. 18.

Answer D is incorrect since the officer has a statutory entitlement to ordinary and additional maternity leave; the protection does not end two weeks after she has given birth, it ends when she returns to work.

Whilst this case may amount to a breach of s. 18, sex discrimination does not apply to treatment of a woman insofar as it is in the protected period, or it is for a reason mentioned in s. 18(3) or (4). Answer B is therefore incorrect.

General Police Duties, paras 4.20.3.6, 4.20.3.7

Answer 20.8

Answer **C** — Under s. 26 of the Equality Act 2010:

(1) A person (A) harasses another (B) if—
    (a) A engages in unwanted conduct related to a relevant protected characteristic, and
    (b) the conduct has the purpose or effect of—

(i) violating B's dignity, or

(ii) creating an intimidating, hostile, degrading, humiliating or offensive environment for B.

(2) A also harasses B if—

(a) A engages in unwanted conduct of a sexual nature, and

(b) the conduct has the purpose or effect referred to in subsection (1)(b).

The behaviour referred to involves unwanted conduct which is related to a relevant characteristic and has the purpose or effect of creating an intimidating, hostile, degrading, humiliating or offensive environment for the complainant or of violating the complainant's dignity (which is described clearly in this question).

In deciding whether conduct has the effect referred to in s. 26(1)(b), the perception of B, the other circumstances of the case, and whether it is reasonable for the conduct to have that effect, must be taken into account (s. 26(4)).

Therefore, while the investigating officer *may* take into account the perception of other members of the team weighing up the evidence against the sergeant, he or she must take into account the victim's perception of what happened.

Answers A, B and D are therefore incorrect.

General Police Duties, para. 4.20.3.8

Answer 20.9

Answer **D** — Section 27 of the Equality Act 2010 states:

(1) A person (A) victimises another person (B) if A subjects B to a detriment because—

(a) B does a protected act, or

(b) A believes that B has done, or may do, a protected act.

(2) Each of the following is a protected act—

(a) bringing proceedings under this Act;

(b) giving evidence or information in connection with proceedings under this Act;

(c) doing any other thing for the purposes of or in connection with this Act;

(d) making an allegation (whether or not express) that A or another person has contravened this Act.

This would mean that generally, if a person makes a claim, he/she could still be the subject of victimisation at some time in the future, regardless of whether the claim was substantiated. Answer B is therefore incorrect.

However, in *Bayode* v *Chief Constable of Derbyshire* [2008] UKEAT 0499 07 2205, the tribunal held that the complainant, a police constable who was a black African and Nigerian by national origin, had *not* been victimised where his colleagues recorded any problems they encountered with him in their PNBs for fear that he might make a race discrimination claim at some future date. Previous unsubstantiated discrimination claims had been made by the complainant. Answer A is therefore incorrect.

Direct discrimination is an entirely different matter to victimisation, and generally involves employers treating one group of people less favourably than others based on protected grounds, such as their racial origin, marital status, sex, religion or belief or sexual orientation. It is out of context in this scenario, and for that reason answer C is incorrect.

General Police Duties, para. 4.20.3.10

Answer 20.10

Answer **C** — Section 42 of the Equality Act 2010 states:

> (1) For the purposes of this Part, holding the office of constable is to be treated as employment—
> (a) by the chief officer, in respect of any act done by the chief officer in relation to a constable or appointment to the office of constable;
> (b) by the responsible authority, in respect of any act done by the authority in relation to a constable or appointment to the office of constable.

The Equality Act 2010 makes provisions for chief officers *and* 'responsible' authorities to be liable for acts done by them towards their staff. Answer B is therefore incorrect.

This liability is not limited to discrimination by members of staff towards people outside the force; it can include discrimination by members of staff towards people within the force and therefore answers A and D are incorrect.

The chief officer of police is also vicariously liable for acts of race discrimination by staff under his/her direction and control. The statutory defence that an employer took all reasonable steps to prevent the acts of discrimination complained of is also available to chief officers (s. 109(4)).

General Police Duties, paras 4.20.4, 4.20.6

Answer 20.11

Answer **B** — Under s. 39 of the Equality Act 2010, it is unlawful for an employer to discriminate against or victimise employees and people seeking work. It applies where the employer is making arrangements to fill a job, and in respect of anything done in the course of a person's employment.

There are a number of exceptions and defences to the provisions of the Act, but two of the more relevant defences in relation to discrimination or victimisation in employment are 'genuine occupational requirement' and 'positive action'.

'Positive action' refers to measures to alleviate disadvantage experienced by people who share a protected characteristic, reduce their under-representation in relation to particular activities and meet their particular needs (s. 158). It allows for measures to be targeted to particular groups, including training to enable them to gain employment, but any such measures must be a proportionate way of achieving the relevant aim.

An employer may also take a protected characteristic into consideration when deciding whom to recruit or promote, where people having the protected characteristic are at a disadvantage or are under-represented (s. 159).

However, this can be done only where the candidates are as qualified as each other. Therefore, if the three people with BME backgrounds had scored the same as MARLER in the assessment centre, the force has used positive action correctly, but if they had scored fewer marks, the force has not. The aim is to help employers achieve a more diverse workforce by giving them the option, when faced with candidates of *equal merit*, to choose a candidate from an under-represented group.

Answers A, C and D are therefore incorrect.

General Police Duties, para. 4.20.5

Answer 20.12

Answer **A** — Section 109 of the Equality Act 2010 states:

> (1) Anything done by a person (A) in the course of A's employment must be treated as also done by the employer.
> (2) ...
> (3) It does not matter whether that thing is done with the employer's or principal's knowledge or approval.

Where acts amounting to discrimination take place outside the workplace, the employer and employees may still be caught within the framework of the legislation. So, for instance, where police officers engage in inappropriate sexual behaviour towards a colleague at a work-related social function, a tribunal may be entitled to hold that the function was an extension of the workplace and so hold the chief officer liable for the acts of his/her officers at that function (see *Chief Constable of Lincolnshire* v *Stubbs* [1999] IRLR 81). Answer D is therefore incorrect.

This case deals with a specific example of behaviour where the officers were at a work-related function, which was an 'extension of the workplace'. The decision does not therefore mean that any behaviour can be included in such a claim (although it is worth noting that discrimination and victimisation are included in the Code of

Conduct for police officers, which may include the conduct of an off-duty officer). Answer C is therefore incorrect. Lastly, this case did not specify that the location of the function was important, merely that it was an off-duty function and an extension of the workplace. Answer B is therefore incorrect.

General Police Duties, para. 4.20.6

Question Checklist

The following checklist is designed to help you keep track of your progress when answering the multiple-choice questions. If you fill this in after one attempt at each question, you will be able to check how many you have got right and which questions you need to revisit a second time. Also available online; to download visit www.blackstonespolicemanuals.com.

	First attempt Correct (✓)	Second attempt Correct (✓)
1 The Police and the Policing Family		
1.1		
1.2		
1.3		
1.4		
1.5		
1.6		
1.7		
1.8		
1.9		
1.10		
1.11		
1.12		
1.13		
1.14		
1.15		
2 Complaints and Misconduct		
2.1		
2.2		
2.3		
2.4		

	First attempt Correct (✓)	Second attempt Correct (✓)
2.5		
2.6		
2.7		
2.8		
2.9		
2.10		
3 Unsatisfactory Performance and Attendance		
3.1		
3.2		
3.3		
3.4		
3.5		
3.6		
3.7		
3.8		
3.9		
3.10		
3.11		
4 Human Rights		
4.1		
4.2		

	First attempt Correct (✓)	Second attempt Correct (✓)
4.3		
4.4		
4.5		
4.6		
4.7		
4.8		
4.9		
4.10		
4.11		
4.12		
4.13		
4.14		
5 Powers of Arrest (including Code G Codes of Practice) and Other Policing Powers		
5.1		
5.2		
5.3		
5.4		
5.5		
5.6		
5.7		
5.8		
5.9		
5.10		
6 Stop and Search		
6.1		
6.2		
6.3		
6.4		
6.5		
6.6		
6.7		
6.8		
6.9		
6.10		
6.11		

	First attempt Correct (✓)	Second attempt Correct (✓)
6.12		
6.13		
7 Entry, Search and Seizure		
7.1		
7.2		
7.3		
7.4		
7.5		
7.6		
7.7		
7.8		
7.9		
7.10		
7.11		
8 Hatred and Harassment Offences		
8.1		
8.2		
8.3		
8.4		
8.5		
8.6		
8.7		
8.8		
8.9		
8.10		
9 Anti-social Behaviour		
9.1		
9.2		
9.3		
9.4		
9.5		
9.6		
9.7		
9.8		

	First attempt Correct (✓)	Second attempt Correct (✓)
9.9		
9.10		
9.11		
9.12		
9.13		
9.14		
9.15		
9.16		
10 Offences Involving Communications		
10.1		
10.2		
10.3		
10.4		
10.5		
10.6		
10.7		
10.8		
10.9		
11 Terrorism and Associated Offences		
11.1		
11.2		
11.3		
11.4		
11.5		
11.6		
11.7		
11.8		
11.9		
11.10		
11.11		
12 Public Order, Processions and Assemblies		
12.1		
12.2		
12.3		
12.4		

	First attempt Correct (✓)	Second attempt Correct (✓)
12.5		
12.6		
12.7		
12.8		
12.9		
12.10		
12.11		
12.12		
12.13		
12.14		
12.15		
12.16		
12.17		
13 Sporting Events		
13.1		
13.2		
13.3		
13.4		
13.5		
13.6		
13.7		
13.8		
13.9		
14 Weapons		
14.1		
14.2		
14.3		
14.4		
14.5		
14.6		
14.7		
14.8		
14.9		
14.10		
14.11		
14.12		

	First attempt Correct (✓)	Second attempt Correct (✓)
14.13		
14.14		
14.15		
14.16		
14.17		
14.18		
15 Domestic Violence and Trade Disputes		
15.1		
15.2		
15.3		
15.4		
15.5		
15.6		
15.7		
15.8		
15.9		
15.10		
16 Protection of People Suffering from Mental Disorders		
16.1		
16.2		
16.3		
16.4		
16.5		
17 Offences Relating to Land and Premises		
17.1		
17.2		
17.3		
17.4		
17.5		
17.6		
17.7		
17.8		
17.9		
17.10		
17.11		
17.12		
17.13		

	First attempt Correct (✓)	Second attempt Correct (✓)
18 Licensing and Offences Relating to Alcohol		
18.1		
18.2		
18.3		
18.4		
18.5		
18.6		
18.7		
18.8		
18.9		
18.10		
18.11		
18.12		
18.13		
18.14		
18.15		
18.16		
18.17		
18.18		
18.19		
18.20		
18.21		
18.22		
18.23		
18.24		
18.25		
18.26		
18.27		
18.28		
18.29		
18.30		
18.31		
18.32		
18.33		
19 Offences and Powers Relating to Information		
19.1		
19.2		
19.3		

	First attempt Correct (✓)	Second attempt Correct (✓)
19.4		
19.5		
19.6		
19.7		
19.8		
19.9		
19.10		
19.11		
19.12		
19.13		
19.14		
19.15		
19.16		

	First attempt Correct (✓)	Second attempt Correct (✓)
20 Equality		
20.1		
20.2		
20.3		
20.4		
20.5		
20.6		
20.7		
20.8		
20.9		
20.10		
20.11		
20.12